DICTIONARY **OF**
Curious
Phrases

LESLIE DUNKLING

HarperCollins*Publishers*

HarperCollins*Publishers*
P.O. Box, Glasgow G4 0NB
www.**fire**and**water**.com

First published 1998

Reprint 10 9 8 7 6 5 4 3

© Leslie Dunkling 1998

ISBN 0 00 472060 1

A catalogue record for this book is available from the British Library

Printed and bound in Great Britain by
Caledonian International Book Manufacturing Ltd, Glasgow G64

Contents

Introduction

There are many phrases in English which are not meant to be taken literally. If we hear that someone has 'kicked the bucket,' for instance, we don't think that the person concerned has actually kicked a bucket. We know that the reference is to someone who has died. Most of the time we use such phrases without much thought, but there comes a time when we ask ourselves – why do we say that? Why do we 'let the cat out of the bag,' 'get down to brass tacks,' take a 'busman's holiday'? This book sets out to explain the origins of these and similar metaphorical phrases, showing how they have evolved through the centuries.

Some people might argue that such phrases should be avoided by a careful speaker or writer because they are clichés. This comment usually implies that a hackneyed phrase has been used in a lazy way, that a more original way of expressing the thought could have been found. But frequency of use does not automatically create a cliché. Just as one word correctly describes a specific object or idea, so a particular phrase may be the correct one to use in specific circumstances. Formulaic phrases such as 'Good morning,' 'How do you do?' 'Merry Christmas,' 'Many happy returns of the day' are, in one sense, hackneyed phrases or clichés which are constantly used, but it would be absurd to say that every speaker should find another way to express such ideas. A great many other phrases are also prompted by situations that regularly occur. The children's misbehaviour once again makes it necessary 'to read the Riot Act.' An approaching examination means that one must 'keep one's nose to the grindstone.'

It is phrases of this type which some would call clichés. Others see them as the linguistic equivalent of philosophical shrugs, an acceptance that familiar circumstances, albeit unpleasant ones, have once again arisen. The familiar words that are used can be rather comforting to both speaker and listener. The underlying message is: at least we are not dealing with the unknown; this is a well-enough known human situation to have its own linguistic convention.

Children learn a number of set phrases at an early age which enable them to cope with recurring situations. 'Finders keepers!' traditionally establishes ownership of something they stumble across. If they are taunted in the playground because they are too clever or too stupid, too tall or too small, too fat or too thin, cry too easily, have red hair, wear glasses or generally offend others by being different in some way, they need to be able to respond quickly with a suitable retort. This may be no more than 'Same to you with knobs on,' 'Do me a favour – drop dead,' or 'Sticks and stones may break my bones, but names will never hurt me.' Only the verbally gifted will be able to rely on the inspiration of the moment and say something original. The average child will be content to use any appropriate phrase which deflects the verbal attack and perhaps gives him the last word. Situational phrases, in other words, are recognised as being useful from a very early age. Genuine clichés are probably those phrases which contribute nothing to the meaning of what is being said and give no psychological comfort to speaker or hearer. Some people constantly preface a sentence with 'I must admit that,' 'I must confess that,' 'To tell you the truth,' 'The fact is,' 'As a matter of fact,' or 'Let's face it.' These are merely verbal tics which distract and irritate the listener. While such phrases should be avoided, a large number of metaphorical idioms have an essential part to play in spoken and written English. Many of them are as interesting as they are useful, and, as the literary quotations in this book demonstrate, they can often be used imaginatively by good writers and speakers. The stories which lie behind their origins also reveal much about our social and linguistic history. These are phrases which thoroughly justify their role in the language, and there is certainly no reason to be ashamed of them.

Achilles Heel

Achilles was a legendary warrior, the chief hero on the Greek side in the Trojan War. He had been plunged into the Styx by his mother while still an infant, making him invulnerable except in the heel by which he was held. When Paris was told by Apollo of this one weakness, he shot an arrow into Achilles' heel and killed him. The story is recalled in the name of the Achilles tendon, which is just above the heel.

Samuel Taylor Coleridge made metaphorical use of the Greek tale, referring in 1810 to 'Ireland, that vulnerable heel of the British Achilles!' Since then the phrase has been generally applied to any weakness in someone or something that is otherwise strong. In one of his letters, for example, George Bernard Shaw says that 'divorce is the Achilles heel of marriage.' In 1972 the *Catholic Herald* was of the opinion that 'it is this refusal to condemn which is the Achilles heel of contemporary Christian psychology.' The Achilles heel of the American physicist Julius Oppenheimer, according to one commentator, was his 'overriding loyalty to his friends.' Another writer said of Trotsky: 'By his verbal artifices, he only discloses his own Achilles' heel.'

Apple of One's Eye

In modern times it is usually children who are referred to in this expression. 'He had an heir of his own,' writes Trollope in *Doctor Thorne*, 'who was the apple of his eye.' In Nancy Mitford's *Love in a Cold Climate* a daughter is described as 'such a treasure, so much the apple of their eye.' A thousand years earlier a writer might have expressed the same idea by using exactly the same phrase. It occurs, for instance, in King Alfred's translation of Boethius, made in the 9th century. It can also be found in all the early translations of the bible. We can safely say that 'apple of one's eye,' meaning one's most cherished possession, is one of the oldest phrases in the English language.

In spite of this, a young girl who happens to remark in Elizabeth Gaskell's *Wives and Daughters* that 'the squire looks upon him as the apple of his eye', is given a stern lecture. 'Molly! Molly! pray don't let me hear you using such vulgar expressions. When shall I teach you true refinement – that refinement which consists in never even thinking a vulgar, commonplace thing! Proverbs and idioms are never used by people of education. "Apple of his eye!" I am really shocked.' This is meant to demonstrate the pretentiousness of the speaker, not reflect Mrs Gaskell's own views.

The phrase seems to compare the object of one's affection with a Cox's pippin, say, but its origin is rather different. It goes back to the days when our ancestors referred to the pupil of the eye, which was thought to be not only round but solid, as the eye's apple. The apple of the eye was its essential part, making sight possible. Those who first described a person as the apple of their eye were therefore saying that the person was as dear to them as their ability to see. Modern parents who use the phrase would probably not argue with that.

As Cool as a Cucumber

'As cool as a cucumber' is a well-used phrase, both in everyday speech and in literature. John Gay recorded it in 1732, referring to it as a 'new simile.' In the 19th century it is found in the works of writers like Thomas de Quincey and Oliver Wendell Holmes. H.G.Wells, in *Kipps*, has: 'The way you caught on about that slop was something worth seeing. Bif! Right off. Cool as a cucumber.' Mary McCarthy mentions 'Hen sitting opposite, cool as a cucumber' in *The Groves of Academe*. A character in Vera Caspary's *Laura* says: 'She was as cool as a cucumber when the boys got there. Opened the door and pointed to the body so calmly you'd have thought it was an everyday thing for her to find her boss murdered.'

The earlier expression applied to a person, especially a woman, was 'cold as a cucumber.' The reputation cucumbers had in the 16th century was summed up by Sir Thomas Elyot in *The Castle of Health*. He reported there that eating them gave rise to a 'cold and thick humour,' which in turn 'abated lust.' Since cucumbers are notoriously associated with flatulence, that may also have acted as a damper on passion. For whatever reason, cucumbers continued to be the vegetable equivalent of a cold shower throughout the 17th century. A young man in Beaumont and Fletcher's play *Cupid's Revenge* refers to young maids as 'cold as cucumbers.' As late as 1736 we find in W.R.Chetwood's *The Voyages, Travels and Adventures of W.O.G.Vaughan*: 'I have, once more, made my Addresses to Isabella, but she's as cold as a cucumber.' At this time the normal pronunciation of cucumber was *cow-cumber*. Although there is no connection between the animal and the vegetable, it is possible that the

3

renowned placidity of cows affected the way people thought about cucumbers.

In modern times there has been a further development. 'There's my friend Jo, calm as a cucumber, just went for her two weeks' holiday and came back with a baby,' says someone in Susan Barrett's *Moses*. Truman Capote uses the same simile in *My Side of the Matter*: 'So just as calm as a cucumber I arose.' This may have been influenced by the phrase 'cool, calm and collected.' The abbreviated form 'cuke,' for half a cucumber, has also given rise in modern times to the occasional 'as cool as a cuke.'

'As cool as a cucumber' remains by far the most frequently-used form, so much so that some writers look for alternatives. 'As cool as you please' is possible. Harold Pinter in his *Birthday Party*, has: 'Why is it that before you do a job you're all over the place, and when you're doing the job you're as cool as a whistle?'

As Dead as a Door-nail

In D.H.Lawrence's *Sons and Lovers* there is a scene where a man says: 'Tha'd drop down stiff, as dead as a door-knob.' 'Why is a door-knob deader than anything else?' asks his son. 'Eh, I dunno; that's what they say,' is the reply. The earlier expression, already in use in the 14th century, was 'as dead as a door-nail.' This was the phrase known to Shakespeare, put into the mouth of Jack Cade in *Henry the Sixth Part Two*. The rebel leader comes face to face with Alexander Iden, and tells him: 'I have eat no meat these five days, yet come thou and thy five men and if I do not leave you all as dead as a doornail, I pray God I may never eat grass more.' Dickens also made use of this form in *A Christmas Carol*, where it is said that 'old Marley was as dead as a door-nail.'

Door-knob or door-nail, the question posed by Paul in *Sons and Lovers* still applies. Perhaps any word beginning with d- which named an inanimate object would have served, since alliteration has always been important in such similes. Door-nails were more familiar to our ancestors than they are to us: they were the studded nails used to strengthen and decorate outer doors in former times. Some scholars believe that the specific door-nail referred to in the saying was the one used as a striker plate for the door-knocker. Since this was constantly being struck on the head it was thought to be deader than most things. The later change to 'door-knob' reflects the increasing rarity of studded doors and door-nails.

As Sure as Eggs is Eggs

This roundabout way of saying that something is certain has been used since the early 19th century, normally in its ungrammatical form. 'I shall come out bottom of the form as sure as eggs is eggs,' says a pessimistic schoolboy in *Tom Brown's Schooldays*, by Thomas Hughes. Earlier, in Dickens' *The Pickwick Papers*, Sam Weller quotes the phrase. Sam's understanding of grammatical rules is hazy, but there may be another reason for the 'is' that occurs where the 'are' should be. It has been suggested that the original statement was mathematical – 'as sure as X is X' – and that this was misunderstood by those to whom algebra was even more of a mystery than grammar.

Some writers spoil the fun of the phrase by 'correcting' it. Richard Barham, in his *Legend of Jarvis's Jetty*, writes: 'If you should jump from off the pier, you'd surely break your legs Perhaps your neck, then Bogey'd have you, sure as eggs are eggs'.

This saying could be extended to say that egg-like objects are not always eggs. This is of some concern to seaside golfers, whose balls are likely to disappear mysteriously from the fairway. In some cases they have been carried away by seagulls who have made an embarrassing mistake.

As the Crow Flies

Mary Lavin writes, in *A Memory*: 'It was just possible Emmy knew nothing of his existence. Yet he doubted it. As the crow flies he was less than two miles away.' This expression has been used since the beginning of the 19th century, obviously based on the idea that crows always use the shortest straight-line route between two points. As motorists constantly discover to their cost, twenty miles 'as the crow flies' can easily become thirty when they are obliged to follow the roads. Aircraft would seem to have an advantage in this respect, but even they follow air lanes which may take them out of their way.

The only question that arises with this useful phrase is: does a crow really use the shortest route? Technically, say the bird-experts, a 'crow' is a carrion-crow, which is not particularly renowned for its sense of direction. It is the rook which appears to fly in a straight line when it heads for home. Both the carrion-crow and the rook belong to the genus *Corvus*, as do the raven and jackdaw. Laymen are likely to refer to any of them, especially rooks, as 'crows,' but pedants – and bar-room smart alecs – might insist that this phrase should really be 'as the rook flies.'

Many country people are more concerned with the height at which rooks are flying, rather than their direction. It is commonly said that when they fly high in the evening, the next day's weather will be fine. Low-flying indicates that wind and rain are on the way.

At a Loose End

A Frenchman in Nancy Mitford's *Love in a Cold Climate* says: 'Now I am at a loose end with time on my hands. Do I not know wonderful English?' He can certainly claim to have a good knowledge of English phrases. 'Loose ends,' referring figuratively to anything left undecided or unfinished, have been talked about since the 16th century, the metaphor probably drawn from weaving or the making of nets. These are the loose ends we still commonly refer to, often implying that something needs to be done about them. Colin Wilson writes in *The Outsider*: 'The reader is left feeling oddly up in the air about it all. No happy finale, no dramatic tying up of loose ends.' John Buchan had said earlier in *Mr.Standfast*: 'By the middle of 1915 most enemy spies had been gathered in. But there remained loose ends, and somebody was very busy combining these ends into a net.'

Since the middle of the 19th century the singular 'loose end' has been used of a person who has nothing special to do at the moment. Such a person is, as it were, dangling in the wind, serving no particular purpose. Early speakers and writers, especially Americans, were likely to say that someone was 'on a loose end,' but by 1860 George Eliot was writing in *The Mill on the Floss*: 'When I've left off carrying my pack, and am at a loose end.' 'At a loose end' is now the usual form in this sense, while 'loose ends' are what need to be tidied. Henry Miller, in *Plexus*, seems to combine the two phrases and give them a new sense when he writes: 'He's at loose ends. Hates his work, loathes his wife, and

7

the kids bore him to death. All he thinks of now is tail. And boy, does he chase it!'

At Loggerheads

'Loggerhead' probably means 'with a log-like head,' a log being taken as the type of something thick and shapeless. Metaphorically, a person described in the 17th century as a loggerhead was stupid, a blockhead. 'You whoreson loggerhead,' says Berowne in Shakespeare's *Love's Labours Lost*, 'you were born to do me shame.' He is speaking to Costard, whose name in itself – derived from a large type of apple – would have indicated to an Elizabethan audience that he was thick-headed. At one time there were British pubs called 'The Three Loggerheads,' with signs that showed two wooden heads. The stranger who was unwise enough to ask at the bar what had happened to the third loggerhead soon discovered that the joke was on him.

As with most insulting terms, loggerhead could become almost affectionate when used between intimates. 'Let us retire, and lay our two loggerheads together,' says a speaker in Samuel Richardson's *Sir Charles Grandison*. In *The Antiquary* Sir Walter Scott writes: 'I have been following you in fear of finding your idle loggerhead knocked against one rock or other.' Sheridan's *A Trip to Scarborough* has Tom Fashion saying to his servant: 'Come, Lory, lay your loggerhead to mine, and let us contrive his destruction.' Lory replies: 'Here comes a head, sir, would contrive it better than both our loggerheads, if she would but join in the confederacy.'

Loggerhead came to have another association with pubs in the 18th century. It was the name given to a poker with a thick head which was used to mull drinks such as flip, a mixture of beer and spirits. Oliver Wendell Holmes remarks in *Elsie Venner* that 'three or four loggerheads (long irons clubbed at the end) were always lying in the fire in the cold season, waiting to be plunged into sputtering and foaming mugs of flip.' Larger versions of these pokers, with a ball or bulb at the end, were used outside the pub to liquefy tar and pitch.

Various large-headed animals, fish, moths and birds have earned the unofficial name of loggerhead. There was also at one time a game called loggerheads, a loggerhead in this context being 'a spherical mass of wood, with a long handle, and the game consisted of an attempt to hurl this towards a fixed stake, in such a manner as to leave it as near as possible.'

In ordinary English speech, 'loggerhead' has survived most strongly in the phrase 'at loggerheads,' used to describe people who disagree about something. In one of his *Times'* articles, Alan Coren mentioned a radio programme in which two people 'argued the fraught toss over the RAC's advice to family motorists in this jammed holiday season to avoid taking motorways to their destinations.' As he pulled into a motorway service area, wrote Coren, the two speakers were 'still at shrill loggerheads.' In the 18th century such a statement would probably have indicated that the people concerned had come to blows. Tobias Smollett writes in *Gil Blas*: 'I expected every moment to see them warm, and to go to loggerheads, the usual end of their dissertations.'

Other 18th century references make it clear that to be at loggerheads formerly meant to be engaged in a physically violent quarrel. The most likely origin of the phrase, therefore, is that the contenders made use of the loggerheads which mulled alcoholic drinks, or perhaps the wooden loggerheads of the game, to threaten or strike one another. At the very least, as F.D.Downey expressed it in *Our Lusty Forefathers*, when they were 'at loggerheads' they were metaphorically 'shaking flip-irons in each other's face.'

At One's Wits' End

`By three o'clock on a Saturday,' says a character in Wilfrid Sheed's *The Critic*, 'I'm at my wit's end.' He makes use of a phrase which has been serving a useful purpose since the 14th century. It occurs, for example, in William Langland's famous poem *Piers the Plowman*, a revised version of which dates from 1377. It is common in literary texts from then onwards. Coverdale's translation of the Old Testament, in 1535, rendered a passage in Isaiah 20 as: 'They shall be also at their wits end,' though a recent translation makes this: 'They shall be dismayed and confounded.' Randle Cotgrave, editor of a French-English dictionary in the early 17th century, equated the phrase with being 'bedunced,' which was another way of saying that one was utterly perplexed about what to do next.

Something that perplexes authors is whether to write 'wit's end' or 'wits' end.' Some simply avoid the issue and omit the apostrophe. Most modern dictionaries advocate 'wits' end,' but many writers clearly feel that a person it at the end of his wit, using the word in the sense of 'ability to think.' The alternative view is that if someone no longer has his wits about him, he is no longer able to use his mental faculties. Fanny Burney, in *Cecilia*, becomes thoroughly confused and speaks of two ladies who 'are quite, as one may say, at their wit's ends.' The implication is that they have only one wit between them.

Eric Partridge disapprovingly lists both wit's end and wits' end in his *Dictionary of Clichés*, but the phrase usefully sums up a despairing state of helplessness in the face of severe problems. The English are rather fond of the expression, as they reveal in an unusual way. In many a suburban street a house can be found that is named Witsend, Wytzend, or something similar. The householders seem to accept that life constantly poses problems, but suggest that sometimes the only thing to do is smile in the face of adversity.

B

Baker's Dozen

By tradition, a 'baker's dozen' is thirteen. The first known reference to the phrase occurs in John Cooke's play *Tu Quoque*, published in 1599. It is then found in later writers such as John Cleveland and Henry Fielding. One 19th century scholar explained the origin of the phrase by saying that market traders 'on purchasing their bread from the bakers, were privileged by law to receive thirteen batches for twelve, and this would seem to have been the extent of their profits.' A different explanation was offered by John Hotten in his *Dictionary of Modern Slang*, another 19th century publication. His entry reads: 'Baker's dozen, this consists of thirteen or fourteen; the surplus number, called the inbread, being thrown in for fear of incurring the penalty for short weight.'

Modern traders probably think of the baker's dozen principle in terms of good customer relations. The giving away of a something extra with a large purchase has certainly survived into modern times, even if 'baker's dozen' itself is less often heard. At one time it was commonly used in contexts where 'a dozen or so' might now be preferred. A report in the magazine *Field* in 1891, for instance, said that 'a baker's dozen struggled on to the finish, but if our deer had stood up for another mile or two, the number would have been still further reduced.' *Blackwood's Magazine* had earlier used the phrase in more dramatic fashion: '"The Pacha has put twelve ambassadors to death already." "The devil he has! and I'm sent here to make up the baker's dozen!"'

Beat About the Bush

To 'beat about the bush' is to approach a subject in a roundabout way and avoid getting to the point. The allusion is to bat-fowling, or bird-batting as it was also known. This involved hunting birds at night when they were roosting in bushes. The bushes would be disturbed by bats or clubs and the birds netted or stunned as they tried to escape. Henry Fielding describes the activity in *Joseph Andrews* for those of his readers who may be 'ignorant of it (as perhaps if thou hast never travelled beyond Kensington, Islington, Hackney, or the Borough, thou mayst be).' It is, he says, 'performed by holding a large clap-net before a lantern, and at the same time beating the bushes: for the birds, when they are disturbed from their places of rest, or roost, immediately make to the light, and so are enticed within the net'.

The beaters would no doubt disturb many bushes before lighting upon one that contained the birds. They would have been beating about the bush until they discovered the bush that really mattered. The fact that the person who beat the bush was not necessarily the one to catch the birds led to another metaphorical expression which has not survived. 'Beat the bush' at one time meant 'to do work for the benefit of others.' There is also a clear connection between bat-fowling and the proverbial 'a bird in the hand is worth two in the bush.'

For the bush-beaters it was a case of trial and error, but 'beat about the bush' often implies that a speaker is deliberately evading the issue. The phrase has been in frequent and constant use since the 15th century, and literary examples are found on all sides. 'Would you introduce her to your wife?' asks Lord Augustus, in Oscar Wilde's *Lady Windermere's Fan*. He continues: 'No use beating about the confounded bush. Would you do that?' 'There didn't seem much point in beating about the bush. In a way it was a relief to say it to someone', is in John Welcome's *Stop At Nothing*. Similar instances occur in Lucky Jim, by Kingsley Amis, A.J.Cronin's *Shannon's Way*, Zane Grey's *Betty Zane* and *The Penny Box*, by Alice Dwyer-Joyce. 'It's no good beating about the bush, Penn,' says the villainous character in the latter story. 'You know what I'm after.'

Bee in One's Bonnet, A

To have 'a bee in one's bonnet' is a relatively modern way of describing an idea that is something of an obsession. Joanna Trollope, in *The Rector's Wife*, has: 'He got a bee in his bonnet about her the minute he got here.' A character in Peter Cheyney's *Call it a Day* asks: 'What's the matter with you, Johnny? Have you got some other bee in your bonnet?' In the 16th century the equivalent expression was 'bees in the head' or 'bees in the brain.' 'Who so hath such bees as your master in his head?' asks someone in Nicholas Udall's *Ralph Roister Doister*, a comedy which had been staged by 1553. Other speakers at the time referred instead to 'maggots in the brains' or 'maggots in the head.' 'Are not you mad, my friend?' says a character in John Fletcher's *Women Pleased*. 'Have not you maggots in your brains?' Evidence that this version was well used is found in 18th century dictionaries. By that time a slang meaning of 'maggot' was 'a whimsical fellow, full of strange fancies.' Maggots rather than bees still prevailed in the early 19th century. Sir Walter Scott, in *The Antiquary*, has: 'For a' the nonsense maggots that ye whiles take into your head, ye are the maist wise and discreet o' a' our country gentles.'

To 'have a bee in one's bonnet' is first recorded in 1845, in the works of Thomas de Quincey, though it was probably used in speech well before that time. It has now completely displaced references to maggots. Some writers hint at how many bees are involved. 'Hindemith,' wrote a music critic in the 1930s, 'is young and impetuous enough to have one or two bees in his musical bonnet.' Sinclair Lewis, in *Babbitt*, feels no need to mention the bonnet at all: 'Ted's new bee,' says a character, 'is he'd like to be a movie actor.'

Lewis is right to assume that his readers will know what is meant by 'bee' in this context. To have 'a bee in one's bonnet' must be one of our best known expressions, conjuring up a rather more amusing and acceptable image than the earlier 'maggots in the brains.' In German, incidentally, one would speak about having a 'grass-hopper in the head.' Probably every language needs a phrase that refers to a whimsical obsession. As Ince says in C.P.Snow's *The Affair*: 'Everyone's got some bee in his bonnet.'

Before You Can Say Jack Robinson

'Before you can say Jack Robinson,' meaning 'in a short space of time,' seems to be disappearing from everyday speech, though it was still to be found in literary texts of the 1950s. 'If I tell him you're our man, you'll get a letter from him before you can say Jack Robinson' says an elderly character in C.P.Snow's *The Affair*. Nancy Mitford's *Noblesse Oblige* has: 'That picture will appear at

Christies before you can say Jack Robinson, though there is no necessity whatever for such a sale.'

The phrase was well-used for two hundred years on both sides of the Atlantic. The earliest printed record occurs in Fanny Burney's *Evelina* (1778), where Captain Mirvan announces that he is willing to 'lay ten pounds to a shilling' that he could throw the foppish Mr Lovel headfirst into a public bath. Another man present says: 'Done! I take your odds!' The captain then says: 'Why, then, 'fore George, I'd do it as soon as say Jack Robinson.' Mr Lovel manages to escape his ducking, and soon afterwards makes sneering remarks about the unintelligibility of the captain's 'sea-phrases.' This is the only hint we have that 'before you can say Jack Robinson' may originally have been a naval expression. Nothing else is known of its origin. Searches have failed to reveal any notable person called John or Jack Robinson who lived in the 18th century. In the absence of any suggestions worth treating seriously, one can only suppose that the name was chosen at random.

In America the phrase seems to have been associated with rural life rather than sailors. *The Oxford English Dictionary* quotes 'If I was to sick them on your old hoss yonder, they'd eat him up afore you could say Jack Robinson' from a text of 1845. *Log of a Cowboy*, published in 1903, has: 'Before you could say Jack Robinson our dogies were running in half a dozen different directions.' Mark Twain, in *The Adventures of Huckleberry Finn*, writes 'a magician could call up a lot of genies, and they would hash you up like nothing before you could say Jack Robinson.'

An alternative phrase with the same meaning is 'before you can say knife.' This first appears in 1893, in Rudyard Kipling's *Many*

Inventions: 'We'll pull you off before you can say knife.' It is possible that this began as a jokey replacement of 'jack knife' for 'Jack Robinson,' but it has taken on a life of its own. In *Both Ends Meet*, a play by A.Macrae, a character remarks: 'With a couple like that you'll be in a lawsuit before you can say knife.' Malcolm Muggeridge says in *Infernal Grove*: 'Like alcoholics after taking the cure – never another drop; well, just a taste perhaps, and then, before you could say knife, back on the meths.'

Other writers have found more personal ways of expressing the thought contained in this phrase. In *The Tempest*, when Prospero asks for some people to be brought before him, Shakespeare has Ariel say:

> Before you can say come, and go,
> And breathe twice, and cry so, so,
> Each one, tripping on his toe,
> Will be here with mop and mow.

A less poetic version in George Colman's *John Bull* is 'before you can say parsnips.' P.G.Wodehouse's Bertie Wooster says what one might expect, and in *Eggs, Beans and Crumpets* we find: 'You have simply got to get your atmosphere right. Chance your arm with the *mise en scéne*, and before you can say what ho, you've made some bloomer.'

Beg the Question

In his discussion of logic, Aristotle uses the phrase *petitio principii* when he refers to basing an argument on an assumption that is not yet proved. In the 16th century the Latin words were sometimes translated as 'petition of principle,' but this clearly meant little to English readers. Later writers treated the original phrase as if it were *petitio quaesiti* and made it a 'begging of the question.' This again is hardly satisfactory. 'Begging' is normally associated with asking for alms, and it is difficult to see how its meaning can be stretched to 'take for granted without good cause.'

The Latin word *petitio* is a noun derived from the verb *petere*. In different contexts this can variously mean 'aim at, attack, make for, seek, look for, ask, stand for office, lay claim to.' The last of these meanings would seem to be more appropriate in *petitio principii*, but 'beg the question' has been in use for centuries and is clearly here to stay.

Be in the Same Boat

What appears to be the first example of 'we're in the same boat,' with the figurative meaning of 'we're in the same position or circumstances,' occurs in *The Cricket on the Hearth*. This was published by Charles Dickens in 1845. Later, but not earlier, instances of the phrase in one form or another are easily found. For example, when the young hero of *Tom Brown's Schooldays*, by Thomas Hughes, protests that his face is muddy he is told: 'Oh, we're all in one boat for that matter.' Dickens almost certainly originated the phrase, though in his poem *The History of Judith*, published in 1584, Thomas Hudson has the lines:

> Have ye pain? so likewise pain have we;
> For in one boat we both imbarked be.

This is presumably the coincidental use of a metaphor, anticipating what was later to become familiar in a simpler form.

Some modern writers extend the boat reference in one way or another. An elderly man in E.F.Benson's *Miss Mapp* tells his friend:

'We're in the same boat: I don't say I like the boat, but there we are.' Anthony Trollope, in *Doctor Thorne*, makes a character say: 'We are in the same boat, and you shan't turn me overboard.' Other writers clearly have a rather large boat in mind when they use this phrase. In *A Travelling Woman*, John Wain writes: 'The admission only puts you in the same boat as everyone else.' 'We are all in the same boat, old and young,' says someone in E.M.Forster's *Howards End*. Sean O'Faolain, in *Lovers of the Lake*, has: 'We are all in the same old ferryboat here.'

A similar slang phrase that came into use at the end of the 18th century was to 'row in the same (or in one) boat.' This had the meaning 'to conspire unfairly with other people'. An author who made use of the saying in 1801 felt obliged to add in parentheses: 'pardon the vulgarity of the expression!' The phrase was later abbreviated to 'row in,' as in Peter Allingham's *Cheapjack*: 'I think these boys had better row in with us. We may as well stick together.' The *Daily Telegraph* had earlier reported in 1897: 'It's very likely the sellers and the general public concerned in auction sales are anything but satisfied with the results of sales by auction where a "knock-out" is arranged, and especially where the auctioneer "rows in" with the crew.'

Below Par

Most of us would think of 'below par' as a golfing expression, but it only became so at the beginning of the 20th century. It was then that an American golfer from Plainfield, New Jersey, devised the golf handicapping system, which is based on a par score. Earlier, 'below par' was a phrase mostly used in financial circles. Shares and bills were below par if they were being sold below their nominal value. In Swift's *Gulliver's Travels*, for instance, there is a reference to exchequer bills that 'would not circulate under nine per cent below par.'

The 'par' in this expression represents a Latin word meaning 'equal.' The same word led to French *pair*. A girl who is working as an *au pair* is supposedly on terms of equality with, on a par with, the members of the family.

By the 18th century, 'below par' was being used more generally of anything that was not up to its normal standard. A speech by a member of parliament, or an author's new novel, might be below par. The phrase was also commonly applied to a person's health, sometimes in the form 'under par.' 'Sir James is certainly under par,' writes Jane Austen, in *Lady Susan*. This usage continues, as indicated by Aldous Huxley in *Brave New World Revisited*: 'Whenever anyone felt depressed or below par, he would swallow a tablet or two of a chemical compound called Soma.'

`Below par' is thus a negative expression in many contexts, and slightly ambiguous when applied to golf. A golfer who has had a bad day may be entitled to say that his round was below par, even though his score was well above par. This development of widely different meanings in individual words and phrases is by no means unusual. One might almost say that it is par for the course.

Between the Devil and the Deep Blue Sea

The origin of this proverbial saying seems obvious enough. It sums up the position of someone who must choose between two courses of action, neither of which will lead to a satisfactory outcome. The 'blue' of the saying, incidentally, is a relatively modern addition: in earlier forms it is simply 'deep sea' or even 'dead sea.'

Laurence Urdang, in his *Picturesque Expressions*, suggests that the origin of the phrase is more complicated than it seems. 'Devil' was formerly a nautical term, referring to the seam in the hull of a ship which ran along the water line. Urdang therefore suggests that a sailor who was ordered to do repair work to the 'devil' was placed in a very perilous position. This may be so, but he did not have to make an impossible decision, as the saying has always implied. There is probably no need of such a fanciful explanation. For our ancestors, the thought of being cast into the arms of the devil as they imagined him was as unwelcome as the thought of drowning.

Beyond the Pale

The general relaxation of social conventions in recent years means that this phrase is now seldom heard. In former times, a man who was told that he was 'beyond the pale' had broken the unwritten rules of society. By behaving badly he had metaphorically stepped outside a boundary fence, marked by a 'pale' or stake. Alfred Jingle in *The Pickwick Papers*, a man who has little respect for decorum, is told by Mr Pickwick: 'I consider you a viper. I look upon you, sir, as a man who has placed himself beyond the pale of society, by his most audacious, disgraceful, and abominable public conduct.'

A minor variant of the expression is 'outside the pale.' Richmal Crompton, in *William Again*, has: 'He was a pariah, outside the pale, one of the "swanks" who lived in big houses and talked soft.' Ivy Compton-Burnett also prefers this form in *A House and its Head*: 'You have put yourself outside the pale of other men.'

Big If, A

A character in *Face To Face*, by Edward A.Rogers, says: 'If, and this is a big if, we have some product for you to throw in which they'll swallow.' Similarly, someone in *Proteus*, by Morris West, tells a colleague: 'I'm trying to spring Rodolfo Vallenilla from gaol in Argentina. If I can – and that's a big "if" – I've still got to get him out of the country.' This 'big if' is now commonly used and is an interesting phrase, not merely because it makes the point that the condition introduced is an important one which may not easily be met. The expression is a complex mixture of spoken and written language. When someone talks about a 'big if,' 'if' must be visualised as if printed in capital letters, for emphasis. This actually happens in *No Thoroughfare*, a work on which Charles Dickens and Wilkie Collins collaborated. It includes the passage: 'I have spoken with Mrs Goldstraw, both in his presence and in his absence, and if anybody is to be trusted (which is a very large IF), I think she is to be trusted to that extent.'

We also make this connection between speech and writing when we specify that a word we are using begins with a small or capital letter. Generally speaking, 'small letter' indicates a more general or less serious use of the word; 'capital letter' makes it specific. It is a way of distinguishing between 'conservative', say, and 'Conservative', 'catholic' and 'Catholic', 'liberal' and 'Liberal'. The examples that follow illustrate a further range of uses:

'When I say the truth about evil, I don't mean to give the word a capital E. I don't mean to speak as if I thought there was such a thing as Evil, a disembodied absolute capable of existing on its own.' (John Wain, *A Travelling Woman*.) 'At least he was fighting on the right side.' 'Do you mean right or Right?' (Mary Wesley,

The Camomile Lawn.) 'Oh, 'tis a fine little voluble tongue, mine host, that wins a widow.' 'No, 'tis a tongue with a great T, my boy, that wins a widow.' (Thomas Middleton, *A Trick to Catch the Old One*.) 'Kate had mentioned that her aunt was Passionate, uttering it as with a capital P.' (Henry James *The Wings of the Dove*.) 'You're not out of trouble but I'm just beginning to spell it with a small t.' (W. Garner, *Big enough Wreath*.)

Bird, The

To be 'given the big bird' was originally actors' slang. It compared the hissing noise made by an audience to the sound made by a flock of geese, and indeed was sometimes referred to as 'being goosed.' Hissing, as it happens, was not always a criticism of poor acting – in melodrama it could be a compliment on an actor's portrayal of a villain – but 'the big bird' seems always to have referred to genuine disapproval. The phrase lives on in actor's language, though the word 'big' has been dropped. Modern audiences also tend to boo rather than hiss, but they leave the actor in no doubt as to their feelings.

Outside the theatre, to give someone the bird took on the general meaning of 'be derisive or dismissive.' If your partner had 'given you the bird,' then he or she had probably ended the relationship. An employee could be given the bird by being sacked. As for expressing disapproval of someone in a general way, to give someone the bird in American slang now refers to an obscene gesture rather than a noise. It is the equivalent of 'the finger,' whereby the middle finger is held up while the others are folded down.

Bite the Bullet

`Bite the bullet' was a well-known phrase in the first half of the 20th century, but it is now seldom used. In Rudyard Kipling's *The Light that Failed*, one man says to another: 'Bite on the bullet, old man, and don't let them think you're afraid.' The expression derives from the practice of giving a wounded soldier a bullet to clench between his teeth in order to distract him from the pain he was feeling elsewhere. Metaphorically the phrase came to mean 'accept a difficult situation without showing emotion, put a brave face on things.' This was at a time when every Englishman was taught to keep a stiff upper lip and not betray his feelings.

The phrase is now rather old-fashioned, more likely to be found in literature than heard in conversation. Readers of the ever-popular P.G.Wodehouse, for instance, would find two examples of it in *The Inimitable Jeeves*. In chapter two occurs: 'Brace up and bite the bullet. I'm afraid I've bad news for you.' Chapter three has: 'The blighter's manner was so cold and unchummy that I bit the bullet and had a dash at being airy.' Not every writer seems to have understood the origin of the phrase. In *Miss Mapp*, E.F.Benson writes as if the bullet in the expression refers to the one that has caused the pain: 'She bit on the bullet of her omission from the dinner-party this evening, determining not to mind one atom about it.' This conjures up the strange image of a person biting on a bullet that is lodged in his or her body.

Bite the Dust

Thanks to its use by countless screen-writers, this graphic phrase suggests the Wild West, with white men defending themselves against the encircling Indians. A shot rings out and another redskin tumbles from his horse. It comes as a surprise to find Tobias Smollett using the expression in his novel *Gil Blas*, published in 1750: 'We made two of them bite the dust, and the others betake themselves to flight.' Smollett himself was simply varying the well-established phrase 'bite the ground,' used by poets of warriors who were killed in battle. In Dryden's translation of the *Aeneid*, for example, occurs: 'so many valiant heroes bite the ground.' Joseph Addison, in his play *Cato*, has a character say: 'I saw the hoary traitor grin in the pangs of death, and bite the ground.' Other poets who use this version of the phrase include Thomas Gray and Lord Byron.

In modern times we are unlikely to use 'bite the dust' to refer to someone's death. The expression is used figuratively of humiliating defeat or failure. Someone's pet project may 'bite the dust' if it fails to materialise. A business may 'bite the dust' by going bankrupt. Confusingly, the editors of Collins *Cobuild English Dictionary* choose to illustrate the phrase with the sentence: 'My vacuum cleaner's finally bitten the dust,' though dust-biting could be regarded as a vacuum cleaner's normal function.

Blessing in Disguise

In *The Importance of Being Earnest*, the Reverend Chasuble says to Jack: 'I would merely beg you not to be too much bowed down by grief. What seem to us bitter trials are often blessings in disguise.' Oscar Wilde was obviously right to give this speech to a clergyman. In 1907, a few years after Wilde's play was first staged, the *Westminster Gazette* commented acidly: 'Religion would gain greatly if the clergy would make a more sparing use of the blessing-in-disguise argument.'

As one might expect, it was a Church of England clergyman who first used the phrase 'blessing in disguise.' James Hervey, rector of Weston Favell, Northamptonshire, was the author of *Meditations and Contemplations*, as well as many other religious works. They are described in *Everyman's Dictionary of Literary Biography* as 'characterized by overwrought sentiment, and overloaded with florid ornament.' 'Blessing in disguise' was one of Hervey's 'ornaments.' In his *Reflections on a Flower Garden* (1746) he included a hymn *'Since All the Downward Tracts of Time.'* It contained the words: 'E'en crosses from his sov'reign hand are blessings in disguise.'

This useful way of explaining away a misfortune was seized upon by Hervey's clerical colleagues. It remains an essential part of religious language, though it is also well used in general situations where an unexpected benefit arises from what at first appears to be a calamity. 'I think I should go mad in prison,' says a character in Eric Linklater's *Poet's Pub*. 'Didn't it embitter you against everything?' 'It was a blessing in disguise' is the reply.

Hervey could have found the inspiration for his phrase in the works of earlier poets. George Villiers, duke of Buckingham, had written:

> Nor is it wit that makes the lawyer prize
> His dangled gown: 'tis knavery in disguise.

Jacob Tonson, editor of *Poetical Miscellanies*, had quoted in 1709 as a 'celebrated poetical beauty': 'praise undeserv'd is scandal in disguise.' No doubt Hervey in his turn has inspired others. A few years after his 'blessings in disguise' had appeared, Dr Johnson wrote in the *Rambler*: 'None can tell whether the good that he pursues is not evil in disguise.'

Blow One's Own Trumpet

A flourish of trumpets has long been used to draw attention to an important person or announcement. It has always been considered distasteful, however, for someone to draw attention to himself in a noisy way. The New Testament, Matthew 6.2, has: 'When you give alms, sound no trumpet before you, as the hypocrites do in the synagogues and in the streets, that they may be praised by men.' In other words, do not blow your own trumpet. Not everyone agrees with this philosophy. 'I will sound the trumpet of mine owne merites,' said a 16th century author, while W. S. Gilbert, in *Ruddigore*, has: 'You must stir it and stump it, And blow your own trumpet.'

The more conventional view appears in *Jennings and Darbishire*, by Anthony Buckeridge: 'I vote we're not allowed to vote for ourselves because my father says it's swanking to blow your own trumpet.' When a boy does this in George Douglas's *The House With The Green Shutters*, the author remarks that 'being boys, they could not prick his conceit with a quick rejoinder. It is only grown-ups who can be ironical; physical violence is the boy's repartee.'

In *Australia* (1873), Trollope noted that 'in the colonies, when a gentleman sounds his own trumpet he "blows".' Mrs. Praed published her *Australian Life* a few years later and confirmed the usage: 'He was famous for "blowing," in Australian parlance, of his exploits.'

Blow One's Stack

To 'blow one's stack,' meaning 'to become angrily excited,' came into use as an American slang term from the 1940s onwards. 'Last night, says a character in Budd Schulberg's *Waterfront*, 'you were blowing your stack because you believe something that too many of us only go through the motions of.' A journalist in the 1950s commented that 'when Andrew Carnegie received the minutes and read them he blew his stack a mile high.' An expression of similar meaning is 'blow one's top.' Robert L. Chapman, in his *Dictionary of American Slang*, says that other variants include 'blow one's topper' and 'blow one's cork.'

Several of these expressions compare an angry person who loses control of himself to the sudden eruption of a volcano or oil well. The last example conjures up an image of champagne bursting out of the bottle, the person concerned having previously 'bottled himself up.' The same idea of releasing internal pressure in an emotional outburst makes us talk about people 'letting off steam,' or say that an angry person has 'steam coming out of his ears.'

These are simply newish ways of expressing old ideas. In former times people who were 'unable to contain themselves' were said to 'vent' or 'give vent to' their emotions. They might vent their spite or malice on someone, or vent their spleen, since for reasons best known to themselves, our ancestors believed that the spleen was the seat of violent passions. We know better than that, but we continue to think of ourselves as gas-filled containers, likely to explode.

Blue Murder

We probably owe the phrase 'blue murder' to an English misunderstanding of *morbleu*, a French oath dating from at least the 17th century. *Morbleu* itself was formerly used in Cornwall, where the phrase 'sing out morbleu' is recorded in the 19th century. The Cornish expression referred to the noise a boy might make when being flogged. To cry, shout or scream 'blue murder' has a similar meaning.

Morbleu appears to mean 'blue death,' but the bleu was merely a euphemistic substitution for *Dieu*. The original meaning of the oath was therefore 'death of God.' Apart from the fact that *Dieu* and *bleu* sound vaguely similar in French, there is no special association between blueness and death, though perhaps those who translated *morbleu* as 'blue murder' were influenced by the tale of Bluebeard. They managed, at all events, to create a truly colourful phrase which continues to appeal to English-speakers.

Typical usage is seen in Angus Wilson's *Anglo-Saxon Attitudes*: 'A few of his utterances are liable to make our union chaps cry blue murder.' Bernard Malamud, in *The Natural*, has: 'Max swore blue bloody murder as Roy howled with laughter.' 'He and Daddy have been yelling blue murder' occurs in *Surfeit of Lampreys*, by Ngaio Marsh. In *Maggie*, by Lena Kennedy, it is a baby who starts 'to scream blue murder.' George Bernard Shaw did not mean to be complimentary when he wrote in a review of Stanford's Irish Symphony that 'what it does end in is blue murder.'

Blue-stocking

In her novel *Giant*, Edna Ferber writes: 'the second sister was, as the term went, a blue-stocking. She was forever reading books, but not the sort of books which other Southern young women consumed like bonbons as they lay in the well-worn hammock under the trees. Leslie Lynnton had opinions of her own, she conversed and even argued with her distinguished father and his friends on matters political, sociological, medical and literary just as if she were a man.'

This is a good explanation of the modern meaning of 'blue-stocking,' a term that was much used in the days when intelligent women were regarded as unusual. The description arose in London around 1750, when a Mrs Montague, Mrs Vesey and Mrs Ord became bored with the card games which were then considered to be the most suitable feminine recreation at evening parties. These ladies preferred intelligent conversation, and chose male and female guests who shared their unconventional views. Some of the men who attended these gatherings cared as little for conventional ideas about dress. Benjamin Stillingfleet, for example, habitually wore grey or blue worsted stockings instead of the black silk stockings considered essential for gentlemen. This caused Admiral Boscawen to make a derisive remark about 'the Blue Stocking Society.' The term was taken up; women who relished intelligent conversation became known as blue stockingers or blue stocking ladies. By the end of the 18th century, when the origin of the term had been largely forgotten, the women became blue-stockings, or blues.

In a curious development, 'blue-stocking' was then translated into French as *bas-bleu* and used as if it had been borrowed from that source by the English. 'The aristocratic *bas-bleus*,' said the Times newspaper in 1842, 'are at present very much devoted to the abolition of slavery.' In the original version of *Don Juan*, Byron comments rather obscurely:

> By measuring the intensity of blue;
> I'll back a London *bas* against Peru.

This comes in a passage where Byron says 'heaven knows why' the stockings of 'learned ladies' are blue. He adds:

> I knew one woman of that purple school,
> The loveliest, chastest, best, but – quite a fool.'

This is a typical male comment of the time. Early references to blue-stockings by male writers were almost invariably sneering. 'I have an utter aversion to blue-stockings,' wrote William Hazlitt, in his *Table-talk*. De Quincey talked of 'a blue-stocking loquacity.' *Blackwood's Magazine* laughed at 'the tawdry blue-stockingship of a young lady from the manufacturing district.' Dickens was equally unimpressed. In his *American Notes* he says: 'blue ladies there are, in Boston; but like philosophers of that colour and sex in most other latitudes, they rather desire to be thought superior than to be so.' Other faults of scholarly women were proclaimed. The *Edinburgh Review* spoke of 'a blue-stocking contempt for household cares,' while an anonymous writer in 1838 punned that 'ladies who are very blue are apt to be rather green.' This was meant to be a comment on social immaturity, though in a different interpretation it is something that might be said today. Most intelligent women are indeed 'green,' in that they care a great deal about the environment.

Bone up on Something

In Budd Schulberg's *Waterfront* we are told that 'Runty had boned up on his Rules of Order.' Mordecai Richler's *The Incomparable Atuk* has the similar: 'Manley had decided to bone up on Marx before joining the C.P. under a cover-name.' 'Bone up on' a subject also occurs in British sources, such as the *Daily Telegraph*. The newspaper reported in 1968 that 'Robert Powell wastes no opportunity to bone up on his hobby – Romanesque architecture.'

This expression began as an American student joke. The Bohn publishing company used to publish the *Bohn Classical Library*, designed to help students get through their examinations. A student who was 'Bohning' was indulging in a brief, intensive period of swotting. Bohn, corrupted into 'bone' because of its sound, was the family name of Henry George Bohn, the publishing company's founder, born in London in 1796 of German parents. It would be interesting to know whether he ever discovered that a form of his name had become part of American slang, both as 'bone' for 'a diligent student,' and 'bone up on' something for 'learn the facts about' a subject.

Build Castles in the Air

In his *Mosses from an Old Manse*, Nathaniel Hawthorne writes: 'She endowed him with an unreckonable amount of wealth. It consisted of half a million acres of vineyard at the North Pole, and of a castle in the air, and a chateau in Spain.' The 'chateau in Spain' is a partial translation of the French expression, *batîr des châteaux en Espagne* 'build castles in Spain' which suggested our 'castles in the air.' Some early French writers referred to building castles in Asia or Albania, proving that 'Spain' had no special significance. To the French of the 14th century it was an example of an alien, Moorish country where a Christian would be foolish to build anything at all. To build a castle in Spain was therefore to 'waste one's time thinking about an impractical plan.'

'Build castles in Spain' was used in this sense by some English writers in the 16th century; others used the phrase 'castles in the sky (or skies).' It was Sir Thomas North, in his translation (1580) of Plutarch's *Lives*, who wrote: 'They built castles in the air, and thought to do great wonders.' North's book was extensively read, by Shakespeare amongst others, and it is surprising that 'castles in the air' does not occur in the plays. Examples are easily found in other 17th century works, one of which comments that such castles are built with whims and dreams.

There appear to be as many day-dreamers today as there were in the 17th century, since this phrase remains in constant use. 'As a girl she built the usual castles in the air; but all her girlish hopes and aspirations have long been dead' writes Henry Lawson, in *The Drover's Wife*. Samuel Butler, in *The Way of all Flesh*, links such castle-building with the consumption of alcohol rather than being young: 'Thus do we build castles in the air when flushed with wine.' The phrase is also well enough known to allow the merest allusion. In *The Old Curiosity Shop*, for instance, Dickens remarks that 'night is kinder than day, which too often destroys an air-built castle at the moment of its completion, without the smallest ceremony or remorse.' In a letter to Swift, John Gay once remarked: 'I am every day building villakins and have given over that of castles.'

Bury One's Head in the Sand

In his short story, *Rawdon's Roof*, D.H.Lawrence refers to the owner of a 'pretty posterior burying her face in the bedclothes, to be invisible, like the ostrich in the sand.' Normally, references to this supposed habit of the ostrich are metaphorical. When Ruth Rendell, in *Talking To Strange Men*, says 'You must have been living with your heads buried in sand,' she means that the people concerned have been hoping that a problem would go away or solve itself if they ignored it.

Experts tell us that ostriches do not actually bury their heads in sand in times of danger, as if they believe that being unable to see what is threatening them will make them safe. If they did behave in such a foolish way they would suffocate. All they do is lie on the ground with their necks stretched out, in a sensible effort to avoid detection. To a human observer at a distance it probably seems as if they have buried their heads, hence the common belief which leads to the phrase.

The latter is so well established that allusions to it are possible in various ways. In *The Limits of Love*, for example, by Frederic Raphael, there is a reference to 'head in the sand Utopianism.' Elsewhere in the novel the author has: 'The trouble is, most people think they can be ostriches until the last minute.' Jeremy Brooks, in *Henry's War*, writes: 'It may prise a few ostrich heads out of the sand.' John Sherwood, in *The Half Hunter*, has: 'Why does Stella try to keep it from her? That sort of ostrich policy always ends in disaster.'

The phrase can be applied to a whole nation. 'America cannot be an ostrich with its head in the sand,' proclaimed Woodrow Wilson in 1916. The *Sheffield Star* matched this in 1976 by saying: 'The people of England should not bury their heads in the sand and say it can't happen here.' These are down-to-earth statements, but a great poet can make even a phrase that borders on cliché into something special. Louis MacNeice once asked 'whether it would not be better to hide one's head in the warm sand of sleep.'

Busman's Holiday

In Ruth Rendell's novel *To Fear a Painted Devil*, a doctor who is at a party meets one of his patients. The man begins a conversation by saying: 'I've been meaning to ask you for ages. It's about a lump I've got under my arm.' The doctor, says Ruth Rendell, 'prepares for a busman's holiday.' There is a similar example in Muriel Spark's *The Fancy*, where two men meet at a rabbit show. 'Are you judging today?' asks one of them. The other shakes his head. 'Busman's holiday,' he comments. He is doing in his spare time what he normally does professionally.

This phrase first appeared in a British magazine at the end of the 19th century. Its use seems to have spread to America, since the *Observer* reported in 1927 that 'the U.S.A. Secretary for War said, "No, I did not go to see the military manoeuvres. Busmen's holidays do not give me any delight".'

The origin of the phrase is uncertain. As far as its meaning is concerned, it could just as easily be 'busyman's' or 'businessman's holiday.' It has been suggested, however, that in the days when buses were still horse-drawn, at least one London driver used to ride his own bus on his day off to make sure that his horses were not ill-treated. If a story about such a conscientious busman was circulating in the 1890s, it has not been traced. A simpler explanation is that busmen did indeed become bus-passengers when on holiday, but only because they needed, like everyone else, to get from one place to another.

A colloquial phrase that was in circulation before 'busman's holiday' was 'blind man's holiday.' From the 16th century onwards this referred to dusk, the twilight hour when it was too dark to read or work but was not yet dark enough for candles to be lit. The phrase describing this natural break in the working day became obsolete when electric lighting arrived. If the horse-loving busman ever existed, one wonders what he did in his free time once the motor-bus had come on the scene.

By the Skin of One's Teeth

This expression is always used to talk about a narrow escape from disaster. In *Down Among the Women*, Fay Weldon writes: 'He's only just kept his mother away from this party by the skin of his teeth.' Since teeth have no skin, the implication is that the escape has been an especially narrow one.

The oddity of the phrase has no doubt helped to keep it in common use for centuries, but it also had an impeccable source. There is little about it to suggest biblical language, yet it occurs at Job 19:20 in the Old Testament. It is a literal translation from Hebrew when Job, who is saying that he has been near to death, adds: 'I am escaped with the skin of my teeth.' It is easy to imagine the impact this image had on early church congregations. It became part of everyday speech in the 17th century and is still well used.

Othello escaped from many situations by the skin of his teeth, but he used a different expression when telling Desdemona of his adventures. Shakespeare tells us that he

> spake of most disastrous chances,
> Of moving accidents by flood and field;
> Of hair-breadth scapes i' th' imminent deadly breach.

A hair-breadth, or hair's-breadth, according to one early writer, was the fortieth part of an inch.

Call a Spade a Spade

In Oscar Wilde's *The Picture of Dorian Gray*, Lord Henry remarks that he hates 'vulgar realism in literature.' The man who calls a spade a spade, he adds, 'should be compelled to use one. It is the only thing he is fit for.' Robert Burton makes it clear in his *Anatomy of Melancholy* that he disagrees: 'I am a loose, plain, rude writer, I call a spade a spade.' This argument about the merits or otherwise of speaking plainly has continued since the 16th century, when 'call a spade a spade' appeared in Nicholas Udall's translation of Erasmus's Latin. Erasmus had himself translated the Greek of Plutarch, making a mistake as he did so. Where Plutarch had used a word meaning 'bowl, trough, boat' in a phrase which should have become something like 'to call a boat a boat,' Erasmus had understood it as a Greek word derived ultimately from 'to dig.' By following the Latin of Erasmus, Udall invented a new English idiom.

Modern writers make frequent use of 'call a spade a spade,' and have recorded the more emphatic form that is now sometimes heard. Mary Webb usefully glosses the original expression in *Gone To Earth*: 'You call a spade a spade, Mr Reddin; you are not, as our dear Browning has it, mealy mouthed.' This is after Reddin has announced that the woman living with him is his 'keep', his 'kept woman' rather than his wife. The alternative version of the phrase occurs in Nigel Balchin's *Mine Own Executioner*: 'Sometimes I get so fed up with all the mumbo-jumbo and abracadabra and making of holy mysteries about simple things that I like to call a spade a shovel.' This becomes slightly stronger in W.Somerset Maugham's short story *Appearance and Reality*, where the writings of Rabelais are described as 'the ribaldry that likes to call a spade something more than a bloody shovel.' Similarly Ruth Rendell, in *Talking To Strange Men*, has: 'That was coming out into the open, Charles thought. That was what he had once heard his father say wasn't calling a spade a spade but a bloody shovel.'

There is an interesting derivative of the phrase in Derek Jewell's *Come In No.1 Your Time Is Up*. A woman is said to be 'a believer in spade-calling, proclaiming to the world that she was no respecter of persons.' As for Maurice Edelman, in *The Minister*, the slang meaning of 'spade' – a black person – leads to a punning speech which is meant to offend those who hear it: 'M'landa – he's the nigger in the woodpile. You will observe, sir, that my views on Africa are not shrouded by any sophisticated considerations. I don't feel any great compulsion to call the black members of our Empire our coloured brothers. I want to make it clear that when I speak of M'Landa and his ilk, I believe in calling a spade a Spade.'

It is curious that this slang use of 'spade,' which alludes to the playing-card suit and the phrase as *black as the ace of spades*, is the result of another mis-translation. The original word was Spanish *espada*. It is obvious why this became 'spade,' but the Spanish word actually means 'sword.'

Catch Someone Red-handed

In the 16th century a Scottish legal term referred to being 'taken red-hand.' The meaning was the same as 'caught red-handed,' apprehended while committing a crime or with the evidence of the crime still on one's person. Needless to say, the phrase had originally been suggested by a victim's blood on the hand of a murderer, but it had quickly acquired the meaning within the law of 'clear evidence of guilt,' applied to any crime. 'If he be not taken red-hand,' wrote an early authority on Scottish legal matters, 'the sheriff cannot proceed against him.' A suspected criminal who was not 'taken red-hand' was said to be 'without red-hand.'

It seems to have been Sir Walter Scott, in *Ivanhoe*, who first used the form 'red-handed' and made the term known to a wide public. Scott referred in Scottish style to a man being *taken* red-handed, but the 19th century English writers who followed him generally preferred *caught* red-handed. Once again the phrase could be used in cases where a criminal's hands were not literally red with blood. 'A notorious thief was caught red-handed in the act of breaking open a lock' said a typical report of the time.

E.F.Benson had fun with the phrase in *Miss Mapp*, where the heroine suspects that her servants are using the telephone to make their own calls. 'Miss Mapp paused by the door to let any of these delinquents get deep in conversation with her friend: a soft and stealthy advance towards the room would then enable her to catch one of them red-mouthed.'

Cat's Pyjamas, The

`We really have to watch him with the girls,' says a character in John Stroud's *On the Loose*. 'The trouble is they all think he's the cat's pyjamas.' Sinclair Lewis, in *Martin Arrowsmith*, has 'This kid used to think Pa Gottlieb was the cat's pyjamas.' This curious phrase came into being in the 1920's, when the idle rich were amusing themselves by inventing slang expressions based on animals. Apart from 'cat's pyjamas,' 'cat's whiskers' and 'bee's knees' have survived, all in the sense of 'wonderful, excellent.' According to a report in the *Times* (1958), Lord Montgomery used to believe 'that to label anything the "cat's whiskers" was to confer on it the highest honour, and the "bee's knees" was not far behind it as a compliment.'

`Cat's whiskers' seems to have some justification, since cats often show considerable pride in them. The rhyme of 'bee's knees' obviously appealed, but 'cat's pyjamas' came into being for a different reason. Pyjamas (usually spelt 'pajamas' in American English) were introduced to the West as night-wear at the beginning of the 20th century. Earlier the word applied only to the loose trousers worn by both sexes in some Asian countries. By 1910 fashionable Americans were throwing 'pajama parties,' the garments still having novelty value. Perhaps there were even some cat-owners who dressed their pets in night-wear. Even then, it is difficult to understand the thinking behind this expression. It might make more sense if it referred to a 'cat in pyjamas.'

Cheesed Off

Hunt and Pringle, in their *Service Slang* (1943), tell us that 'cheesed off' means 'more than brassed off; yet not entirely browned off.' This explanation would probably baffle American readers, to whom these phrases are unfamiliar. All three expressions seem to have come into being during World War Two, and were originally thought of as military slang. 'Cheesed off' remains in colloquial use to some extent and is found in the works of British authors. In

The Taste of Too Much, for instance, by Clifford Hanley, a woman says: 'You said half past six. I got cheesed off waiting.' In *Tropic of Ruislip*, by Leslie Thomas, a character says: 'I get cheesed off with the game.' At one time this expression was common enough to be used in an abbreviated form. 'I'm cheesed' meant that the speaker was bored, irritated or depressed.

`Cheesed off' is likely to have been inspired by too much cheese on wartime military menus, which made them very boring. 'Brassed off' was certainly a reference to brass-cleaning duties, which most servicemen regarded as an unnecessarily time-wasting occupation. 'Browned off' may have referred to an older saying, to be 'in a brown study,' which meant to be in a state of gloomy distraction. The colour brown has long been associated in a general way with gloom.

Chip off the Old Block

What many would consider to be the 'normal' use of this expression is shown in *Seven Tales and Alexander*, by H.E.Bates: 'He's my son, and he's a chip off the old block, and I'm proud of him.' Thomas Wolfe's *Look Homeward, Angel* has a mother say: 'He's a chip off the old block. His father over again.' 'Chip off the old block,' however, is often applied to relations other than father and son. Somerset Maugham, in *Creatures of Circumstance*, writes: 'His heir was a nephew – not a bad boy, but not a chip off the old block, no, sir, far from it.' In *George Beneath A Paper Moon*, by Nina Bawden, a mother is speaking about her daughter when she says: 'Chip off the old block, you know. Took me right back, hearing her rant on like that. I had much the same thing from Claire when she wanted to marry Sam.' Another permutation is shown in Fay

Weldon's *Leader of the Band,* where a father describes his daughter as a 'chip off the old block.' The reference in all cases is to similarities in character and behaviour between one generation and the next. The metaphor is self-explanatory; a piece of wood chipped from a block shares its basic characteristics.

Edmund Burke is frequently said to have been the originator of this phrase, having famously applied it in the House of Commons to Pitt the Younger. By that time, however, the expression had been in circulation for well over a century. It was probably coined by Bishop Robert Sanderson, one of whose sermons asked: 'Am not I a child of the same Adam, a vessel of the same clay, a chip of the same block, with him?' Fifteen years later, in 1642, John Milton was writing: 'How well dost thou now appear to be a chip of the old block.' 'Of' rather than 'off' the old block remained the standard form until the 19th century.

After confidently crediting Burke with this phrase, Edwin Radford, in *Crowther's Encyclopaedia of Phrases and Origins*, adds: 'It is, of course, associated with the "family tree".' We may make such an association today, but is was not in the minds of those who first spoke of 'chips of old blocks.' The notion of a 'family tree' appears only at the beginning of the 19th century, nearly two hundred years after Bishop Sanderson first used the chip and block metaphor.

Cloud-Cuckoo-Land

'Cloud-Cuckoo-Land' is an ideal, imaginary place, a dream land where one builds castles in the air. The phrase translates Greek *Nephelococcygia*, the name of an imaginary town in Aristophanes' comedy *The Birds*. The town is supposedly built in the air by the birds to help separate the gods from men. In English the phrase is normally used of someone who is perhaps day-dreaming, or not thinking realistically. 'Obviously you were away off in Cloud-Cuckoo-Land' says a teacher to a young girl, in *The Diviners*, by Margaret Laurence.

In *Blimey!* David Goddard uses the phrase to mean an unreal world. He writes: 'King's Road beckons the well-heeled traveller into a cloud-cuckoo-land of high-priced tat and gear.' In former times 'cloud-cuckoo-town,' which is nearer to Aristophanes' intention, was sometimes preferred. An article in an English newspaper (1903) talked of 'our new school of economists (sort of cloud-cuckoo-town).'

Clutch at Straws

We clutch at straws when, in sheer desperation, we put our hopes in something that is very unlikely to succeed. 'You know how it is at times like this,' says a character in John Le Carré's *The Honourable Schoolboy*: 'Clutching at straws, listening to the wind.' He is referring to an investigation where evidence will be almost impossible to find. Robert Shaw, in *The Hiding Place*, has: 'Towards evening a new solution to his problems occurred to him – he was clutching at straws now: could he find another guardian while he was away?' The hero of George MacDonald Fraser's *Flashman* says: 'I didn't understand, then, how the news of Kabul and Gandamack would make England shudder, and how that vastly conceited and indignant public would clutch at any straw that might heal their national pride.'

To 'clutch at straws' is a shortened and perhaps mis-heard version of a 17th century proverb, quoted by Samuel Richardson in *Clarissa*: 'A drowning man will catch at a straw.' Few of the writers who followed Richardson bothered to mention the 'drowning man.' By 1823 Sir Walter Scott was saying, in *Quentin Durward*, that 'love, like despair, catches at straws.' It is also probable that in ordinary speech 'clutch' rather 'catch at straws' had become the usual form. That is certainly how the expression was known to careful users of the language such as Elizabeth Gaskell and Thomas Carlyle. Minor variants of the phrase, such as 'grasp at straws,' are also occasionally found. The anonymous writer of an official document in 1793 was determined to go his own way. He referred to the 'impulsion from which a drowning man catches at a twig.'

Cock-and-bull Story, A

A 'cock-and-bull story' is a foolish tale that insults our intelligence, often offered as an excuse. It derives ultimately from the French expression *coq à l'âne* 'cock to the donkey,' which came into English in the 17th century as 'cockalane.' This was used of a story or conversation which passed illogically from one subject to another. Sir George Etherege gives an example in his play *The Man of Mode*, performed in 1676: 'What a cockalane is this? I talk of women, and thou answerest tennis?'

English writers soon changed 'cockalane' into 'cock-and-bull,' which was at first used of any long and pointless account – a kind of shaggy-dog story without even a feeble punch-line. The modern meaning of 'cock-and-bull story,' an incredible tale which is supposedly true, is recorded from the end of the 18th century. Charles Dickens, in *The Pickwick Papers*, has: 'He was bribed by that scoundrel Jingle, to put me on a wrong scent, by telling a cock-and-bull story of my sister and your friend Tupman.' The phrase is still well used, as more recent literary sources indicate. 'You don't go for that cock-and-bull story about their colonel having been kidnapped by Russian agents?' says a character in Mordecai Richler's *The Incomparable Atuk*. Frank Yerby, in *A Woman Called Fancy*, writes: 'I'm going to invite them in – let them search the place. Give them a cock and bull story about sending the boy away with one of the servants.'

Eric Delderfield, in his *Introduction to Inn Signs*, relates that stage-coach passengers who broke their journey at the 'Cock' and 'Bull' inns, both at Stony Stratford in Buckinghamshire, 'exchanged jokes and stories, thus giving rise to the expression 'cock-and-bull stories.' This is nonsense of course, but is at least an excellent example of a cock-and-bull story.

Cold Turkey

This American phrase is mainly used in the context of drug or alcohol abuse. Someone who has managed to stop smoking, for instance, might say that he 'kicked his habit cold turkey.' He would mean that he did not try to cure himself by gradually reducing the number of cigarettes smoked in a day, or resorting to aids such as nicotine substitutes. He simply refused to smoke another cigarette. Use of the word 'simply' will be queried, perhaps, by anyone who has suffered acute withdrawal symptoms when trying to deal with an addiction. A cold turkey cure is neither easy or pleasant.

Most American commentators link the phrase to the kind of unprepared meal that is based on left-overs from a feast. Like a cold turkey cure, it involves little or no preparation. A far more fanciful theory links the appearance of a drug addict's skin as he experiences withdrawal, with the flesh of a cold plucked turkey. The 'left-overs' theory is far more likely.

Come a Cropper

'Come a cropper' was originally a slang term used of a hunter who was thrown head first from his horse. The earlier and more formal version of the expression probably referred to being pitched 'neck and crop,' or 'completely.' The latter phrase was often used of a forcible removal, as when drunks were thrown out of a public house. In *Clayhanger*, Arnold Bennett has: 'Who's master here? D'ye think as I can't turn ye all out of it neck and crop, if I've a mind?' The fact that 'crop' is coupled with 'neck' in this saying leads some scholars to argue that 'crop' refers to the 'craw' of a bird. It is more likely to allude to the 'head,' since the earliest meaning of 'crop' was the top of a herb.

In modern times, to 'come a cropper' is used metaphorically more often than literally. Writers seem to be especially fond of applying it to relationships between men and women, perhaps because of the original 'hunting' connotations. In *The Way We live Now*, Anthony Trollope writes: 'He would be coming a cropper rather, were he to marry Melmotte's daughter for her money, and then find that she had got none.' A character in Terence Rattigan's *Who is Sylvia?* says: 'We bachelors welcome competition from married men. We so much enjoy watching them come the inevitable cropper.' Mary McCarthy makes a man say, in *The Group*: 'That's where I come a cropper with women. Women expect an affair to get better and better, and if it doesn't, they think it's getting worse.'

Cook Someone's Goose

James Robertson Planché's play *The Golden Fleece* was first performed in 1845. It contained the line: 'To save my bacon I must cook his goose!' This is the first instance of 'cook someone's goose' known to the *Oxford English Dictionary*, but from 1850 onwards the phrase was appearing on all sides in literary sources. There is no way of knowing how long the phrase had been used in popular speech before being recorded in print, but it is unlikely to have been a great length of time. The phrase is striking enough to appeal to a wide range of writers, and it was probably seized upon fairly quickly.

In *A Hog on Ice*, the American scholar Charles Earle Funk mentions a *Handbook of Literary Curiosities* by somebody called Walsh. He says that Walsh's book contains an anecdote about Eric XIV of Sweden, who came 'to a towne of his enemyes with very little company.' The townspeople, thinking that they had nothing to fear from such a small number of men, hung a goose on the town walls and invited Eric's army to shoot at it. Before nightfall, however, the invaders had set the town's strongholds on fire and the townspeople realised that they must treat the situation more seriously. 'They demanded of Eric what his intent was, to whom he replyed, "to cook your goose".'

This story may be satisfying in itself, but it creates many problems. Internal evidence suggests that the anonymous author was writing in the 17th century, but no one has been able to trace the passage that Walsh claims to be quoting. Then again, it concerns a Swedish king who came to the throne in 1560, but there has never been a phrase in Swedish which would translate literally as 'cook someone's goose.' Nor is there any obvious reason why the saying of a 16th century Swedish king, reported by a 17th century English writer, should suddenly burst upon the scene in 19th century England. There is evidence, on the other hand, that by the early 19th century unsuccessful actors were being 'goosed,' a reference to the hissing noise made by audiences. 'Cook someone's goose' may have extended this idea of making it impossible for someone to continue with whatever he was doing.

Modern speakers and writers may not know the origin of this phrase, but they use it a great deal. 'That almost cooked my goose for good' occurs in *Flashman*, by George MacDonald Fraser. T. S. Eliot's *Murder in the Cathedral* has: 'Leave well alone, or your goose may be cooked and eaten to the bone.' Mary McCarthy, in *The Groves of Academe*, says: 'One direct question from either of you, and Maynard's goose would have been cooked. You had him on the ropes and you didn't know it.' Some authors expand the phrase. Nigel Dennis writes, in *Cards of Identity*: 'The emergence of a tough young rival has cooked his charming and irresponsible goose.' Somerset Maugham, in his short story *Lord Mountdrago*, has: 'I thought it a very good opportunity to cook his goose, and by God, sir, I cooked it. I tore his speech to pieces... If ever a man was made a fool of I made a fool of Griffiths.' Bernard Wolfe, in *The Late Risers*, jokingly reverses the expression: 'The wife's posse is breathing down my neck hard. Don't give out this address, or my cook is goosed.'

Couch Potato

'Couch potato' became a well-known term in the 1980s. It describes the kind of person who spends a great deal of time watching television or videos, probably eating junk food while doing so. Couch potatoes may like watching televised sport, but they are happy to leave violent physical exercise to others. At best they claim to be active mentally. If they are not exactly meditating, they are indulging in transcendental vegetation.

The 'transcendental vegetation' joke was first made by the American cartoonist Robert Armstrong. It was he who, in 1976, picked up on a phrase invented by Tom Iacino and drew a potato lying on a couch watching television. Iacino had punned on an existing American phrase which described someone addicted to the 'boob-tube' as a 'boob-tuber.' The best-known 'tuber' in another sense was the potato, which in turn led to 'couch potato.' The phrase seems set to take a permanent place in the language. Couch-potatoism may be an unhealthy and undesirable way of life, but one suspects that it is here to stay.

Cry One's Eyes Out

In John Updike's *Rabbit Redux* a young man remarks that his mother is in the kitchen, 'crying her eyes out.' The phrase in itself attracts no more comment from the man to whom it is said than it would from other native English-speakers. It is a phrase that everyone has heard hundreds of times, so that its literal meaning fails to register. How else, we might even ask, can you express the thought? To say that someone is 'weeping copiously' might be more accurate, but in ordinary conversation that would sound much stranger than 'crying one's eyes out.'

For Jonathan Swift, nevertheless, 'cry one's eyes out' was still something of an oddity, though his inclusion of the phrase in his *Polite Conversation* shows that it was in frequent use amongst his contemporaries. Swift was by no means the first to record it in print: the *Oxford English Dictionary* quotes an obscure work of 1692 which talks about letting people 'whine on, till they cry their eyes out.'

The expression suggests eyes being washed from their sockets by 'floods of tears,' another exaggeration that passes unnoticed. Its familiarity is hardly surprising, it has been in constant use since the 16th century. It is one of a group of phrases that we use rather lazily, without really thinking about what we are saying. If we were to think about them we might laugh at their absurdity, 'laugh our heads off,' so to speak, at the thought of crying our eyes out.

Dark Horse

'Dark horse' began as racing slang for a horse which ran much better than its previous form suggested. There is an early use of the phrase in Benjamin Disraeli's *The Young Duke*: 'A dark horse, which had never been thought of, rushed past the grand stand in sweeping triumph.' The allusion was not to the colour of the horse, but to the fact that punters had been 'kept in the dark' about its capabilities. The latter expression was in use before the end of the 18th century. In 1792, for instance, Mary Wollstonecraft had stated sarcastically in her *Vindication of the Rights of Women*: 'As blind obedience is ever sought for by power, tyrants and sensualists are in the right when they endeavour to keep women in the dark.'

Soon after its use amongst the racing fraternity had been noted, 'dark horse' was being applied to human beings. The anonymous *Sketches from Cambridge*, published in 1865, says that 'a man may choose to run dark, and may astonish his friends in the final contest of the mathematical tripos.' In the same work occurs: 'every now and then a dark horse is heard of, who is supposed to have done wonders at some obscure small college.'

Modern use of the phrase seems to centre on politics or sexual interest and often implies that the person concerned keeps his own counsel by choice. Typical of the former usage is the 1952 comment in an American newspaper: 'not a front runner, he is a dark horse who might come in first should Taft and Eisenhower cancel each other out.' *Life* magazine had earlier said that 'Dewey, Taft and Stassen will get away fast, but watch out for Dark Horse Vandenberg on the backstretch.' The secretive ladies' man is referred to in Clifford Hanley's *The Taste of Too Much*, where a dialogue runs: '"I don't think you're very interested in girls, are you, Peter?" "Oh, I don't know." "Oh, I bet you're a dark horse all right".' In Elizabeth Jane Howard's *Getting It Right*, a young woman learns that her brother has brought a girl home and exclaims: 'Well, Gavin, I think you're a very dark horse.'

Davy Jones's Locker

In nautical mythology Davy Jones is the spirit of the ocean, while Davy Jones's locker is a reference to the bottom of the sea. In the early 19th century, a sailor who had gone to Davy Jones's locker, or was 'laid in the lockers,' was one who had been buried at sea. There is an example of the latter usage in Sir Walter Scott's *Guy Mannering*, where someone says: 'Brown's dead-shot-laid in the lockers, man.'

The first recorded reference to Davy Jones's locker occurs in George Roberts' description of his *Four Years' Voyage*, published in 1726. He speaks there of 'heaving the rest into David Jones's locker.' The origin of the expression is not known, but it probably began as an allusion to the biblical story of Jonah being saved by the whale after being thrown overboard. This tale would have been known to every seaman in the early 18th century. It seems likely that the name 'Jonah,' formerly 'Jonas,' was converted into 'Jones' before being given a suitably Welsh first name. 'Locker' was simply the standard naval term for a chest.

Davy Jones was never regarded as a benevolent spirit. As early as 1751 Tobias Smollett was saying, in *Peregrine Pickle*: 'This same Davy Jones, according to the mythology of sailors, is the fiend that presides over all the evil spirits of the deep.' A naval writer recorded in 1790 that 'the great bugbear of the ocean is Davie Jones. At the crossing of the line they call out that Davie Jones and his wife are coming on board and that every thing must be made ready.' In *Bleak House,* Dickens has a character say: 'If you only have to swab a plank, you should swab it as if Davy Jones were after you.' Robert Louis Stevenson, in *Treasure Island*, has the interesting: 'And you have the Davy Jones's insolence to up and stand for cap'n over me!'

Donkey's Years

This expression seems to appeal to writers. 'The only active duty the army had seen in donkey's years,' writes Mordecai Richler, in *The Incomparable Atuk*, 'was when two divisions were hired out to one Hymie Slotnick to make a Western.' Richard Gordon, in *The Face-maker*, has: 'I'm beginning to think that life resembles something I haven't experienced for donkey's years – it's like Saturday night in an old-fashioned public-house.' The author adds, by way of explanation: 'It gets better towards closing-time.' J.I.M. Stewart, in *The Guardians*, writes: 'It was donkey's years since he had been in an English train.'

The origin of the expression was mentioned by E.V.Lucas in *The Vermilion Box* (1916): 'Now for my first bath for what the men call "donkey's ears," meaning years and years.' This makes more sense, since although donkeys are not especially known for living to a great age, their ears are certainly long. The change from 'ears' to 'years' had occurred by the 1920's, and was natural in view of the closeness in sound of the two words as well as the meaning of the phrase.

Dutch Courage

Dutch courage, the false courage induced by drinking alcohol, used to be known in English as 'pot-valour.' This was before the rivalry between England and the Netherlands in the 17th and early 18th centuries caused many derisive remarks about the Dutch to become current in English. 'Dutch courage' is one of those insulting expressions which remains current. The obvious inference is that the Dutch themselves are only valiant after they have been drinking, although as it happens, there is another possible explanation for the phrase. It may be that when the English soldiers went to the Netherlands and discovered gin, a Dutch invention, they made use of it to bolster themselves.

In *Woodstock* (1826), by Sir Walter Scott, there is a reference to 'laying in a store of what is called Dutch courage.' This seems to indicate that the phrase had only recently been introduced to English. Trollope's *Doctor Thorne* has a conversation which runs: 'Do you think I can't work without Dutch courage?' 'Scatcherd, I know there is brandy in the room at this moment, and that you have been taking it within these two hours.' Modern speakers and writers use the phrase in the same way, but the words have become formulaic and there is no thought of insulting Dutch people. Richard Gordon writes in The Face-Maker: 'The coming interview had blunted his appetite for food while sharpening it for the drink, leaving him flushed and muzzy. Not that he needed Dutch courage, he told himself.'

Easy Street

The first known mention of 'Easy Street' occurs in a story by the American writer G.W.Peck, *Peck's Red-Headed Boy*, published in 1901. It is not clear whether he invented the phrase or simply recorded something that had recently come into use, though the latter is more likely. The expression had the advantage of being self-explanatory. The person who lived on Easy Street, as American writers usually expressed it, was in a comfortable financial position, able to live a life of ease. 'Little Stevie doesn't have to worry any more,' says someone in Thomas Wolfe's *Look Homeward, Angel*, 'he's on Easy Street.' It is curious that in Britain people were far more likely to speak about those who had lost all their money and were residing in Queer Street.

Easy Street is treated either as a proper name, in which case it takes capital letters, or as an ordinary verbal phrase, as when P.G.Wodehouse writes, in *The Adventures of Sally*: 'Honestly, it's the chance of a lifetime. It would put you right on easy street.' The expression is still more likely to be used by an American speaker or writer, though by the 1930s it was clearly known in other English-speaking countries. When someone in *The Master of Jalna*, by Mazo de la Roche, is asked 'Are you sure you can spare it?', the reply is: 'I hope so – after the sale! I'm in Easy Street.' L.P.Hartley, in *The Hireling*, has: 'He knew that she lived in Easy Street, but then so did most, if not all, of his customers.'

Eleventh Hour, The

'The eleventh hour' is commonly used to refer to a period which falls just within a time-limit. Occasionally it means the same as 'last-minute,' as when the *Baltimore Sun* reported that 'the fireworks bill was passed by the Senate tonight despite eleventh-hour attempts to sabotage it or delay enactment.' It can also mean 'late': an article in the *Listener* declared that 'to commit a boy to preparing for either examination deprives the eleventh-hour developer of a chance of an award.'

The phrase originally occurs in the parable of the labourers in the vineyard, told at Matthew 20 in the New Testament. The kingdom of heaven is compared to a householder who pays the same wages to labourers taken on at the eleventh hour and those who have worked all day. When 19th-century writers first began to make use of 'eleventh hour,' they usually showed an awareness of its Christian source. Southey's *All for Love*, for example, has: 'Though at the eleventh hour Thou hast come to serve our Prince of Power.' C.M.Flandrau, in his *Harvard Episodes*, writes: 'So, in response to John's eleventh-hour prayers, he did what he could.' By the beginning of the 20th century the biblical connection had apparently been forgotten. In 1904 the *Daily Chronicle* was referring to 'an eleventh-hour alteration in the arrangements for the return of Queen Alexandra from Copenhagen.' In recent times the phrase has come to suggest a point of crisis. When a threatened strike is avoided, for example, it is usually at 'the eleventh hour.'

Englishman's Home is his Castle, An

This is the modern form of a saying that is first recorded in the 16th century. William Lambarde published a book in 1588 describing the office of a Justice of the Peace. It included the statement: 'Our law calleth a man's house, his castle, meaning that he may defend himselfe therein.' Sir Edward Coke restated this principle in 1600: 'The house of every man is to him as his castle and fortresse, as well for his defence against injury and violence, as for his repose.' By the mid-19th century, in Edward Freeman's work *The History of the Norman Conquest*, this had become: 'An Englishman's house is his castle.'

More recently, 'house' in this saying has tended to become 'home' and the phrase has acquired a less specific legal sense. There is now often the thought that we are entitled to do whatever we feel like doing in the privacy of our home. We can relax and be ourselves. Samuel Butler, discussing a typical clergyman in *The Way of All Flesh*, says that he is expected 'to be a kind of human Sunday'. leading a stricter life than other people. 'But,' adds Butler, 'his home is his castle as much as that of any other Englishman, and with him, as with others, unnatural tension in public is followed by exhaustion when tension is no longer necessary.'

In *The Pickwick Papers*, Dickens has the constable Daniel Grummer burst in on the Pickwickians at dinner. 'This is a private room, sir,' says Mr Snodgrass indignantly. Mr Grummer shakes his head. 'No room's private to his Majesty when the street door's once passed. That's law. Some people maintains that an Englishman's house is his castle. That's gammon.'

Face the Music

Someone who 'faces the music' faces up to the consequences of his actions, accepts responsibility for them and stands ready to take his punishment. 'I am willing to face the music. It was my fault', says a character in *Sylvester*, by Edward Hyams. R.F.Delderfield, in *Theirs Was The Kingdom*, has: 'Stay put man, and face the music. You're in this as deep as me.' A character in Alan Sillitoe's *Saturday Night and Sunday Morning* says: 'What a daft thing to do, to get a girl into trouble. He'll just have to face the music.' A similar reason prompts the use of the phrase in Henry Miller's *Tropic of Cancer*: 'I ought to go back and face the music. If anything should happen to her I'd never forgive myself.'

No one is sure what 'music' refers to in this phrase, which was first recorded in American sources in the mid-19th century. One suggestion is that it alludes to a performer going on stage to face the pit-orchestra and the audience. Another theory makes it the bugle call to which a soldier responds. In neither of these instances, however, is someone showing a willingness to admit publicly to an offence. It is more likely that 'music' in this expression is used ironically: the person who has offended is going to be subjected to loud and angry condemnation. Someone is going to make a 'song and dance' about what has happened, and that is the 'music' that has to be faced.

Falling in Love

We have been speaking about people 'falling in love' since the early 16th century, but 'fall' seems rather a strange word to use. Being in love normally brings a feeling of elation, of 'walking on air.' As Nancy Thayer says in *Nell*: 'When they walked along the water, holding hands, talking, embracing, saying elaborate things to one another: if that had not been love, at least it had been lovely.' Love, in other words, is associated with an uplifting of the spirits, yet *falling* in love seems to suggest that we become downcast. Nancy Thayer tries to grapple with this paradox, insisting that falling in love is 'an apt phrase.' This, she says, is because her heroine 'did feel like Alice in Wonderland, falling down the rabbit's hole.' The 18th century novelist Laurence Sterne took a less romantic view. 'To say a man is fallen in love,' he writes, in *Tristram Shandy*, 'carries an idiomatical kind of implication that love is a thing below a man.'

This implication was not apparent when the phrase 'fall in love' was first used. At that time, 'fall' did not necessarily refer to some kind of descent; applied to people it could be used of a sudden change from one mental or emotional state to another. The word still has that sense in 'fall asleep,' a phrase which is even older than 'fall in love.' There too the usual meaning of 'fall' in modern times influences our thinking. We talk about a *deep* sleep and assume that 'falling asleep' refers to reaching a lower level of consciousness.

'Falling in love' is like 'falling asleep' in that a person passes from one state to another without being consciously aware of the change taking place. Nancy Thayer's comparison of the 'fall' to Alice's tumbling down the rabbit-hole may seem apt, but it is difficult to maintain. As well as falling in love, we can just as easily fall out of it.

Feet of Clay

In *Ulysses* James Joyce writes: 'They discovered that their idol had feet of clay, after placing him upon a pedestal.' There is a similar comment in Angus Wilson's *Hemlock and After*: 'Eric is sad because his idol has feet of clay.' A person who has been greatly admired, in other words, is revealed as having a basic weakness or fault. The allusion is to the Old Testament, Daniel 2.31, where Daniel describes and interprets a dream that has been troubling King Nebuchadnezzar. The king has dreamed of an image, the head of which 'was of fine gold, its breast and arms of silver, its belly and thighs and bronze, its legs of iron, its feet partly of iron and partly of clay.' Daniel interprets the feet of iron and clay as a divided kingdom brought about by marriage. It will not hold together, 'just as iron does not mix with clay.' A statue made of the strongest metals in its upper parts will still be toppled if there is a weakness at its base; a kingdom will likewise collapse if a fundamental weakness is introduced.

Although the phrase makes a metaphorical reference to 'feet of clay,' writers in their various ways often choose to take it literally. Mary McCarthy, for example, in *The Group*, writes: 'She had taken Kay up for all she was worth, because Kay, as she said, was "malleable" and "capable of learning." Now she claimed to have detected that Kay had feet of clay, which was rather a contradiction, since wasn't clay malleable?' Peter de Vries, in *Comfort Me With Apples*, has a husband tell his wife: 'Do you think I don't know how you feel? The man you've lived with all these years turning out to have feet of clay...' The wife replies: 'Feet! It's your head that's clay!'

Oscar Wilde also chooses to play with the phrase in *The Picture of Dorian Gray*. Lord Henry remarks: 'She is very clever, too clever for a woman. She lacks the indefinable charm of weakness. It is the feet of clay that makes the gold of the image precious. Her feet are very pretty, but they are not feet of clay. White porcelain feet, if you like. They have been through the fire, and what fire does not destroy, it hardens.'

Flash in the Pan

'Flash in the pan' is the kind of phrase an amateur golfer might use about a particularly good round. Today he may have been brilliant, but he knows from past experience that next time he goes out on the course he will probably experience the usual disasters.

The phrase might now make one think of a flaming frying-pan, but at the beginning of the 19th century it referred literally to the 'pan' of an old-fashioned gun, which held the priming. Sometimes the priming would flash in the pan without igniting the charge. This might look spectacular, but it achieved no real result. Figuratively, therefore, 'flash in the pan' came to mean an aborted attempt to do something, especially one which seemed to begin well but then failed. It has this meaning in Robert Shaw's *The Hiding Place*: 'President Truman made it clear that today's blow was no flash in the pan. The showering of high explosive on the power plants was described as a "new policy of getting tough with the Reds".' The attacks, in other words, would not fizzle out. They would continue in the way they had begun, with the same intensity.

Bernard Malamud, in *The Natural*, applies the phrase directly to a person, a baseball player: 'The companies were suspicious he might be a flash in the pan.' Again there is the idea of beginning spectacularly well, but not being able to sustain the effort. In modern times, though, this expression is used about a spell of brilliant success that occurs briefly at any time, not necessarily at the beginning of something. The 'flash' of the phrase now dominates its meaning, rather than the charge which fails to ignite.

Fleshpots of Egypt, The

Collins *Cobuild English Language Dictionary* defines 'fleshpot' as 'a place such as a strip club, massage parlour, or brothel, where people go for sexual pleasure.' This is no doubt the meaning Mordecai Richler has in mind when he says, in *The Incomparable Atuk*: 'How he had yearned for the flesh-pots of Toronto.' *The Concise Oxford Dictionary* prefers to believe that 'fleshpots' is still used simply as a metaphor for luxurious living. This was true in former times, when people were generally more familiar with biblical texts. In the 18th century, when Jonathan Swift wrote to Laurence Sterne, saying: 'I expect to hear the two ladies lamenting the fleshpots of Cavan-street,' Sterne would instantly have recognised the allusion to Exodus 16.3: 'And the whole congregation of the people of Israel murmured against Moses and Aaron in the wilderness, and said to them, "Would that we had died by the hand of the Lord in the land of Egypt, when we sat by the fleshpots and ate bread to the full; for you have brought us out into this wilderness to kill this whole assembly with hunger".'

The fleshpots referred to in the Bible were pots in which meat was cooked. From this, a reference to the 'fleshpots of Egypt' came to mean a comfortable life-style, with plentiful food and drink. When Carlyle, in the 19th century, talks in *Frederick the Great* of 'the Law, with its high honours and deep fleshpots,' he is not implying that members of the legal profession are regular patrons of massage parlours. It is the modern assumption that 'sins of the flesh' are always of a sexual nature that causes the ambiguity.

Morris West makes use of the *Exodus* story in *Proteus*. A man who is trying to make the world a better place is told: 'Like all zealots, my dear Spada, you miss the point. You make a choice too trenchant for normal folk. When Moses led the Israelites out of servitude, were they grateful? Never! They cried for the onions and the fleshpots of Egypt. Freedom was a luxury they could neither understand nor afford.'

Flog a Dead Horse

When we tell someone that he is 'flogging a dead horse' we are using a phrase that has only been current since the late 19th century. At that time the expression seems to have appealed to British members of parliament. It would be muttered in the chamber if one of their number was stressing the need for reduced expenditure or something equally unpopular. A milder version of the phrase was 'mount on a dead horse.' This had the same meaning of 'waste one's time with something that cannot possibly succeed.'

Since the 17th century a 'dead horse' had metaphorically represented anything that had ceased to be of use. Henry Fowler demonstrated such usage in his *Modern English Usage*: 'The old trade union movement is a dead horse, largely due to the incompetency of the leaders.' 'Dead horse' also had a specific meaning related to wages paid in advance. E.C.Wines, in his 1832 book *Two Years in the Navy*, writes: 'Most of us had not worked out our dead horses – debts due to the purser on account of advances of pay.' *Yachting* magazine was later to explain: 'The common sailor was advanced one month's pay at the time of signing the articles. This usually went to his boarding-house keeper for alleged debts. During the first month out, he was said to be 'working off the dead horse'; and at the end of this period it was the custom to make an effigy of a horse and throw it overboard with suitable ceremonies.'

Fly a Kite

'Fly a kite' has several metaphorical meanings, though it mainly refers to making a tentative proposal in order to see how others react to it. Flying a kite, after all, is one way to find out 'which way the wind is blowing.' 'I'm not aware the President has come to any conclusion on the Security Council,' says a diplomat in *The Touch of Innocents*, by Michael Dobbs. He continues: 'It's just a kite being flown by some of his advisers.' *Nature* magazine reported in 1971: 'The solution, the committee suggests – and it is plainly flying a kite and not laying down policy – may be a more selective way of choosing the departments to which studentships will be allocated.'

One meaning of 'fly a kite' in criminal slang is 'issue a worthless cheque.' In the past it has also meant to sell worthless stocks and bonds, or raise money on fraudulent accommodation bills. For prisoners the phrase could refer to smuggling a letter or verbal message into or out of the prison. At one time it referred specifically to writing a mournful letter to a charitable institution or sympathetic individual. In most of these activities the criminal was 'trying it on,' putting a paper object into the wind to see whether it happened to be blowing in a favourable direction. With luck, something would come from nothing.

'Go fly a kite' can also be an irritated remark by one person to another. It means much the same as 'go jump in the lake.' The reference to kite-flying presumably has no special significance; it is merely something that will cause you to go away.

Fly in the Ointment

This phrase was probably made popular by Charles Lamb, in his *Essays of Elia* (1840). He says there that 'a Poor Relation is the most irrelevant thing in nature, a lion in your path, a frog in your chamber, a fly in your ointment.' There is an earlier reference in a 17th century sermon – 'there is ever some dead fly in our box, which marreth our ointment' – but the phrase was not in general use at that time. Like Charles Lamb, the sermon-writer was alluding to the Bible, *Ecclesiastes* 10.1: 'Dead flies make the perfumer's ointment give off an evil odour.' The biblical passage continues: 'So a little folly outweighs wisdom and honour.' In modern times we think in a different way of the 'fly in the ointment.' It is used to describe whoever or whatever spoils an otherwise satisfactory situation.

The 'ointment' referred to in the Bible was used by the ancient Hebrews after washing. It was made of oil and various sweet-smelling substances and could be used on the hair and beard as well as the skin, which it was thought to keep soft. To put ointment on ('anoint') the feet of a person was to pay him special honour.

Modern writers seem to visualise an actual fly when they use this expression. For some writers, the size of the fly reflects the importance of the problem. The *Daily Express* once reported that 'the insurance of school fees has now become so general that it is as well to point out to parents that there is a rather large fly in the ointment.' J.I.M.Stewart, in *A Use of Riches*, has: 'He felt a little bad, perhaps, that he and poor old Hugo Petford-Smith belonged to the same regiment. Still, it was only a small fly in the ointment.' Others are more concerned with how many flies there are: 'That, from my point of view, is the one fly in the ointment' writes Harry Farjeon, in *Exit*. P.G.Wodehouse, in *Cocktail Time*, offers the philosophical comment: 'in every ointment there is a fly, in every good thing a catch of some sort.'

Fly on the Wall

Some writers are fortunate enough to come up with a striking phrase that becomes part of the language. By an odd coincidence, there are two such phrases in English, both traceable to an individual author, which are based on the word 'fly.' In his 18th century novel *Tristram Shandy*, Laurence Sterne says of his uncle Toby: 'He was of a peaceful, placid nature, no jarring element in it, all was mixed up so kindly within him; my uncle Toby had scarce a heart to retaliate upon a fly. Go, says he, one day at dinner, to an over-grown one which had buzzed about his nose, and tormented him cruelly all dinner-time, and which after infinite attempts he had caught at last, as it flew by him; I'll not hurt thee, says my uncle Toby, rising from his chair, and going across the room, with the fly in his hand, I'll not hurt a hair of thy head: – Go, says he, lifting up the sash, and opening his hand as he spoke, to let it escape; go, poor devil, get thee gone, why should I hurt thee? – This world surely is wide enough to hold both thee and me.'

Although Sterne does not actually say that Uncle Toby 'would not harm a fly,' there is little doubt that it was this famous passage which enabled subsequent writers and speakers to use such a phrase. Edna O'Brien, for example, writes in *The Country Girls*: 'He didn't like people to think he was brutal. He had the name of being a gentleman, a decent man who wouldn't hurt a fly.' Similarly, in Edith Pargeter's *Most Loving Mere Folly*, a mother says of her son and his partner: 'I don't say anything about *her*, but he wouldn't hurt a fly.'

When Nancy Mitford published her *Love in a Cold Climate* in 1949, she described a scene where two other women in the room with the young narrator were deep in conversation. 'I had been throwing an occasional glance in their direction,' she wrote, 'wondering what it could all be about and wishing I could be a fly on the wall to hear them.' The novel was widely read, and the 'fly on the wall' remark seems to have made a great impression. It perfectly summed up the idea of an inconspicuous eavesdropper. It is now a commonplace for someone to say something like: 'I wouldn't mind being a fly on the wall when they get together.' People are also sometimes invited to be a 'fly on the wall,' to sit in on a committee meeting, say, in order to listen and observe what happens without actually taking part in any discussion. In the world of radio, television and films, the phrase has taken on a specific sense of uninvolved documentary. *City Limits* reported in 1986: 'This is a film that has tried hard not to impinge its identity on its subject, using a fly on the wall approach.' It is clear that the imagination of an individual writer can still make a great impact.

For a Song

Anything that is bought 'for a song' is a bargain, bought below its true value. We may be quoting Shakespeare when we use the expression, since it is first recorded in his works. In *All's Well That Ends Well* the Clown is talking about Bertram, who is 'a very melancholy man'. The Clown then adds that he knows another man who, in a fit of melancholy, 'sold a goodly manor for a song.'

The phrase was later expanded, since Francis Grose, in his *Classical Dictionary of the Vulgar Tongue* (1785), lists it as 'for an old song.' 'I wish I had bought it myself,' says Mrs Weston, in E.F.Benson's *Queen Lucia*, 'for he got it for an old song.' This was also the form known to Byron. He describes an architect in *Don Juan* who:

> produced a plan whereby to erect
> New buildings of correctest conformation,
> And throw down old, which he call'd *restoration*.
> The cost would be a trifle – an 'old song,'
> Set to some thousands ('tis the usual burden
> Of that same tune, when people hum it long).

By coincidence it is a builder in George Douglas's *The House With The Green Shutters* who says to his client: 'There's not a thing in your house that a man in your position can afford to be without, and ye needn't expect the best house in Barbie for an old song!'

'For a song' is now the usual form. At Angmering, in Sussex, there is a house called 'Arches' which its owner Bud Flanagan liked to say was bought 'for a song.' He and his partner Chesney Allen made a small fortune from 'Underneath the Arches.' Flanagan used part of his share to buy the house.

For Pete's Sake

A child is likely to ask 'who is Pete?' when an adult uses this exclamatory phrase. The expression is obviously the equivalent of 'for God's sake,' 'for Christ's sake,' 'for heavens' sake,' or 'for goodness' sake.' The religious nature of these sayings causes many commentators to say that it must be Saint Peter who is referred to. Saints, however, are not generally referred to by diminutive forms of their names.

Writers seem to be uncertain as to whether 'Pete' in this phrase really is a name. Those who favour the name idea tend to use a capital letter. 'For Pete's sake, sit down,' occurs in Bernard Malamud's *The Natural*. Elizabeth Jane Howard, in *Getting It Right*, has: 'What on earth did they think you were made of, for Pete's sake?' By contrast Judith Guest, in *Ordinary People*, writes: 'Watch, for pete's sake, watch!' Similarly, Michael Rumaker's *Exit 3* has: 'For pete's sake, don't start that again.'

As far as the origin of the phrase is concerned, the word rather than name presents the strongest case. 'For pity's sake' was much used in former times, and it seems likely that it was this which became, deliberately or accidentally, 'for Pete's sake.' But even if this is what happened, 'pity' was transformed into a name, not another word. 'Pete' deserves its capital letter.

Full Monty, the

New phrases can be introduced to the language at any time.

A recent example is the full Monty, an expression which was unknown to most English-speakers until 1997. It then burst upon the scene as the title of an acclaimed film in which a group of Yorkshire working men parodied the Chippendales. Most people would now agree that the phrase means 'the whole thing', but there is little agreement as to the origin of the expression.

The phrase was first used in the north of England. It was listed, for instance, in *Street Talk*, a book published in 1968 which derived in its turn from the scripts of Coronation Street, the TV soap opera about life in a northern English town. This, together with the fact that the phrase was unknown at that time in the USA, means that a suggestion made by Tony Thorne, linking the expression with an American card game called 'monte', can almost certainly be discounted.

Several other possible origins have been suggested by writers such as Nigel Rees and Michael B. Quinion. They include:

(a) a corruption of the phrase 'the full amount'. However, there is no obvious reason why 'amount' should have become 'monty'. It is also probably significant that early printed occurrences tend to treat 'Monty' as a name, capitalised.

(b) a reference to Field Marshall Montgomery wearing all his medals. This distinguished soldier was certainly known as Monty throughout the British Army, but that was in the 1940s. He would have meant little or nothing to a new generation of the 1980s.

(c) a reference to a television advertisement for Del Monte fruit juice, supposedly shown in Britain in the 1980s and featuring someone asking for 'the full Del Monte.' Evidence to support this reference is lacking.

(d) a reference to the hire of formal clothes for a wedding from the British firm of outfitters Montague Burton's, now known more simply as Burton's. This would mean that the full Monty would originally have referred to someone being dressed to the nines, wearing everything. The connection with clothes is appealing, since the film that made the phrases known is about men who take off every item of clothing. That may be coincidence, but in the absence of any hard and fast evidence, this explanation of the phrase remains the most convincing.

Full of Beans

In Edna Ferber's *Giant* a man arrives home in high spirits. His wife 'thought she had never seen him so pleased with himself and the world.' After a moment, using a metaphorical phrase that has been in use since the mid-19th century, she asks him: 'What makes you so full of beans?' Robert Surtees, in *Handley Cross*, seems to have been the first writer to record this expression. He speaks of "ounds, 'osses, and men, in a glorious state of excitement! Full o' beans and benevolence!'

It was natural for Surtees to include horses in his comment. 'Full of beans' was originally applied to a horse, like the one Puck refers to in Shakespeare's *A Midsummer Night's Dream*:

> I jest to Oberon, and make him smile
> When I a fat and bean-fed horse beguile,
> Neighing in likeness of a filly foal.

A 'bean-fed' horse was later described in slang as 'beany' or 'full of beans.' It had plenty of energy and was ready to be exercised. From this developed the additional notion of general good health and high spirits. 'She's strong and well and full of beans' says a character in W.Somerset Maugham's *Here and There*.

In American slang the phrase has acquired a second and less pleasant meaning. A person who is thought to be talking nonsense can be told insultingly that he is 'full of beans,' 'full of prunes' or 'full of hops,' the reference in each case being to something which has laxative qualities. 'Full of bull' also occurs, where 'bull' is for 'bullshit.' The blunter versions of the phrase are 'full of shit' or 'full of crap,' referred to euphemistically as 'full of it.'

Funny Bone

The *Oxford English Dictionary* defines 'funny bone' as 'the popular name for that part of the elbow over which the ulnar nerve passes, from the peculiar sensation experienced when it is struck.' That is all right as far as it goes: the 'peculiar sensation' is the tingling which shoots down the forearm to the fingers if we knock our elbow against a hard surface. But the OED definition makes no mention of the joke that is inherent in the name 'funny bone.' It was clearly influenced by the fact that the bone of the upper arm is called the humerus, from the Latin word *(h)umerus* 'shoulder.' This suggested the word 'humorous,' derived from an entirely separate Latin word, which together with the tingling sensation suggested 'funny bone.'

Rapping our funny bone against something hard is unlikely to make us laugh, but the phrase is sometimes interpreted figuratively as if that is what happens. The *Daily Chronicle* reported that 'two principal figures and a few carefully careless scratches – that is all Mr. Raven-Hill uses in the pointing of his joke, but he hits the universal funny-bone with his pencil.' In his 1965 novel *Road to Gundagai*, G. McInnes wrote: 'Kennedy hit our funny-bones because he was a man who used long words with an extremely sober face.'

Funny-peculiar or Funny-ha-ha

Ian Hay, in his light comedy *Housemaster*, has a character say:

'That's funny.' The reply is: 'What do you mean, funny? Funny-peculiar, or funny ha-ha?' The ambiguity of the word 'funny' justifies the question, and Hay's wording of it obviously struck a chord. The many examples of the phrase found in print after 1938, the year in which Hay's play was first staged, show that it quickly came into general use.

It is slightly odd, not to say funny-peculiar, that each half of the expression is also used on its own. 'It felt funny-peculiar, walking down the street alone,' writes Budd Schulberg, in *Waterfront*. Stella Gibbons, in *Westwood*, has: 'You said her conscience forced her into being a you-know-what. It sounds awfully funny-peculiar.' In such instances the 'funny' appears to be unnecessary, adding nothing to the sense. Similarly, Mary McCarthy in *Charmed Life* writes that 'his art-school training rendered him funny-ha-ha to the cognoscenti.' When it is not being used to clarify which meaning of 'funny' is intended, 'funny-ha-ha' is a very strange word. It confesses immediately that it cannot do its job of conveying a specific meaning without something being tacked rather clumsily on the end. Miss McCarthy could instead have used a well-established word such as amusing, comical or laughable, especially since she was writing rather than speaking. In ordinary speech, 'funny' will no doubt continue to be the first word that springs to most people's minds. Ian Hay's invention will then come into play to help them explain what they mean.

Get Down to Brass Tacks

The 'brass tacks' in this expression are the 'practical details of the matter being discussed.' 'Let's get down to a few brass tacks!' says a character in Joyce Porter's *Dover One*. 'How did they do it, and where's the body?' Mary McCarthy, in *The Group*, has the interesting exchange: '"Do come down to brass tacks." "The Brass Tack'," Norine said, frowning. "Wasn't that your name for a literary magazine at college?"'

The 'getting down' part of the phrase seems to suggest someone kneeling so that he can get closer to the tacks. Some American linguists have therefore linked it to the cleaning of sailing-ship decks and the exposure of brass nails. A quite different explanation of the phrase's origin was suggested by Julian Franklyn, in *A Dictionary of Rhyming Slang*. He had no doubt that the 'brass tacks' were there to rhyme on 'facts.' He believed that the expression originated with London Cockneys, but was established in the USA by the beginning of the 20th century. By chance, T.S.Eliot makes use of this rhyme in *Sweeney Agonistes* 'Fragment of an Agon':

> Birth, and copulation, and death.
> That's all the facts when you come to brass tacks.

One problem with this explanation is that rhyming slang phrases are usually abbreviated. 'Loaf of bread' is used to rhyme on 'head,' but 'use your loaf of bread' quickly becomes 'use your loaf.' One might have expected the 'brass tacks' saying to have become 'get down to brass.' There is no evidence that this happened, perhaps because 'brass' already existed in rhyming slang as a term for a prostitute. It had begun as 'brass nail,' rhyming on the slang meaning of 'tail.'

Get Hold of the Wrong End of the Stick

The *Oxford English Dictionary* has a quotation from an American publication of 1846, *Swell's Night Guide,* which runs: 'Which of us had hold of the crappy end of the stick?' This supports the claim of Roy Wilder, in *You All Spoken Here,* that 'get the shitty/dirty end of the stick' derives from log-rolling, where two men would lift a log on a pole held by each of them. 'The shitty end of the stick resulted from horseplay, from coating one end of the stick or pole in ordure.' The meaning of 'get the dirty end of the stick,' as it became in its euphemistic form, seems to have been 'come off second best when bargaining.' John Dos Passos, in *The 42nd Parallel,* writes: 'I guess I always get the dirty end of the stick, all right.' P.G.Wodehouse, in *Laughing Gas,* has the similar: 'I mean what's downtrodden and oppressed and gets the dirty end of the stick all the time. That's me.'

The British form of this expression is first mentioned in 1886 by T.L.Kington-Oliphant in *New English*: 'We talk of the wrong end of the stick.' In early use this had the same meaning as the American 'dirty end of the stick,' to fare badly in negotiations, to get less than one's fair share. A writer in 1890 remarked that if you happen to have the arrangement of a bargain with the rural Australian, you will rarely find that the apparently impassive countryman has 'got the wrong end of the stick.' Other variants retain this meaning. Michael Cronin's *Dead and done With* has: 'I've had the rough end of the stick ever since I got here.' Paul Scott writes in *Staying On*: 'Always I have the mucky end of the stick. But then I am only part of the fixtures and fittings.' Other writers talk variously of getting the 'cruddy\thick\short' end of the stick.

By 1930 Evelyn Waugh was writing, in *Vile Bodies*: 'My private schoolmaster used to say, "If a thing's worth doing at all, it's worth doing well." But these young people have got hold of another end of the stick, and for all we know it may be the right one. They say, "If a thing's not worth doing well, it's not worth doing at all".' This moves towards the modern meaning in Britain of 'get hold of the wrong end of the stick,' which is a re-interpretation of the original expression. It now means to 'misunderstand completely a situation or what someone has said.' George Orwell clearly has that meaning in mind in *Coming up for Air*: 'Listen, Hilda. You've got hold of the wrong end of the stick about this business.' It is found also in E.F.Benson's *Trouble for Lucia*, where the heroine blithely tells her friend: 'I shouldn't wonder if you'd got hold of the wrong end of the stick somehow. Habit of yours, Elizabeth.'

Get into a Scrape

We tend to think of young boys getting themselves into a scrape. The difficulties they face are usually their own fault, caused by their own behaviour. The phrase has been in use since at least the beginning of the 18th century. There is a reference in the Tatler magazine of 1709, for instance, to a 'youngster in a scrape.' Later literary examples include 'how in the nation did they ever git into such a scrape?' which occurs in Mark Twain's *Huckleberry Finn*. Anthony Trollope, in *The Last Chronicle of Barset*, has: 'If you don't take care, young man, you will find yourself in a scrape.'

The Book of Days, published in Colorado in 1863, explains the origin of the phrase as follows: 'There is a game called golf, almost peculiar to Scotland, though also frequently played upon Blackheath, involving the use of a small elastic ball, which is driven from point to point with a variety of wooden and iron clubs. In the north it is played for the most part upon downs near the sea. One of the troubles of the golf players is the little hole which the rabbit makes in the sward in its first efforts at a burrow; this is commonly called 'a rabbit's scrape.' When a ball gets into a 'scrape' it can hardly be played. The rules of golfing societies include one indicating what is allowable to the player when he gets into a 'scrape.' Here, and here alone, has the phrase a direct and intelligible meaning. It seems therefore allowable to surmise that this phrase originated among the golfing societies of the north and in time spread to the rest of the public.'

In support of this theory, golf historians report that there was formerly a club called a 'scraper' which was like the modern sand-iron. It was used when a ball had come to rest in a rabbit's scrape. The editors of the *Oxford English Dictionary* nevertheless prefer to explain the phrase in terms of being caught in a narrow place, where one can hardly move without scraping one's shoulders. If 'get into a scrape' does in fact derive from golf, it joins a large group of expressions which have sporting origins.

Get out of Bed on the Wrong Side

In the 16th century there was a superstitious belief that it was lucky, and good for one's temper, to get out of bed on the right side. By 'right' people meant 'right-hand,' as opposed to 'left-hand,' but this meaning gradually seems to have been forgotten. By the 19th century English-speakers were referring to 'getting out of the right or wrong side of the bed,' but were no longer associating 'right' with 'right-hand.'

We could still say of someone who is especially cheerful that he obviously got out of the right side of bed that morning, but as literary examples demonstrate, we are far more likely to use the negative expression. Mary McCarthy's *The Group* has: 'He might have just got up "on the wrong side of the bed," as Mother said; Daddy was cross too, sometimes, in the morning.' 'Got out of the wrong side of bed this morning, did we?' says someone in Tom Sharpe's *Porterhouse Blue*. A 19th century instance occurs in *Mary Jane's Memoirs*, by G.R.Sims: 'I never lived in a family that so often got out of bed on the wrong side, to use a homely expression.'

Get Someone's Goat

This expression was first recorded in America in 1914. That year a writer in the *Saturday Evening Post* mentioned something that 'got my goat.' A few months later, a story in the same magazine included the comment: 'That got my nanny up this time.' Edgar Wallace was later to combine the two forms of the phrase in *The Double*: '"She was most kind and gracious, recognised me in an instant. Didn't mention you, by the way." He dug Dick in the ribs playfully. "That's got your nanny-goat!"'

'Get someone's nanny' is still sometimes found in

contemporary American writing, but 'get someone's goat' – 'make someone irritable or angry' – quickly established itself as the usual form. By 1924 John Galsworthy was writing in *The White Monkey*: 'That had got the chairman's goat! Got his goat? What expressions they used nowadays!' *To Kill a Mockingbird*, by Harper Lee, has: 'He said he was trying to get Miss Maudie's goat, that he had been trying unsuccessfully for forty years.' Later in the same novel occurs: 'No matter what anybody says to you, don't you let 'em get your goat.' Upton Sinclair, in *World's End*, writes: 'They are sharp traders, and that's all right, but what gets your goat is the mask of righteousness they put on.' A young man in John Updike's *Rabbit Redux* tells another man: 'I'm just kidding, right? To get your goat, O.K?'

No one has satisfactorily explained the 'goat' reference in this phrase. Robert L. Chapman, in his *Dictionary of American Slang*, says that it is 'perhaps from depriving a racehorse of its goat mascot.' As an alternative explanation he offers French *prendre sa chèvre* 'take one's goat away,' in the sense of 'take away one's source of milk or nourishment.' No such expression exists in modern French, but there is a seldom-used idiom *rendre quelqu'un chèvre*, literally 'make someone a goat.' This has the metaphorical meaning 'to drive someone up the wall,' rather stronger than 'get someone's goat' but obviously of similar sense. The French phrase suggests that someone is made angry enough to start acting like a goat, butting his head against a wall. It may well be that some such thought was the original inspiration for 'get someone's goat.'

Give Someone Short Shrift

To 'give someone short shrift' means to treat someone curtly, to pay little attention to what they are trying to tell you. The origin of the phrase is a reminder of the brutality and inhumanity of our ancestors. 'Shrift' is from the seldom-used verb 'to shrive,' which has to do with hearing someone's confession and imposing a penance. Another word from the same family is 'shrove,' which is retained in Shrove Tuesday. This was traditionally the day on which people were 'shriven' in preparation for Lent, which begins the following day on Ash Wednesday.

In former times, when a condemned criminal was about to be executed, he would be grudgingly allowed to make a short shrift – a brief final confession in which he asked for God's pardon. 'Make a short shrift,' says Ratcliff callously to Lord Hastings, in Shakespeare's *King Richard the Third*. The Duke of York has announced that he will not eat his dinner that night until the head of Hastings has been brought to him.

The modern sense of 'give someone short shrift' is considerably weaker, but implies that no notice will be taken of anything the person concerned has to say. 'I encountered some obstacles deliberately put in my path by upstart Jacks in office, but I gave them short shrift,' says the formidable aunt in *Abbie*, by Dane Chandos. 'If I'd made a fool of the mother who bore me, my father would have given me short shrift' is said in *Comfort Me With Apples*, by Peter de Vries. Other examples from newspapers and magazines include: 'a man who tries to exercise authority in the manner of a sergeant-major will get short shrift in a progressive school.' 'Every argument tells with still greater force against the present measure, and it is to be hoped that the House of Commons will give it short shrift to-night.' 'Possessing a very large wastepaper basket, I give short shrift to all anonymous correspondents.'

Give Someone the Cold Shoulder

Edwin Radford, in *Crowther's Encyclopaedia of Phrases and Origins*, says that 'when an unexpected visitor is a welcome one, the hostess puts herself to some trouble to prepare a dainty meal for the guest who has made a journey to visit her. But where the visitor is not particularly welcome and is not to be encouraged to pay similar visits in the future, cold meat, the remains of the shoulder which formed the last meal, is usually brought out. To be given the cold shoulder is a pretty plain hint that you are not encouraged by your hostess.'

Mr Radford clearly prefers a fanciful explanation to the simple truth. This expression first appears in *The Antiquary*, by Sir Walter Scott, where we are told: 'The Countess's dislike didna gang farther at first than just showing o' the cauld shouther.' Scott's Glossary to the novel explained that 'to show the cold shoulder' meant 'to appear cold and reserved.' The 'showing' of the shoulder makes it clear that the Countess turned her back on the person she disliked. Unexpected guests and shoulders of meat had nothing to do with it.

Scott used the phrase again in *St Ronan's Well*, published in 1824. It seems to have established itself quickly in everyday speech, either as 'show, give or turn the cold shoulder to someone.' Writers such as Dickens (in *The Old Curiosity Shop*), and Thackeray (in *Lovel the Widower*), used it without comment, expecting their readers to understand what was meant. In *Flashman*, by George MacDonald Fraser, the phrase is condensed into a single verb: 'I cold-shouldered one or two when they came too close.' Thomas Hood does the same thing in *A Drop of Gin*, describing the 'friends and peers of earlier years' who

> But snub, neglect, cold-shoulder, and cut
> The ragged pauper, misfortune's butt.

It was 19th century humorists like Hood who first associated this phrase with cold meat, usually mutton. They would have been surprised at the thought that, by some people at least, their joke would one day be taken seriously.

Go Scot-free

'What happens,' a lawyer asks a client in *Proteus*, by Morris West, 'if you lay a false charge against a guilty man and he sues you for libel or defamation – and goes scot-free at the end of it?' Some speakers and writers might prefer 'get off scot-free.' A man in *The Blinder*, by Barry Hines, tells a friend: 'You can't get married if you don't want to.' 'So you get off scot-free then?' is the rejoinder. James Purdy, in *Eustace Chisholm and the Works*, mixes the two forms: 'Ain't you lucky to be a boy! No matter who makes love to you, you can go off scot-free.'

The 'scot' in this phrase was originally a payment that had to be made, such as the bill in a tavern or a rental charge, as when North mentions in his translation of Plutarch that 'Livius did please them by letting them have the lands scot-free.' Later, however, 'scot' also took on the metaphorical sense of 'punishment, injury.' A 17th century commentator reported that 'Oxford escaped scot-free of the plague.' Since 'scot' in these senses alternated with 'shot,' 'shot-free' is also found inworks by writers such as Shakespeare. In *Henry the Fourth, Part I*, Falstaff is caught up in a battle and puns: 'Though I could scape shot-free at London, I fear the shot here.'

Go the Whole Hog

To 'go the whole hog' means to see something through to the end, do it thoroughly, often with the implication that this means taking a risk. The phrase was much used of Andrew Jackson, during his successful presidential campaign of 1828. A contemporary political commentator explained that 'go the whole hog' – a Virginian saying – became 'a political phrase marking the democrat from a federalist.' Certainly the *Virginia Herald* said of Jackson in 1829 that 'we all know that of late he has shown a disposition to become a "whole hog man".' In 1852 the magazine *Household Words* commented: 'When a Virginian butcher kills a pig, he is said to ask his customers whether they will "go the whole hog," as, in such case, he sells at a lower price than if they pick out the prime joints only.'

For some reason, scholars have been reluctant to accept that it was this which ultimately led to metaphorical use of the phrase. Many point to the fact that by the early 19th century 'hog' was the slang name of a coin, a ten-cent piece, so that the phrase could mean 'to invest all one's money in a project.' Henry Lawson, as it happens, writes in *Stiffner and Jim*: 'I thought I might as well go the whole hog – I might as well die for a pound as a penny, if I had to die.' The *Oxford English Dictionary* suggests instead a complex literary origin, based on the coincidence that 'whole hog' occurs in 'Hypocrisy Detected,' a poem by William Cowper. Cowper's theme is that Mahomet banned his followers from eating part of a hog, without specifying which part. He continues:

> But for one piece they thought it hard
> From the whole hog to be debarr'd.

Eventually, Cowper says, Mahometans are able to convince themselves that each part of the hog is acceptable, so that they can eat the entire animal. The more straightforward association of 'go the whole hog' with butchers in Virginia is far more likely to be its true origin.

In Britain the phrase is sometimes used to mean 'have sexual intercourse.' 'I have tried all sorts of erotic things, but my girlfriend refuses to go the whole hog' occurs in a letter of desperation written to an agony aunt by the young hero of *The Growing Pains of Adrian Mole*, by Sue Townsend.

Grass Widow

The meaning of 'grass widow' has changed through the centuries. In its earliest use it seems to have referred to an abandoned mistress, especially an unmarried woman with a child. Parallel expressions in Dutch and German suggest that 'grass' alluded to meetings in the fields rather than the marital bed. German villagers would formerly lay chopped straw before the door of a woman who 'anticipated conjugal life,' in the words of Professor Ernest Weekley. If the woman then married while obviously pregnant she would carry straw instead of flowers. In 17th century England there was a slang expression 'to give a girl a green gown.' A modern young man might speak instead of having a 'roll in the hay' with the girl in question.

'Grass widow' possibly changed its meaning in the 19th century among the Anglo-Indians, the original sense of 'grass' no longer being evident. By this time it was popularly believed that 'grass widow' was a corruption of 'grace widow,' though it is difficult to know how the meaning of 'grace' can be stretched to support this.

'Grass' may also have been reinterpreted as a reference to being 'at grass,' which at one time could mean 'to be on holiday.' Edwin Radford, in *Crowther's Encyclopoedia of Phrases and Origins*, is more specific. He mentions 'the custom of European husbands in India sending their wives to the cool hills during the hot season, while they remained behind in the parched cities. On the hills, in the cool, the grass grew greenly, hence a "grass" widow.' Radford is clearly unaware that 'grass widow' had existed since the 16th century in an earlier meaning, and therefore wrongly claims this as the origin of the phrase.

The *Oxford English Dictionary* does have quotations from 19th century writings which demonstrate Anglo-Indian usage of 'grass widow.' John Lang's *Wanderings In India*, for instance, published in 1859, has: 'Grass widows in the hills are always writing to their husbands, when you drop in upon them.' Other quotations, however, show the phrase to have been in use at this time elsewhere in the English-speaking world. A woman writer who visited gold diggings in Australia reported in 1853 that the miners were away for long periods. She added: 'the wives thus left in town are termed grass widows – a mining expression.' Quotations from late-19th century newspapers, meanwhile, show that 'grass widow' and 'grass widower,' in the modern meaning of a wife or husband temporarily separated from his or her partner, were already familiar terms to American readers.

'Grass widower' continues to be used alongside 'grass widow.' Ruth Rendell writes, in *To Fear a Painted Devil*: 'I'll nip indoors and make the poor grass widower a nice cup of tea.' The phrase has also developed other variants, such as 'grass widowhood.' William J.Locke, in *Stories Near and Far*, writes: 'She could never resolve the problem whether she would have been happier or unhappier in a grass-widowed state.' An American magazine once reported: 'She and her husband lived charmingly apart, grass-widowing here and there.' Stephen Vincent Benét, in *Everybody Was Very Nice*, refers to 'grass bachelors,' but he applies the phrase with no justification to divorced men. A 'grass bachelor' would more accurately describe an unmarried man whose regular partner was temporarily absent.

Great Guns

In former times the 'great guns' were cannons, the most important weapons used in battles, especially at sea. As symbols of great force and power they gave rise to several metaphorical expressions. Important people, for example, were 'great guns.' 'None of the great guns were at Madame de Coligny's,' wrote Lady Granville in a letter to a friend in 1815. Sir Walter Scott, ten years later, mentions 'a worthy clergyman, one of the great guns, as they call them.' This metaphor was often extended. An 1885 article in the *Manchester Examiner* remarked : 'The Opposition are anxious to have their great guns in the Upper Chamber pounding away at the same time.' More recently, the *Times Literary Supplement* warned: 'We must now brace ourselves to receive broadsides from the great guns of science and technology.'

In modern times we might instead speak of important people as 'big guns.' This form was already in use by the late 19th century. Benjamin Disraeli, in his novel *Endymion*, writes: 'I do not despair of its being done. But what I want is some big guns to do it.' A further development in American speech has led to 'big gun' becoming 'big shot,' a term often used ironically.

The rushing noise of balls fired from cannons led to the use of 'great guns' to describe howling winds. 'It blows great guns indeed,' says a character in Dickens's *Barnaby Rudge*. 'There'll be many a crash in the forest to-night.' Dylan Thomas was obviously familiar with this usage. *Under Milk Wood* has: 'But with blue hazy eyes the fishermen gaze at that milkmaid whispering water with no ruck or ripple as though it blew great guns and serpents and typhooned the town.'

'To blow great guns' is now seldom heard, any more than 'great guns!' used as an exclamation. 'Great guns! is he her uncle?' occurs in Mark Twain's *Huckleberry Finn* and in other works of the late 19th century. 'Go great guns' in the sense of 'proceed with great momentum' is a more recent phrase which is still current, especially in sporting contexts. Early use is found in *Field* magazine in 1913: 'Louvois shot out, passed Sanquhar and Fairy King, and going great guns beat the favourite by a head.' More recent examples from the *Times* newspaper include: 'Local partisanship will no doubt run high between Bristol, who are going great guns so far, and their old rivals Gloucester.' 'Arsenal, going great guns in their functional, efficient way, must see the league title within their sights.'

Great Scott

'Great Scott!' is an inoffensive substitute for 'Great God!' It is natural to think that its original use was inspired by some famous person called Scott, and there is a good candidate. Sir Walter Scott, who died in 1832, can almost certainly be ruled out, since this phrase only began to be used in the mid-19th century, and in America rather than Britain. Robert Falcon Scott, the explorer, was not born until 1868. A famous Scott in America, however, was General Winfield Scott (1786-1866), otherwise known as 'Old Fuss and Feathers.' The nickname alluded to his notorious vanity and pomposity. It may well have been the latter that led to 'Great Scott! being used ironically, as if 'Scott' was a synonym for 'God.'

'Great Scott!' is now seldom heard in conversation, but occurs in American literature. Stephen Vincent Benét, in *Everybody Was Very Nice*, has: 'Great Scott, I can remember when I was just a kid and the Prentisses got divorced. They were pretty prominent people and it shook the whole town.' 'He doesn't recognize me,' says a woman about her husband, in *Comfort Me With Apples* by Peter de Vries. 'Great Scott, he's denying you,' says her brother. The ejaculation has also been turned into a verb. In a sketch published in *Harper's Weekly*, Mark Twain wrote: '"Ger-reat Scott!" ejaculated the Major. The secretary said, wonderingly: "Why, what are you Great-Scotting about, Major?"' P.G.Wodehouse, in *Stiff Upper Lip, Jeeves*, has the similar '"You don't mean that old crumb was there?" I said, Great-Scott-ing.'

Future generations of 'Trekkies' may perhaps revive this phrase, associating it with Lieutenant Commander Scott of the Starship *Enterprise*. He has already had a minor impact on the language. In the American television series 'Star Trek', first shown 1966-9, Captain Kirk would usually at some stage issue the command 'Beam me up, Scottie.' He would then disintegrate and magically reappear on board the *Enterprise*. 'Beam me up, Scottie' is sometimes used jokingly to mean 'Get me out of here.'

Green with Envy

It is said of a young woman, in Mary McCarthy's *The Group*, that 'her room-mates were green with envy.' The statement would have surprised readers in the 16th century, who associated envy with the colour yellow. That is the point of Nym's comment in *The Merry Wives of Windsor*: 'I will possess him with yellowness.' He means that he intends to make Page jealous.

It is surprising, then, that Shakespeare refers in *The Merchant of Venice* to 'green-eyed jealousy.' Later he has Iago expand on this in *Othello*:

> O beware, my lord, of jealousy;
> It is the green-ey'd monster which doth mock
> The meat it feeds on.

Iago is saying that jealousy is like a cat which plays with, or mocks, the mouse it intends to kill, 'the meat it feeds on.' Jealousy, in other words, does to love what a cat does to a mouse. It makes a mockery of love, even though it feeds on love.

This single dramatic speech seems to have been responsible for our association of greenness with envy. 'Green with envy' is a common saying; references to 'green-eyed' or the 'green-eyed monster' also occur. 'I never thought he'd come the old green-eyed monster' says a character in C. Watson's *Hopjoy was Here*.

'Yellow,' in the meantime, has gone on to become a symbol of cowardice. This may have arisen through a series of mistakes. When costard apples were commonly sold by costard-mongers, the later coster-mongers, 'costard' was a slang word for the head. Children used to taunt a fearful child with 'cowardy, cowardy costard.' This was rather like calling him 'cowardy head,' much as a modern child might call another 'bighead' or 'fathead.' After costard apples had disappeared from the scene, children assumed that the now meaningless word 'costard' was 'custard.' They duly amended their taunting to 'coward, cowardy custard,' associating cowardice with something very yellow.

Hair of the Dog that Bit You, A

Anyone suffering from a hangover is likely to be told that he or she needs 'a hair of the dog that bit you.' The narrator of *Consenting Adults*, by Peter de Vries, says at one point: 'That does it. I'll never touch another drop of the stuff. Except for a hair of the dog, of course, the efficacy of which is known of old. I would resist Cyril Connolly's dictum that a tuft of the dog was even better.'

There is a widespread belief that drinking a little more of whatever caused the problem in the first place will make one feel better. This is rather like saying that petrol should be used to put out a fire, but foolish as they are, such beliefs are very ancient. The *Iliad* tells us that a wound caused by the spear of Achilles could be cured with an ointment that included rust from the same spear. There was also a Latin tag *similia similibus curantur* 'likes are cured by like', the basis of Hahneman's theories of homeopathy.

'Hair of the dog' stems from the belief that if you were bitten by a mad dog, a hair of the dog that bit you, laid across the wound, would heal it. In other words, catch the dog, snip off one of its hairs, apply the hair to the wound and all will be well. Needless to say, anyone trying to do such a thing would run a grave risk of being bitten more severely, and no amount of dog hairs would heal the wounds.

By the 16th century, the phrase 'hair of the dog' was being applied metaphorically to hangover cures. John Heywood includes it in his *Proverbs in the English Tongue*, published in 1534. Dickens was later to quote it in *Barnaby Rudge*: 'Drink again. Another hair of the dog that bit you, captain.' Modern writers usually leave the phrase unfinished. Margaret Mitchell's *Gone With the Wind* has: 'Do you think Miss Pittypat would be having any brandy in the house? The hair of the dog...'

According to Mary McCarthy, in *The Groves of Academe*, the most famous literary reference to 'the hair of the dog' occurs in the works of Byron. She writes: '"And now for God's sake, hock and soda-water," laughed the very handsome curly-haired youth who had spoken at this morning's session. Anna knew her Byron and knew what this meant; it was the *locus classicus* of the hair of the dog in literature.'

Miss McCarthy is thinking of *Don Juan*, where Lord Byron several times comments on his own favourite hang-over cure. Canto Two, for instance, has:

> Ring for your valet – bid him quickly bring
> Some hock and soda-water, then you'll know
> A pleasure worthy Xerxes the great king;
> For not the blest sherbet, sublimed with snow,
> Nor the first sparkle of the desert spring,
> Nor burgundy in all its sunset glow,
> After long travel, ennui, love, or slaughter,
> Vie with that draught of hock and soda-water.

This would only be an example of the 'hair of the dog' if it were hock and soda water that had made Byron drunk in the first place. The phrase is not properly applied to hangover cures in general.

Hang by a Thread

We often use this expression about someone whose life is in danger, as when a character in John Welcome's novel *Stop at Nothing* remarks: 'Mantovelli's life is hanging by a thread. He'll be lucky if he lasts a month.' This proves to be true, for the man concerned dies next day.

The saying conjures up an image of someone hanging over a precipice, suspended by a rope which is no thicker than a thread, but it alludes to a story which is rather different. Cicero relates that Damocles, who lived in the 4th century BC, used to flatter his royal master, Dionysius. At one point he told him how happy he must be to have such wealth and power. Dionysius responded by inviting Damocles to a banquet, so that he could see for himself what it meant to be in his position. At the banquet Damocles discovered that a sword was hanging over his head, suspended by a single thread. It is doubtful whether he enjoyed the meal, but by the end of the evening he had grasped the fact that a powerful position is also a precarious one.

Thomas Wolfe alludes to this story in *Look Homeward, Angel* when doctors announce that a man is terminally ill. 'She had brought him home, the shadow of his death was suspended over them like a Damoclean sword.'

Hanky-panky

When 'hanky-panky' first began to be used in English its meaning was very similar to 'hocus-pocus,' which refers to the trickery of a magician. 'Hocus-pocus' itself was an incantation used by stage magicians, the words being meaningless but meant to sound like Latin. In popular speech hocus-pocus became hoky-poky; it is this which may in turn have led to hanky-panky. In modern times, the phrase has come to mean any kind of funny business, though it is often applied to slightly improper sexual behaviour. In Daphne du Maurier's *Rule Britannia*, a man offers a woman a case of Californian wine. He adds: 'No hanky-panky, I promise you. It's all above board. No duty to pay. We're to import it in large quantities, and this happens to be the first consignment.' Edna Ferber's *Giant* has a husband who says to his new wife: 'You were tucked away in the library with that Rorik guy. What kind of hanky-panky was going on?'

English-speakers are rather fond of rhyming phrases, which perhaps recall their childhood. Young children instinctively play with words and names, creating Georgie-porgie, Jimsy-wimsy, footsy-wootsy and similar combinations. It was a little girl asking J.M.Barrie to be her friendy-wendy that inspired him to invent Wendy as a girl's name for use in *Peter Pan*. Other phrases of the hanky-panky type include airy-fairy, argy-bargy, arty-crafty, big-wig, boogie-woogie, brain drain, chock-a-block, clap-trap, even-stevens, flibberty-gibberty, fuddy-duddy, heebie-jeebies, helter-skelter, hi-fi, higgledy-piggledy, high and dry, hob-nob, hodge-podge, hoity-toity, hotch-potch, hot-shot, hugger-mugger, hurdy-gurdy, hurry-scurry, itsy-bitsy, jeepers-creepers, lovey-dovey, namby-pamby, nit-wit, no go, okey-dokey, palsy-walsy, pell-mell, pot-shot, rag-bag, rat-tat, shilly-shally, silly-billy, sin-bin, teasy-weasy, teeny-weeny, walkie-talkie, wear and tear, wheeler-dealer, willy-nilly.

Hardly the Word

We use this phrase when we want to amend something that has just been said, either by ourselves or by someone else. 'He had a weakness for writing edifying literature,' says a man in *The Lost Inheritance*, by H.G.Wells. He then adds: 'Weakness is hardly the word – downright mania is nearer the mark.' Thomas de Quincy, in *Reminiscences of the English Lake Poets*, has: 'He read to me a passage from Fairfax's *Tasso*, ending pretty nearly with these words – Amidst the broad fields and the endless wood, The lofty lady kept her maidenhood. I thought that, possibly, he had his sister in his thoughts. Yet "lofty" was hardly the right word. Miss Wordsworth was too ardent and fiery a creature to maintain the reserve essential to dignity.' Kingsley Amis writes, in *Stanley and the Women*: 'You've some idea of how difficult she can be. Difficult, that's hardly the word. It's a full-time job just keeping an eye on her.'

'Hardly' in this context means 'not quite, scarcely,' though its original sense was 'in a harsh manner.' By the 17th century the word had come to mean 'not easily, with difficulty.' An early translation of the New Testament, Luke 18, ran: 'How hardly shall they that have money enter into the kingdom of God?' It is easy to see how a statement like 'he can hardly survive' could then be interpreted as 'he can only just survive.'

Have a Chip on One's Shoulder

Occasionally we come across a person whose general attitude is resentful and defiant, who seems to be convinced that everyone is prejudiced against him. We say that such a person has a chip on his shoulder. 'Like all martyrs, when you get to know them, he turns out to have quite a chip on his shoulder' says someone in Mary McCarthy's *The Groves of Academe*. Berta Ruck, in *Ancestral Voices*, writes: '"One forgives that rather – well, brusque manner."

"Yes, as if she had a chip on her shoulder about something".'
In *Waterfront*, Budd Schulberg has the interesting: '"You looking
for me?" Terry asked. His voice had a chip on its shoulder.'

   The *Oxford English Dictionary* quotes the *Long Island Telegraph* of
May 20, 1830: 'When two churlish boys were determined to fight,
a chip would be placed on the shoulder of one, and the other
demanded to knock it off at his peril.' Eric Partridge hints, in his
Dictionary of Historical Slang, that the chip of wood may have been
suggested by the slang phrase 'chip at someone,' meaning to
quarrel with or adversely criticise that person. By the end of the
19th century the chip on the shoulder had become purely
metaphorical. Somerset Maugham summed up the meaning it
had acquired in one of his short stories: 'He was a man with a chip
on his shoulder. Everyone seemed in a conspiracy to slight or
injure him.'

Have a Frog in One's Throat

Margaret Laurence writes, in *The Diviners*: 'Her voice comes out
like a croak. She clears her throat. "Sorry. Frog in my throat." Frog
in the throat? What a gruesome expression. Who could ever have
thought that one up? Ugh. Those clammy clambering teeny
saurian legs in your *gullet*, for God's sake?' We have no way of
knowing who 'thought up' this expression, though it was
obviously suggested by the sound a person makes when the
throat is partly blocked by phlegm. 'I was in wonderful voice last
night,' wrote Charles Dickens to a correspondent in 1868, 'but
croak a little this morning.' Frank Richards, in *Old Soldiers Never
Die*, has: 'One was speaking very thickly and the other lost his
temper and told him to pull the bloody frog out of his throat.'

The phrase is one that appeals to the imagination of children, though as with Margaret Laurence it may conjure up an unpleasant image. As it happens, in former times it was usually children who were said to have a disease in the throat called 'the frog.' This was another name for the thrush, the infectious disease which produces white patches in the mouth and causes the throat to swell.

Have Someone or Something Taped

Employees who are asked by the boss whether they can handle a particular task may well say that they 'have it taped,' meaning that they have it under control. In Britain, especially, someone might also talk about having another person taped. It's the sort of thing a policeman might say to someone suspected of a crime, and it would mean: 'I know the kind of person you are and what you've been doing.' James Joyce used the phrase in that way in *Grace*: 'I never saw such an eye in a man's head. It was as much as to say: I have you properly taped, my lad.'

Most people would guess that the 'taping' referred to had something to do with a recording. It seems to suggest someone or something that has been captured on audio or video-tape, then studied in great detail so that it is thoroughly understood. The problem with this is that the phrase existed before such recordings were possible. Those who originally used it had a simpler kind of tape in mind, the one a tailor might use to take someone's measurements. In early 20th century slang, then, saying that you had something or someone taped was a fashionable way of saying that you had sized up a situation, or that you had somebody's measure.

Have Two Strings to One's Bow

John Lyly told the readers of his *Euphues,* in 1579: 'My counsel is that thou have more strings to thy bow than one.' This would have been sound advice for a military archer, but the phrase seems always to have been used metaphorically. As a general comment on the advisability of having something to fall back on in an emergency, to have another possible course of action if the first one fails, it has been much repeated through the centuries. 'It's as well to have a second string to your bow,' writes Winifred Holtby, in *South Riding.* Fittingly, perhaps, there has been an alternative way of expressing this thought since the 17th century. Those who preferred a more domestic image than archery have been able to say: 'don't put all your eggs in one basket.'

The spare bow-string image has proved popular, however. Even Jane Austen, who normally makes her characters express their dislike of such phrases, remarks in *Mansfield Park* that 'Miss Bertram might be said to have two strings to her bow.' Mary McCarthy, who by contrast crams every idiomatic phrase ever invented into her novels, says in *The Group*: 'Libby decided that she must have another string to her bow.' Libby wants to do something else besides book-reviewing. If there comes a time when book-reviews are no longer offered to her she will then be able to turn to her 'second string' and still have a source of income.

'Second string' has taken on a life of its own with the meaning of 'back-up, stand-in, substitute.' 'The man who may take over as second string to Tony Lock is Mike Allen,' reported the *People* newspaper in 1958. The phrase can alsobe applied to a reserve team. 'On Saturday, Archie kept goal for the Rochdale second string' said a report in *Sport* magazine. In theory there could be a 'third string,' 'fourth string,' and so on. Although two strings to one's bow are normally mentioned, John Heywood was already referring to 'many strings' in the 16th century. In a more recent work Edward A.Rogers, in *Face To Face*, has: 'I wonder if he really left Hollywood because of the chance you gave him, or because he had played out almost every string he had in his bow out there?' The 'played out' may be coincidental, but it is almost as if Rogers is mistakenly thinking that this phrase refers to a violin bow.

Hell-for-leather

Rudyard Kipling, in *The Story of the Gadsbys* (1889), writes: 'Here, Gaddy, take the note to Bingle and ride hell-for-leather.' This is the first recorded instance of this strange phrase, which seems to refer in some way to the leather harness of a horse. 'In leather' is sometimes used for 'in harness,' as in a sentence like 'the horse goes quietly in leather.' To ride hell-for-leather means to ride all out, as quickly as possible – ride like hell in leather, as it were. However, Professor Ernest Weekley suggested that the expression might be a corrupt form of 'all of a lather.' This is highly ingenious, though 'all in a lather' was the more usual form. Mary Martha Sherwood, in *The History of Henry Milner*, writes: 'Miss Bell had already exercised her mare so well, that, to use a jockey term, she was all in a lather.' This novel was published in 1837, long before the first use of 'hell-for-leather.'

Writers such as Mary Webb, in *Gone To Earth*, use hell-for-leather in a horse-riding context: 'Here have I been going hell-for-leather up and down the country.' Others merely use it in a more general way to mean 'as fast as possible.' 'We saw a swarm of figures running hell-for-leather' is in George MacDonald Fraser's *Flashman*. *The Times* reported in 1963 that 'Australia's plan was to make 90 during the afternoon, if they could, without losing too many wickets and to go hell-for-leather afterwards.'

Hide One's Light Under a Bushel

Mary McCarthy writes, in *The Group*: 'She had put Helena, who was not one to hide her light under a bushel, on the board of the literary magazine.' Helena, in other words, is neither shy nor modest about admitting that she is talented. Samuel Butler, in *The Way of All Flesh*, has: 'he liked being seen and being congratulated on growing up such a fine-looking and fortunate young fellow, for he was not the youth to hide his light under a bushel.' The phrase occurs again in Derek Jewell's *Come In, No.1, Your Time Is Up*. 'Is he as much of a financial genius as they make out?' asks someone. 'The best finance director in the country,' is the reply. 'He doesn't exactly hide his light under a bushel.' D.H.Lawrence uses a slight variation in *Rawdon's Roof*: 'Alec Drummond, whatever else he did, didn't hide his prowess under a bushel.'

There is a hint of disapproval in all these instances, since not hiding one's light under a bushel smacks of arrogance. In the New Testament, where the phrase originally occurs, there appears to be a more positive attitude. Matthew 5.14 relates that Jesus told his disciples, in the Sermon on the Mount: 'You are the light of the world. A city set on a hill cannot be hid. Nor do men light a lamp and put it under a bushel, but on a stand, and it gives light to all in the house. Let your light so shine before men, that they may see your good works and give glory to your Father who is in heaven.'

The 'bushel' referred to is a wooden container used to measure a bushel (equivalent to eight gallons) of grain or fruit. Two thousand years ago it would have been a familiar every-day object. As for the biblical message, it is reinforced at *Mark* 4.21: 'Is a lamp brought in to be put under a bushel, or under a bed, and not on a stand? For there is nothing hid, except to be made manifest; nor is anything secret, except to come to light.' *Luke* 11.33 also has: 'No one after lighting a lamp puts it in a cellar or under a bushel, but on a stand, that those who enter may see the light.' None of this, of course, refers to boasting about one's own abilities: the light that should not be hidden is that of Christian faith.

Hit the Nail on the Head

Most people who have tried to a hit a nail on the head, only to give themselves a resounding blow on the thumb, would easily understand why this phrase came to have the metaphorical meaning of 'get to the exact truth of the matter.' Nevertheless, some speakers and writers in the 19th century preferred to imagine a number of nails in a line, all needing to be driven home. The person who identified the correct answer to a problem when a number of solutions presented themselves was, in their view, hitting the *right* nail on the head. In Dickens's *Oliver Twist*, Noah Claypole tells Charlotte that he wants to embark on a life of crime and is disconcerted when he realises that Fagin has overheard him. Fagin immediately reassures him: 'You've hit the right nail upon the head, and are as safe here as you could be.' By contrast, a character in Arthur Murphy's play *The Way to Keep Him* is told: 'You have not hit the right nail on the head.'

What was probably the earliest form of this expression occurs in a religious play of the mid-15th century: 'Now be myn trowthe ye hytte the pynne.' Other early variants talked of hitting the mark or needle, but by 1529 John Skelton was writing in *Colyn Cloute* that 'yf that he hyt the nayle on the hede, it standeth in no stede.' The underlying idea seems to have been that, when trying to hammer home a pin-like nail, it was easier to miss than score a direct hit. A text of 1700 says: 'At last they ignorantly hit the nail on the head, saying that the Devil was in him.' 'He was rash,' says Elizabeth Gaskell in *Wives and Daughters*, 'hitting the nail on the head sometimes.' Straightforward modern use of the phrase is demonstrated in Mary McCarthy's *The Group*, when Mr Davison says: 'I mean exactly that. You've hit the nail smack on the head.'

Hobson's Choice

Many people associate 'Hobson's choice' with the 1954 David Lean film, in which Charles Laughton played the part of Hobson, a shoe-seller and tyrannical father. He was eventually presented with 'Hobson's choice' by his daughter. The film looked back to a stage-comedy by Harold Brighouse, but the phrase itself had already been in use for several centuries. In 1712, Richard Steele explained its origin in *The Spectator*: 'Tobias Hobson, from whom we have the expression, was the first on this island who let out hackney horses. He lived at Cambridge, and observing that the scholars rode hard, his manner was to keep a large stable of horses, with boots, bridles, and stirrups, to furnish the gentlemen at once without going from college to college to borrow, as they have done since the death of this worthy man. Mr Hobson, when a man came for a horse, obliged him to take the horse which stood next to the stable-door. From whence it became a proverb to say "Hobson's choice".'

Steele thought that it was only by 'vulgar error' that this expression had come to mean 'choose what is offered to you or have nothing at all.' In his view, Hobson had insisted on a strict rotation system for his horses in order to make sure that every customer, and for that matter every horse, was fairly treated. In theory, said Steele, 'Hobson's choice' should mean a choice deliberately made with the welfare of others in mind. The popular view has instead made it 'an apparent choice where in fact no real choice exists.' Morris West uses the phrase in such a sense in *Proteus*. A man who believes that he must either commit suicide or die slowly in prison says: 'Hobson's choice: a clean exit or a long slavery.' Either way, in other words, the result will be the same.

`Hobson's choice' was no doubt a Cambridge university joke to begin with. Tobias Hobson was a character, known amongst others to John Milton as a young man. Milton's epitaph for him ran:

> Here lies old Hobson; Death hath broke his girt
> And here, alas! hath laid him in the dirt.

Curiously, in spite of the overwhelming evidence for this man being responsible for 'Hobson's choice,' Professor Ernest Weekley thought this 'very doubtful.' Weekley had come across an allusion in a publication of 1617 to 'Hodgson's choice.' No other such references have been found, and no doubt the memory of Richard Cocks, the writer concerned, was at fault in using Hodgson for Hobson.

Home, Sweet Home

A character in Evelyn Waugh's *Vile Bodies* remarks: 'Lord, I shall be glad when we get to Dover. Home, sweet home, eh?' This rather stretches the meaning of 'home, sweet home,' which originally referred to a person's home rather than his native country, but the phrase has taken on a life of its own. In the sentimental days of the past it was frequently displayed in houses, usually as a piece of framed embroidery. That was also the time when most people could have made an attempt at singing the song from which the words are derived.

'Home, sweet home' was the one and only lasting success of an American, John Howard Payne, who was born in New York in 1791. In his youth he was an actor, billed as The American Juvenile Wonder. He went on to write plays and musical dramas, and in 1822 produced 'Clari, The Maid of Milan.' It was this which included the song 'Home, Sweet Home:'

> Mid pleasures and palaces though we may roam,
> Be it ever so humble, there's no place like home;
> A charm from the skies seems to hallow us there,
> Which, seek through the world, is ne'er met with
> elsewhere.
> Home, home, sweet, sweet home! There's no place
> like home! there's no place like home!

The roam/home contrast was a well established poetic idea when Payne came to it. In 1703, Nicholas Rowe's *The Fair Penitent* had contained the lines:

> We'd teach the saunt'ring squire, who loves to roam,
> Forgetful of his own dear Spouse and Home.

Coleridge's *The Sigh* (1794) had:

> In distant climes to roam,
> A wanderer from my native home.

Byron rhymed the two words in *The Bride of Abydos* (1813), while in the same year Sir Walter Scott wrote:

> As wilder'd children leave their home,
> After the rainbow's arch to roam.

None of these poets could match the simple effectiveness of Payne's 'there's no place like home,' especially when stripped of the 'humble' reference. As the 19th century writer E.J.Worboise pointed out: 'When it is not only humble, but frowsty, you are apt to wish you were anywhere else than at home!' 'Home' nevertheless has long been an emotionally powerful word. In 1951, when the Ministry of Health tried to replace it with appalling officialese, Winston Churchill put them in their place. 'Be it ever so humble,' sang Churchill, 'there's no place like the accomodation unit.'

Hue and Cry

'Hue and cry' now means little more than a noisy protest about something. A government spokesman, for example, makes a statement and the opposition parties raise a hue and cry about it. The phrase once had a more legal sense, referring to the appeal made by the victim of a crime or a constable to apprehend a lawbreaker. When a hue and cry was raised against someone, by a simple shout of 'Stop thief!' or a more formal proclamation, members of the public had a legal obligation to help in the apprehension of the person concerned. In the literature of former times, 'hue and cry' normally has this meaning. 'The old gentleman,' says Dickens in *Oliver Twist*, 'was not the only person who raised the hue-and-cry.' The same novel refers to someone who is 'deeply absorbed in the interesting pages of the Hue-and-Cry.' The reference here is to an official police gazette which was still being published when Dickens wrote his novel. It listed the particulars of offenders and their crimes.

Hue and cry was adapted from the Norman French *hu e cri* in the 13th century. *Hu* is ultimately from a French verb *huer* which means to make a hooting noise, especially when hunting. The word represents a natural non-verbal sound, rather like 'hoy' or 'ahoy' in English. The *Oxford English Dictionary* suggests that it may originally have included noises such as the sound of horns and trumpets, or anything that would attract attention. In spite of all the emphasis on noise that the phrase contains, the idea of a chase still sometimes comes to the surface. 'Then began the hue and cry,' writes Richard Hughes in *A High Wind in Jamaica*. 'Sixteen men flinging about in lofty acrobatics, all to catch one poor old drunken monkey. For he was drunk as a lord, and sick as a cat.'

Hunky-dory

In *Tropic of Cancer* Henry Miller writes: 'For the time being, of course, he was pretending that everything was hunky-dory.' 'Hunky-dory,' in the sense of 'satisfactory, okay, fine,' made its first appearance in America in the middle of the 19th century. Its listing in most contemporary American and British slang dictionaries indicates that it is still in use.

The 'hunky' part of the expression has been linked to Dutch

honk, used in children's games to indicate a home base or safe place. The word was first heard in the New York area when children of Dutch immigrants talked of 'reaching hunk' or 'being on hunk' when playing tag. From this, 'to be hunk' came to have the general meaning of 'to be safe.' By the early 1860's 'hunky' had become a slang word meaning 'to be in good condition, be safe and sound, all right.' 'If I'd took good care of that map,' says a character in K. Munroe's *Golden Days*, published in 1889, 'we'd been all hunky at this minute.'

Within a few years, for reasons that no one has been able to explain satisfactorily, 'hunky' had been extended to 'hunky-dory.' Most commentators fall back on the 'meaningless extension' theory, pointing to expressions like 'okey-dokey' which have grown from okay. At work in such instances is a kind of linguistic playfulness. It can be seen when children convert names into Georgie-Porgie, Petesy-Wetesy. This explanation of hunky-dory might be acceptable if 'hunky' had become *hunky-dunky*, say, since most repetitive phrases have an in-built rhyme. It may be that 'dory,' like 'hunky,' is a corruption of a Dutch word, but scholars have yet to find it.

If the Mountain will not come to Mahomet, Mahomet must go to the Mountain

In *Shannon's Way*, by A.J.Cronin, a doctor goes to the nurses' common-room. One of the nurses exclaims: 'Why, Mahomet has come to the mountain,' and is said to be pleased with herself for making use of the phrase. It alludes to a proverbial saying that was already current in the 17th century. Francis Bacon's essay Of *Boldness* quotes it in the form: 'If the hill will not come to Mahomet, Mahomet will go to the hill.' By 1642 it had become, in the works of the theologian John Owen: 'If the mountaine will not come to Mahomet, Mahomet will goe to the mountaine.'

Mahomet is an early English form of the name that is now usually written Mohammed. When the Arabs asked the Prophet Mohammed to supply miraculous proofs of his teachings, he ordered Mount Safa to come to him. The mountain, needless to say, did not move. 'God is merciful,' said Mohammed. 'Had the mountain obeyed my words it would have fallen on us and destroyed us. I will go to the mountain and thank God.' In modern times, as the A.J.Cronin quotation suggests, an allusion to Mahomet going to the mountain is likely to occur when it becomes obvious that the only way to see someone is to pay that person a visit, not wait for a visit to be made.

In a Nutshell

When we refer to putting something 'in a nutshell' we are remembering Pliny the Elder, a remarkable Roman who lived two thousand years ago. Pliny's attitude to life and his scientific curiosity was summed up in the manner of his death. When Vesuvius erupted in 79 A.D., he wanted to help those who were affected as well as observe the event from near at hand. His enthusiasm led to his becoming one of the volcano's victims.

Of Pliny's many works, only his *Historia Naturalis* survives. In it he mentions a copy of Homer's *Iliad* which was small enough to be enclosed in the shell of a nut. English writers such as Jonathan Swift, in *A Tale of a Tub*, and Thomas Carlyle, in *Past and Present*, make specific reference to this '*Iliad* in a nutshell.' *The Times* also reported in 1865 on 'a whole *Iliad* of finance in a comparative nutshell.' Writers and speakers, however, soon began to use the nutshell image on its own. 'There, sir, is political economy in a nutshell,' says a speaker in Thomas Love Peacock's *Crotchet Castle*, published in 1831.

The phrase is widely used in modern times. Henry Cecil's *Brothers in Law* has: 'That could be a long story, but I'll make it a short one. In a nutshell, I've got too big for my boots.' In *Funeral in Berlin*, Len Deighton writes: 'I say, that's rather good. In an absolute nutshell. I'll write that down. "Expendable hero", that's what Stok is all right.' A man in Margaret Atwood's *Bodily Harm* says: 'The U.S. borrowed too much money. That's the whole problem in a nutshell.' Jeremy Brooks, in *Henry's War*, has someone make the sarcastic comment: 'You've put it in a nutshell the size of the *Queen Mary*.'

The phrase has also spawned a verb. *The National Observer* stated in 1892: 'To add that the hour-glass or Victorian type of figure vies with the high-waisted or Empire is to nutshell the extreme ideals of the moment.' Mark Twain, in *Life on the Mississippi*, has: 'The clerk nutshelled the contrast between the former time and the present.' There is every reason to think that nutshelling of this kind will continue indefinitely.

In Cahoots With

Patricia Highsmith, in *Ripley Under Ground*, writes: 'I suspect him of being in cahoots with the Buckmaster people to earn more money.' The man concerned is in league with the others, in other words, in some kind of illegal partnership. The phrase is used mainly in the USA and usually indicates collusion, a secret collaboration. A typical statement would be that someone is in cahoots with the devil. When first used in the early 19th century the expression was often 'in cahoot with,' but the plural form is now standard. Further examples include: 'Born troublemaker, probably in cahoots with his sister in Michigan,' (James A.Michener's *Chesapeake*); 'He's in cahoots with the union,' (Richard Bissell's *The Pajama Game*); 'Fleck and the professor in cahoots. The professor and the Navy in cahoots,' (Alistair Maclean's *The Dark Crusader*).

French *cahute*, German *Kajüte* and Dutch *kajuit* all mean a 'small hut.' This strongly suggests that 'in cahoots with' derives from pioneer immigrants who shared a frontier cabin. Those living with one another in harsh surroundings would have needed to collaborate closely in order to survive. To be in cahoots with someone still carries a suggestion of protecting a mutual interest against outside intruders.

Indian Summer

The phrase 'Indian summer' was first applied in the 18th century to the late autumn weather of New England. One early writer described it as 'two or three weeks of fair weather, in which the air is perfectly transparent, and the clouds, which float in a sky of the purest azure, are adorned with brilliant colours.' He continued: 'This charming season is called the Indian Summer, a name which is derived from the natives, who believe that it is caused by a wind, which comes immediately from the court of their great and benevolent God Cautantowwit, or the south-western God.' John Bradbury, in his *Travels in the Interior of America*, writes: 'About the beginning or middle of October the Indian summer commences, and is immediately known by the change which takes place in the atmosphere, as it becomes hazy, or what they term smoky.'

In modern times a spell of fine weather late in the year, no matter where it occurs, is called an 'Indian summer.' *The Houston Chronicle*, for example, reported one year that 'a delightfully persistent Indian Summer lingered over Houston, luring people to parks for langorous hours of contentment before looking ahead to winter and the prospect of rain and blue northers.' In 1962 the *Sunday Times* said that 'an Indian summer in the West Country brought peak holiday traffic jams in Devon yesterday.'

As with other terms that denote times of the year, 'Indian summer' is metaphorically applied to a period of a person's life, when a renewed energy and optimism interrupts the decline into old age. Norman del Mar, in his biography *Richard Strauss*, comments on 'the works of his Indian summer when, in the last five years of his life, inspiration came to him once more.'

In Fine Fettle

The English word 'fettle' is little used, other than as part of the phrase 'in fine fettle' – in excellent condition or health. Salman Rushdie, in *Midnight's Children*, has: 'Everything's in fine fettle, don't you agree? Tickety-boo, we used to say.' Mary Lavin says, in *A Memory*: 'This morning he was in fine fettle.' The verb 'fettle' was formerly in dialectal use, meaning 'to make ready, put in order, arrange.' It could also be used in the sense of 'groom a horse,' or 'attend to cattle.' Scholars believe that the word originally referred to some kind of belt, used to gird a man or a horse.

'Fettle' has nearly always been used in a positive way. Variations on 'fine fettle' that occur in literary sources include 'splendid, high, good, first-rate fettle.' In the past it was often possible to indicate someone's good health by saying simply that he or she was 'in fettle.' *The Oxford English Dictionary* nevertheless quotes a dialectal tale of the mid-19th century which says: 'I'm in terrible poor fettle with the toothache.'

In the Frame

A sports commentator might say of a team that is behind in a game, but playing well, that they are still 'in the frame' – they still have a chance of winning. The expression is perhaps a simple variant of 'in the picture,' with the meaning being that the team still 'merits attention.' It could instead be borrowed from snooker or pool, where 'frame' is used to denote an individual game. The allusion is to the racking of the balls in a triangular frame at the start of each game. A snooker or pool player who is 'still in the frame' could yet score enough points to win that particular game.

Another possibility is that 'in the frame' refers to horse-racing, where the names of the horses in each race are displayed in a large frame. The meaning then becomes something like: the team is still 'in the race.'

An innocent person who has been accused of a crime has perhaps been 'framed,' or is the victim of a 'frame-up.' He may even describe himself as being 'in the frame.' The thought behind this kind of 'framing' is that evidence has been fabricated, just as a frame is constructed around a picture. Some speakers may have in mind the framework of a building, but again there is the idea of an artificial structure. American policemen began to hear claims of 'It's a frame-up' in the early years of the 20th century. British audiences were later to become familiar with the expression in countless Hollywood gangster movies.

In Two Shakes

'Come on right over and we'll celebrate,' says someone in *Comfort Me With Apples*, by Peter de Vries. 'I'll be there in two shakes' is the reply. In one form or another, this roundabout way of saying 'immediately' has been in use since the early 19th century. Richard Barham, in *The Ingoldsby Legends*, has: 'He'll be up at the church in a couple of shakes.' 'A brace of shakes' has also been frequently used.

In its earliest form, this phrase seems to have referred to a single 'shake of a hand,' though it is not clear whether this was the normal handshake or the shaking of a dice. References to 'a shake' have continued to occur alongside 'two shakes,' Edith Nesbit being one writer who alternated between them. 'He'll be ready in a brace of shakes,' is in one of her books, while in another she has:

'Wait a shake, and I'll undo the side gate.'

This by no means exhausts the list of possible variants. 'Half a shake' is occasionally found, as well as fancifully extended forms. By the mid-19th century, American authors in particular were writing 'in the shake of a lamb's tail,' 'in two shakes of a lamb's tail' or 'in a couple of shakes of a sheep's tail.' In *Huckleberry Finn*, Mark Twain writes: 'I says to myself spos'n he can't fix that leg just in three shakes of a sheep's tail, as the saying is? spos'n it takes him three or four days?' This is clearly an expression that leaves room for personal preference.

Ivory Tower

This expression was first used (as *tour d'ivoire*) by the French literary critic Charles Augustin Sainte-Beuve. He was discussing the novelist and poet Alfred Victor de Vigny, who had spent the last twenty years of his life in secluded retirement, working in a turret room. The phrase was picked up by other French writers, notably Henri Bergson, winner of the 1927 Nobel Prize in Literature for his philosophical works. An English translation of Bergson in 1911 contained the passage: 'Each member of society must be ever attentive to his social surroundings: he must avoid shutting himself up in his own peculiar character as a philosopher in his ivory tower.'

Henry James, closely acquainted with French literature, then seized on the phrase as the title for a novel, left unfinished at his death in 1916. Since that time 'ivory towerism' has become widely identified with an escape from the harsh realities of life, a policy of seclusion and separation from the world. The person accused of living in an ivory tower is being told that he is aloof, that he lacks understanding of the practical problems faced by ordinary people. To paraphrase G.Vann in his *Water & Fire*, published in 1953, he is 'averting his gaze from the squalors of humanity.' In *Comfort Me With Apples*, Peter de Vries also implies that the language of the ivory tower has little in common with ordinary speech: 'Was he talking like a private eye already? Coming down out of the ivory tower to walk the earth at last? Or was it just your intellectual's oral slumming?'

'Ivory tower' has given birth to a number of derivatives. Nicholas Blake's *Whisper in Gloom*, for example, has: 'I'm going to plunge you into reality, my little Ivory-Towerist.' An article in *20th Century* reported in 1959 that 'British governments have been badly informed and Britain's ivory-towered embassies may have to bear some of the blame.' In 1963 the *Daily Telegraph* asked its readers to 'pity the poor parson! If he eschews all worldly contact, he's accused of being ivory-towerish and out of touch.'

In his *Dictionary of Phrase and Allusion*, Nigel Rees points out that the phrase 'ivory tower' occurs coincidentally in the Old Testament's Song of Solomon. The praises of the 'queenly maiden' are being sung – her 'rounded thighs are like jewels,' her 'two breasts are like two fawns, twins of a gazelle,' and so on. She is also told that her 'neck is like an ivory tower.' The allusion here is clearly to the colour of the skin. Sainte-Beauve, with his *tour d'ivoire*, was thinking of ivory as something rare, as distanced from daily life as the lofty perch on which the Conte de Vigny spent his days.

J

Jay-walking

An American magazine reported in 1917 that Bostonians were referring to 'a pedestrian who crosses streets in disregard of traffic signals' as a jay-walker. There was no need to explain to an American readership the significance of the 'jay', it was a well-established slang term for a country bumpkin, a hick. Jay-walkers were those who acted as if they normally lived in rural areas and were unaccustomed to city ways. 'Jay-walking' identified a phenomenon which was becoming common to all cities, and the term quickly spread throughout the English-speaking world. An official report in 1970 stated: 'A quarter of all London's accidents involve pedestrians – we have no effective jay-walking law.' Peter de Vries, as it happens, responds to this comment in *Comfort Me With Apples*: 'Driving, my dear Mrs Gutman, has become pedestrian. Jay-walking is the last adventure open to man.'

Ultimately the 'jay' in 'jay-walking' is the bird, known for its chattering and bright plumage, but not greatly admired. 'Is the jay more precious than the lark because his feathers are more beautiful?' asks Petruchio, in *The Taming of the Shrew*, as he proves to Kate that she has no need of fine clothes. Shakespeare also has Imogen say, in *Cymbeline*: 'Some jay of Italy hath betray'd him.' This uses 'jay' in one of the slang senses it had already acquired. An Elizabethan audience would have understood the word to refer to a flashily dressed woman, a prostitute. Changes of meaning through the centuries often cause us to have difficulty understanding Shakespeare's English, but one wonders what he, for his part, would have made of 'jay-walking.'

Keep One's Nose to the Grindstone

For some reason, using a grindstone has exemplified hard and boring work for centuries. In Dickens' *Our Mutual Friend*, the villainous Wegg threatens to punish Mr Boffin: 'His nose shall be put to the grindstone for it...I shall not neglect bringing the grindstone to bear, nor yet bringing Dusty Boffin's nose to it. His nose once brought to it, shall be held to it by these hands, Mr Venus, till the sparks flies out in showers.' This seems to imply that Mr Boffin has a metallic nose which Wegg will grind down, but we understand the general sense. Wegg intends to make Mr Boffin slave away at menial tasks.

It is interesting that Dickens still used the expression in the sense that it had in the 17th century. Originally, your nose was always brought or put to the grindstone by an oppressive master, one who treated you with great severity and forced you to do monotonous work. 'Let him be fetched in by the ears: I'll soon bring his nose to the grindstone,' says the Nurse, in Sir John Vanbrugh's *The Relapse*. This meaning of causing someone else to work hard can still be present in modern times. 'Her tribe of brothers and sisters,' writes Mary McCarthy in *The Group*, 'had kept her Dad's nose to the grindstone; if he had not had so many children, he might have been a famous specialist, instead of a hard-worked G.P.'

Use of the expression has nevertheless changed. We now speak about keeping our own nose to the grindstone, voluntarily engaging in a sustained spell of hard work. The nature of that work has also changed – it is more likely to be intellectual than physical. Students who spend a week preparing for an exam consider that they are keeping their noses to the grindstone, but this is a watered-down sense. Charles Dickens would have pointed out that there is no Mr Wegg standing beside them, waiting for the sparks to fly out in showers.

Keep the Wolf from the Door

Our distant ancestors were more familiar with wolves than we are; at one time they roamed wild in the English countryside. According to C.E.Hare, in *The Language of Field Sports*, the last wolf to be killed in the wild in England was in 1682. Before that, several expressions referring to the wolf had become part of the language. One that is still much used, and which dates from at least the 15th century, is 'to keep the wolf from the door.' In modern times this phrase is often used light-heartedly, but there was a time when those who were starving had good reason to think of poverty as a ravenous animal that was anxious to devour them.

The milder use of the expression seems to have begun in the 17th century. The diplomat James Howell, in one of his *Familiar Letters*, comments that if a couple are proposing to marry, 'he or she should have the wherewithal to support both, at least to keep the wolf from the door, otherwise 't'were a mere madness to marry.' Henry Herman, whose novel *His Angel* was published in 1891, remarks: 'It makes a lot of difference to one's happiness if the wolf is not scratching at the door.' P.G.Wodehouse makes a similar allusion to the saying in *Louder and Funnier*: 'Most of these essays were written at a time when the wolf at the door left little leisure for careful thought.'

Keep your Pecker up

This phrase traditionally had an innocent meaning in Britain, where it was commonly used to encourage someone to remain cheerful in spite of difficulties that had to be faced. The 'pecker' was understood to mean the beak of a bird, and the meaning was no more than 'keep your head up.' The expression probably derived from cock-fighting, where the sinking of a game-cock's head would have been an ominous sign that defeat was near. Examples of the phrase used in its 'be brave' sense are easily found amongst British authors from Dickens onwards. In *Five Tales*, for instance, John Galsworthy writes: 'Keep your pecker up, and get off abroad.' Elizabeth Jane Howard, in *Getting It Right*, has: 'When she thanked him again he gave her a cheery wink – as a kind of telegram to keep her pecker up.'

Since 'pecker' in American slang means 'penis,' North American writers who use this phrase interpret it differently, making it specifically sexual. Mary McCarthy, in *The Group*, has: 'You say your husband can't sleep with you because you're a "good woman." I suggest you enlighten him. Tell him what you do with Harald. That ought to get his pecker up.' There are clear signs that the phrase is now taking on this American sense in Britain. Nina Bawden writes, in *George Beneath A Paper Moon*: 'She was pressing against him. Her warm, silky body. A phrase came into his head. It gets the old pecker up. The manager at the supermarket who was turned on by veiled women.' It seems likely that the innocent British meaning will disappear, leaving only a bawdy comment.

Kettle of Fish

Stan Barstow illustrates normal modern usage of this phrase and explains its meaning in *A Kind of Loving*: 'That's a different kettle of fish. That's a different thing altogether.' Later in the novel he applies the expression to a person: 'Right behind Hassop there's Mr Althorpe and he's a different kettle of fish altogether.' Joanna Trollope, in *The Rector's Wife*, has: 'That was all very well at Woodborough Junior but here, I can tell you, the mothers are a very different kettle of fish.'

The first thing that strikes most people as odd about this phrase is the idea of putting fish into a kettle. A 'kettle,' after all, is now usually a container with a spout, lid and handle, which is used to boil water for making tea. In the 18th century, especially in Scotland, the word had a more general meaning; it could be used of a cauldron, or open pot. As a writer explained in 1791, these pots were then used in a popular form of outdoor entertainment: 'It is customary for the gentlemen who live near the Tweed to entertain their neighbours and friends with a Fete Champetre, which they call giving "a kettle of fish." Tents or marquees are pitched near the flowery banks of the river; a fire is kindled, and live salmon thrown into boiling kettles.'

To the Scots, then, 'kettle of fish' came to mean 'riverside picnic.' To English observers, who saw people and utensils scattered in a disorderly way on a river bank, the phrase took on the meaning of 'a confused state of affairs, a great muddle.' English novelists such as Samuel Richardson and Henry Fielding were soon making ironic references to a 'fine' or 'pretty kettle of fish' to indicate a messy situation. In Arnold Bennett's *Clayhanger* occurs: 'We shall be having you ill next, and then there'll be a nice kettle of fish.' This usage continues in modern times. 'I hear you are in a kettle of fish,' says a character in Iris Murdoch's *Under the Net. Maggie*, by Lena Kennedy, has: 'He leaned on the mantleshelf thinking, well here's a pretty kettle of fish. What shall I do?'

The phrase is well enough established for a writer to play with it. John Steinbeck, in *East of Eden*, says: 'Liza Hamilton was a very different kettle of Irish.'

Kicked Upstairs

We have become used to the idea of someone being 'kicked upstairs,' removed from a position where he has become an embarrassment by being promoted. In reality, the new position is a less active one or less influential. For most people the phrase is especially associated with politics, and the elevation of a member of parliament to the House of Lords. Although it sounds very modern, the expression dates from at least the end of the 17th century. Lord Halifax, Chancellor of the Exchequer at that time, may well have originated it. He is reported to have said in 1697 that 'he had known many kicked down stairs, but he never knew any kicked up stairs before.'

Sporadic references to the phrase occur in the 18th and 19th centuries. A letter written in 1750 by the Countess of Shaftesbury mentions that 'the Bedfordian set will be honourably kicked up or down stairs.' John Croker's *Diary* for 1821 says: 'Lord Melville informs me that he is about to be kicked upstairs (his expression) to be Secretary of State for the Home Department.' Croker's comment shows that the phrase was not yet in general use, since he clearly thought that the phrase was Lord Melville's own.

It was perhaps William Cooper, in *The Struggles of Albert Woods*, who re-introduced the phrase in modern times. He writes there that 'Dibdin was to be kicked upstairs and Albert was to take his place.' Dibdin soon afterwards receives a knighthood which he triumphantly believes is 'for my services to the committee.' He has no idea that his fellow committee members considered him a liability. Cooper's novel was published in 1952, since when references to being kicked upstairs have become commonplace. *The Guardian* asked in 1970: 'Which party has kicked more people upstairs?' but it is not only political parties which indulge in this practice. Wherever it occurs, those concerned probably prefer it to being kicked out.

Kick the Bucket

Kick the bucket tends to evoke an image of a suicide kicking away the bucket on which he is standing in order to leave himself suspended, but a little thought soon makes it clear that this cannot be the origin of the phrase. To begin with, it has always been applied to those dying naturally as well as unnaturally. Even amongst suicides, only a small proportion hang themselves, and few of those choose to stand on a bucket rather than a stool or chair.

The true explanation of the phrase depends on the fact that 'bucket' can have another meaning besides 'container for liquid.' Shakespeare, for instance, uses the word to mean 'the beam of a balance or crane.' In *King Henry the Fourth Part Two*, Falstaff refers to 'he that gibbets (hangs) on the brewer's bucket.' Modern

French has *trébuchet* for a pair of scales used to weigh delicate objects. The *-buchet* of this word is from the same source as 'bucket' in its sense of 'beam.' This survived in dialect for the beam from which pigs were suspended while being slaughtered. In that position their heels could be said to be 'kicking the bucket.'

There was also a phrase 'kick the beam' in the 18th century, the time when 'kick the bucket' began to be used. 'Kick the beam' referred literally to a scale of a balance which was so lightly loaded that it flew up and hit the cross-beam when the weight was put on the other side. Figuratively the phrase meant to 'fly in the air.' It has been suggested that the soul of a person 'kicked the beam' in that sense when he died.

'Kick the bucket' is not an elegant phrase, but it is well used colloquially. Literary examples are also common. Alan Sillitoe uses it in *A Tree on Fire* and again in *The Loneliness of the Long-Distance Runner*. James Purdy, *Eustace Chisholm and the Works*, has: 'Should old Maureen kick the bucket, you go call on Reuben.' An earlier example is in Trollope's *Doctor Thorne*: 'You wouldn't do as young Hatherly did, when his father kicked the bucket.' Mark Twain writes, in *Roughing It*: 'One of the boys has gone up the flume, throwed up the sponge, kicked the bucket. He's dead!'

Kill two Birds with one Stone

'Kill two birds with one stone' means to do something that will bring about more than one useful result. The phrase seems to have been unknown to Shakespeare and his contemporaries, but was used by Thomas Hobbes in one of his essays in 1656. There he writes that 'T.H. thinks to kill two birds with one stone, and satisfy two arguments with one answer.' Hobbes is known for the economy and effectiveness of his prose, and the striking phrase could easily have been his own invention. The fact that he chooses to provide a gloss for it makes this more likely. Thereafter the metaphorical meaning of the phrase became well established. By the end of the 17th century the anonymous author of *The Growth of Deism in England* was able to write: 'thereby they kill two or three birds with one stone', in the knowledge that none of his readers would think he was actually discussing the killing of birds.

It is interesting that even in this early use of the expression the number of birds was already being expanded. Two remains the usual number, as when Monica Dickens writes, in *Kate and Emma*: 'It was typical of Molly that even in a crisis she could plan to kill two birds with one stone.' In *Under the Volcano*, Malcolm Lowry has: 'It's a perfectly good idea, a most practical idea. Don't you see it'll kill two birds with one stone?' Later in the same novel, however, occurs: 'I'd discovered I might kill several birds with one stone by coming to Mexico.' Similarly, Margaret Drabble in *The Middle Ground* has: 'She had decided to kill several birds with one stone.' Josephine Tey, in *The Franchise Affair*, begins a chapter with the words: 'Robert had decided to kill a great many birds with one stone by spending the night in London.'

Eric Partridge remarks in passing (in his *Dictionary of Clichés*) that 'kill two birds with one stone' comes from a Latin original, but does not elaborate. Other scholars have been unable to identify such a Latin expression. There is, nevertheless, a French version of the saying, *faire d'une pierre deux coups* 'make two hits with one stone,' which possibly adds some weight to Partridge's claim. In German the equivalent expression refers to hitting two flies with one swat (*zwei Fliegen mit einer Klappe schlagen*).

Kinder, Kirche, Küche

Germaine Greer, in *The Female Eunuch*, writes: 'The women students had not yet formed any clear idea of the disabilities which increasingly encumber women as they move towards Kinder and Küche.' The allusion is to a group of German nouns which *all begin with the letter K*. Taken together they supposedly represent the interests of the traditional housewife. Germaine Greer mentions *Kinder* 'children' and *Küche* 'kitchen.' It is more usual to find a third noun mentioned, *Kirche* 'church.' A 1963 article in the *Economist*, for example, said: 'Her countrywomen are unhappy housewives trapped in the home by an ideal of *Kinder, Küche, Kirche* which is vigorously pressed by American educators and husbands.'

It is not just American husbands who favoured this view of womanhood. Dorothy L. Sayers, in *Gaudy Night*, talks of 'the Nazi doctrine that woman's place in the State should be confined to the 'womanly' occupations of *Kinder, Kirche, Küche*.' Perhaps because of these associations, this phrase is not listed in modern works on German idioms, such as Duden's *Redewendungen und Sprichwörtliche Redensarten*. The order of words is also arbitrary, though they should always be accorded the capital letters that distinguish German nouns. Ruth Rendell does not bother with this convention in *To Fear a Painted Devil*, where the words are applied to a man whose mother was German and is himself said to be very teutonic: 'He was an awfully *kinder, küche, kirche* sort of person, house-proud, passionately neat and tidy.'

The *Kinder, Kirche, Küche* philosophy may have been endorsed by Adolf Hitler and his followers, but it was not their conception. In 1899 the *Westminster Gazette* was already referring to the doctrine, adding a fourth noun, *Kleider* 'clothes,' for good measure: 'She says women have no business to interfere with anything outside the four K's. The four K's are *Kinder, Kirche, Küche,* and *Kleider*.' One wonders which four words might be used to define the existence of a typical woman a century later.

Know Chalk from Cheese

In the early 18th century Nicholas Amherst wrote his 'secret history of the university of Oxford,' which he published under the title *Terrae Filius*. At one point he had this to say: 'There is not (said a shrewd wag) a more uncommon thing in the world than common sense. By common sense we usually and justly understand the faculty to discern one thing from another, and the ordinary ability to keep ourselves from being imposed upon by gross contradictions, palpable inconsistencies, and unmask'd imposture. By a man of common sense we mean one who knows, as we say, chalk from cheese.'

Comments on the necessity of being able to distinguish between chalk and cheese go back to the 14th century. At that time cheese would always have been of the 'cottage cheese' variety, and therefore very similar in colour to chalk. The two words also resembled one another, beginning with the same sound. The phrase made the point that in spite of such similarities, they had very different qualities indeed. Only a fool would confuse them. In modern times we tend to say that two people are like chalk and cheese, meaning that they are very different in character. In Edith Pargeter's *Most Loving Mere Folly* it is a young man and older woman who have fallen in love who are said to be 'as different as chalk and cheese.' The expression is especially apt if used, say, of a mother and daughter, who may physically resemble each other, yet differ greatly in personality.

Land of the Living

If we have not been in touch with someone for a long time we are likely to wonder whether he or she is still 'in the land of the living.' The phrase appears to be a roundabout way of saying 'alive,' but it usually means 'active, in touch with others.' It may be used jokingly of someone who has slept in, for instance, and makes an appearance late in the morning. A typical example of its use is seen in Thomas Wolfe's *Look Homeward, Angel*, where a son writes to his mother: 'Yours of the 11th to hand and must say I was glad to know you were in the land of the living again.' Fanny Burney had earlier written, in *Evelina*: 'I'm glad to see you still in the land of the living.' *The Oxford English Dictionary* quotes a letter from Lady Cave, written in 1708: 'Sir Thomas is glad to hear Col. Oughton is in the land of the living, having not heard a word from him.'

'Land of the living' is a direct translation from Hebrew. It is found in the Old Testament at Jeremiah 11.20, where the prophet is describing a plot against him: 'Then thou shewedst me their doings. But I was like a lamb that is brought to the slaughter: and I knew not that they had devised devices against me, saying, Let us destroy the tree with the fruit thereof, and let us cut him off from the land of the living, that his name may no more be remembered.' This same passage also led to the use of a well-known phrase which refers to innocent obedience. Max Beerbohm, in *Zuleika Dobson*, makes a character say: 'I am going to die for the love I bear this woman. And let no man think I go unwilling. I am no lamb led to the slaughter.' *The Daily Telegraph* reported in 1982 that 'the rank-and-file membership of the union are meekly following their so-called leaders like lambs to the slaughter.'

Last Straw, The

It seems to have been Charles Dickens who gave us a verbal outlet for extreme irritation, allowing us to refer metaphorically to 'the last straw.' Something that in itself is perhaps relatively unimportant, following on a string of other annoyances, pushes our patience and endurance beyond all limits. *Dombey and Son* was published in 1848, and contains the passage: 'As the last straw breaks the laden camel's back, this piece of underground information crushed the sinking spirits of Mr. Dombey.' No earlier reference to this saying has been discovered, though later ones are easily found. Florence Nightingale, for example, in her handbook *Nursing*, says: 'It is the last straw that breaks the camel's back.'

Last straws come in various shapes and sizes. Elizabeth Jane Howard, in *Getting It Right*, makes much of the phrase: 'I have a suspicion that this incident will prove to be the Last Straw,' says someone. This is followed by the comment – 'Mr Adrian specialized in last straws, could even be said to be addicted to them.' '*This* is the straw that broke the camel's back,' occurs in Truman Capote's *My Side of the Matter*. It brings the riposte: 'That's not the only back that's going to be broke.' 'I was thinking of you when I kissed her,' a man tells his sweetheart in *Geordie*, by

David Walker. The young lady concerned is not mollified by this information. She stamps her foot in rage as she says: 'That's the last straw. That's the finish.'

The last straw image seems to satisfy most writers, but Mark Twain goes his own way in *The Adventures of Tom Sawyer*. He writes there that 'this final feather broke the camel's back.' This version of the saying does not seem to have been taken up. Where camels' backs are concerned, straws seem to be rather more appropriate.

Learn Something by Heart

The *Encyclopedia Britannica*, in its edition of 1875, remarked that: 'It was not till the publication of Allan Ramsay's *Ever-green* and *Tea Table Miscellany*, and of Bishop Percy's *Reliques*, that a serious effort was made to recover Scotch and English folk-songs from the recitation of the old people who still knew them by heart.' We all talk in this way about knowing something 'by heart,' though we are well aware that the heart has nothing to do with the memory process. 'At first, being little accustomed to learn by heart, the lessons appeared to me both long and difficult,' says the heroine in Charlotte Brontë's *Jane Eyre*.

To 'learn something by heart' has been a way of talking about memorizing since the 14th century. Since that time the French have also talked about knowing something *par coeur* 'by heart.' In both cases, the expression may reflect ancient medical ideas which made the heart the seat of intelligence, as well as sensitivity and courage. An alternative theory is that the original French phrase was *par choeur*, which sounds exactly the same. This would imply that something was learnt by a choral method, or constant repetition. Unfortunately, no textual references to learning *par choeur* have been found.

Such mis-translations do occur, however, as in the famous case of Cinderella's slipper. In the original French tale the slipper is made of *vair* 'fur.' This sounds the same as *verre* 'glass', and was so translated. The 'glass slipper' that was accidentally created in this way has intrigued children ever since.

Leave Someone in the Lurch

The first references to 'leaving someone in the lurch,' in the sense of abandoning someone to a very difficult situation, occur at the beginning of the 17th century. There was an earlier expression, 'leave someone in the lash,' which had the same meaning. The *Oxford English Dictionary* links the 'lash' in this phrase to a whip-lash, but a more plausible suggestion was made by Ernest Weekley in his *Etymological Dictionary of Modern English*. There he drew attention to the French verb *lâcher*, as in *lâcher un amant* - 'jilt a lover.' In modern French a *lâcheur* or *lâcheuse* is a man or woman who lets people down. The 16th century 'leave someone in the lash' could well have been suggested by such French words.

It seems likely, however, that the 'lash' reference was always obscure to English-speakers, and that it soon became confused with 'lurch,' another word that poses problems as to its origin. It is known that there was a 17th century game called Lurch, which seems to have resembled backgammon. It is also known that the term 'lurch' was used in other games to describe an overwhelming victory, such as one player winning a game without his opponent scoring a point. From this arose the now obsolete phrases 'give someone the lurch,' get the better of someone, 'have on the lurch,' have at a disadvantage and 'be in someone's lurch,' be in someone's power. 'Leave someone in the lurch' could have been another natural development from the sporting term, but there was probably also an assumption that this was the true form of 'leave someone in the lash.'

To add slightly to the confusion there are two other 'lurch' words which are unconnected with the gaming term. One of these means to 'roll to one side, while the other is a variant of 'lurk' and means to 'prowl.' The first of these was nautical in origin, while the second led to the name of the 'lurcher' dog, traditionally used by poachers to catch hares and rabbits.

Whatever its precise origin, people have been consistently 'leaving one another in the lurch,' or insisting that they do not do so, since the 17th century. 'If a woman's in trouble, I don't leave her in the lurch,' says a man in E.M.Forster's *Howard's End*. 'I can't leave her in the lurch after just moving her out here, away from everything she knew and liked in the East,' says the hero of *Face To Face*, by Edward A.Rogers. In *Framley Parsonage*, by Anthony Trollope, occurs: 'Justinia has made me promise, promise, mind you, most solemnly, that I would have you back to dinner tonight, by force if necessary. It was the only way I could make my peace with her; so you must not leave me in the lurch.'

Earlier references include the comment by Boileau in *Lutrin* (1682): 'He had left her in the lurch, and under colour of religion courted another pretty Pigeon.' Rudyard Kipling also made good use of the phrase in his *The Seven Seas*:

> We preach in advance of the Army,
> We skirmish ahead of the Church,

With never a gunboat to help us
When we're scuppered and left in the lurch.

Let the Cat Out of the Bag

To 'let the cat out of the bag' would once have been a sensible thing to do, though in modern times the expression has come to mean 'reveal something that should be kept secret,' usually to someone else's annoyance. 'You could have told me,' says a man in Christopher Short's *The Saint and the Hapsburg Necklace*. 'I was afraid that if I did,' comes the reply, 'you might let the cat out of the bag. You are so impetuous.' Mary McCarthy describes an equally untrustworthy person in *The Group*: 'Kay, who had always been a blurter, had let the cat out of the bag.'

Authors sometimes play with the phrase, as does Joyce Porter in *Dover One*. When someone says: 'I reckon that's let the cat out of the bag, all right!' the reply is 'If it was ever in.' D.H.Lawrence is even more expansive in his short story *Rawdon's Roof*: 'If they were friends, just friends, all right! But then in that case, why start talking about not having a woman sleep under your roof? Pure mystification! The cat never came out of the bag. But one evening I distinctly heard it mewing inside its sack, and I even believe I saw a claw through the canvas.'

In times past there really was a cat in the bag at certain times. This saying is closely connected with 'buying a pig in a poke,' which means to buy something without inspecting it beforehand. In the 17th century, piglets were sold at markets in 'pokes,' or bags. 'Poke' is connected to the French word *poche*, which now means 'pocket' but originally meant a 'little bag.' Traders were likely to put a stray cat into the bag instead of a piglet, which is why at one time it would have been wise to let the cat out, or at least have a look at it, before handing over one's money. Originally, then, it was only in the interest of dishonest traders not to reveal the truth by letting the cat out of the bag.

This unscrupulous practice of selling cats for piglets was clearly not confined to English dealers. There is an expression in French – *acheter chat en poche*, literally 'to buy a cat in a bag' – which means exactly the same as 'buy a pig in a poke.' The latter phrase is less commonly heard in English, but is found in literature. In *The History of Mr Polly*, for instance, H. G. Wells has: 'Wimmin's a toss up,' said Uncle Penstemon. 'Prize packets they are, and you can't tell what's in 'em till you took 'em 'ome and undone 'em. Never was a bachelor married yet that didn't buy a pig in a poke.' A vaguely similar thought is voiced in William J. Locke's *Jaffery*: 'What is the veil but a relic of marriage by barter, when the man bought a pig in a poke and never knew his luck till he unveiled his bride?'

Like a Bear with a Sore Head

Grose's *Classical Dictionary of the Vulgar Tongue*, which appeared in 1785, illustrates the word 'grumble' with the sentence: 'He grumbled like a bear with a sore ear.' Bears with sore ears would certainly have been found in bear gardens, where bear-baiting took place. This was a popular spectator sport in England between the 14th and 17th centuries. A bear was chained to a stake and had to defend itself against the dogs who were set on it. The riotous atmosphere at such events led to 'bear garden' becoming a term to describe a place where confusion reigns. 'Winslow gave a lamentable exhibition last night,' says someone in C.P. Snow's *The Masters*. 'He makes the place a perfect bear-garden.' *Eating*

People Is Wrong, by Malcolm Bradbury, has: '"It's a mad, crazy world we live in." Jenkins nodded sagely. "It's a bear-garden".'

Frederick Marryat seems to have been the first writer to amend Grose's 'bear with a sore ear.' In *The King's Own* he uses the expression 'as savage as a bear with a sore head.' Ten years later, in a work called *Poor Jack*, Marryat changed the simile to 'as sulky as a bear with a sore head.' Marryat's stories were immensely popular in the 19th century, and his words would have been widely noted. He was probably responsible for making most of us think automatically, when someone is behaving with a mixture of savagery and sulkiness, of bears with sore heads. 'Who said I was angry?' asks a character in Jeremy Brooks's *Henry's War*. 'Come off it,' is the reply. 'You've been like a bear with a sore head all day.'

Like the Clappers

'Like the clappers' was first recorded by Eric Partridge in his *Dictionary of Forces' Slang,* published in 1948. Partridge noted that the phrase meant 'very fast,' that it was sometimes extended to 'like the clappers of hell,' and that it was most commonly used by airmen. M.K.Joseph puts the expression into a military context in *I'll Soldier No More*, where he remarks that 'it was raining like the clappers.' In *Vodi*, John Braine has a character say: 'I've got to work like the clappers this morning.' The allusion is presumably to the rapid movements of clappers inside an electric bell. Castanets are also a form of clappers, but there is no reason to suppose that they would have been in the minds of British servicemen in the 1940s.

Also in favour of the bell theory is that they have long been the source of idiomatic phrases in English. In Shakespeare's *Much Ado*

About Nothing, for instance, Don Pedro says: 'He hath a heart as sound as a bell, and his tongue is the clapper; for what his heart thinks, his tongue speaks.' 'As sound as a bell' was already in use when Shakespeare wrote those words, the pure sound of a finely tuned bell being much admired by our ancestors. Thomas Newton had noted as early as 1576: 'They be people commonly healthy, and as sound as a bell.' The image survived well. 'A single man with prospects, an' as sound as a bell, is not to be had every day,' said the *Pall Mall Magazine* in 1898. H.A.Vachell was later to write, in *Some Happenings*: 'Doctors were so ridiculously cocksure! All the same, he felt mildly interested in the vetting. Constitutionally he was as sound as a bell.'

Long in the Tooth

'Long in the tooth' is used informally to describe someone who is 'rather old.' It was the teeth of horses which originally inspired the phrase. They appear to get longer as the gums recede with age. Applied to humans, the expression dates from at least the mid-19th century. Thackeray's *Esmond* has: 'She was lean, and yellow, and long in the tooth; all the red and white in all the toyshops of London could not make a beauty of her.' This seems to have set a fashion for using the phrase of women, examples being found in many modern novelists. Evelyn Waugh writes in *Unconditional Surrender*: 'If you're lucky you get fixed up with a nurse. Cape's got one – a bit long in the tooth but very friendly.' John Braine's *Room at the Top* has: 'A trifle long in the tooth, mark you, but she has style, real style.' Elizabeth Jane Howard, in *Getting It Right*, says: 'If it is a girl you're after, you're not going to meet her in that salon of yours, are you? They all sound a bit long in the tooth there, apart from anything else.' The Irish novelist Patrick Boyle, in *Like Any Other Man*, uses a slight variant: 'The director's wife would be a bit long of the tooth, you could gamble on that.'

There is no reason why 'long in the tooth' should not be applied to a man. This is the case in *The Old Boys*, by William Trevor, where someone says: 'Our own doctor is long in the tooth, behind the times, against modern methods, you know the kind of thing.' The phrase is of course meant to be metaphorical when applied to human beings, but Edward Blishen rather confuses the issue in *A Cack-handed War*. One of his characters says: 'Well over forty, she was. Pots of money. Bit long in the tooth, o'course. But Gawd...she fancied me. Thought she'd eat me, Ted. Those big teeth. Biting, an' all that.'

Look a Gift-horse in the Mouth

'One does not bite the coin of an honoured stranger,' says an Afghan, in George Macdonald Fraser's *Flashman*. The hero explains that this means 'you don't look a gift horse in the mouth.' Charles Dickens says in *David Copperfield* that looking a gift-horse in the mouth 'is not a gracious thing to do.' An earlier version of the saying referred to a 'given horse,' but the idea was the same. A gift of any kind should be accepted uncritically, not examined minutely in the way that a horse might be examined by a potential buyer. In the latter case the horse's mouth would indeed be looked into, since its teeth give the surest indication of its age. There is another allusion to this fact in the expression 'straight from the horse's mouth,' referring to information that is completely reliable.

In his novel *Blue Dreams*, William Hanley writes: 'He was looking no gift horses in the mouth. (Or, as George Brady had once said in perverse variation, never kick a gift horse in the teeth).' However, circumstances may well arise which make it necessary to think very carefully about the wisdom of accepting a gift. Andrew Rawnsley made the point in an *Observer* article in October, 1996. Discussing the revelation that an MP had accepted various gifts in return for promoting the cause of a businessman, he concluded: 'the moral of this is that politicians should always look a gift horse in the mouth, especially when it has halitosis.'

Lose One's Marbles

A letter to the *Times* newspaper in August 1996 complained about the decline in quality of the exhibits at the Royal Academy's Summer Exhibition. The writer of the letter, Roy Barley, asked: 'what has happened to the art of painting? Surely the selection committee have lost their way (if not their marbles)?'

This colloquial way of referring to a loss of mental faculties was first recorded in America. *American Speech* reported typical usage in 1927: 'There goes a man who doesn't have all his marbles.' The phrase was later popularised by P.G.Wodehouse in novels such as *Cocktail Time*, where he writes: 'Do men who have got all their marbles go swimming in lakes with their clothes on?' In the 1960s the crime novels of John Wainwright also featured the phrase strongly. *Web of Silence* has: 'Have you lost your marbles, Pewter? Have you gone for a complete loop?' In *Take-Over Men* is: 'You lost your goddam' marbles? You gone completely crazy, you nutty slob?'

Robert L. Chapman, in his *Dictionary of American Slang*, says that this phrase is ultimately 'from a story about a boy whose marbles were carried off by a monkey.' That does little more than raise a few questions about where Dr Chapman's marbles are hiding themselves these days. Nor does Tony Thorne help us much in his *Dictionary of Contemporary Slang* by relaying the suggestion that 'marbles have been seen as a synonym for the bearings which allow a machine to operate.'

The evidence for a different explanation of how 'marbles' came to be equated with mental faculties lies in the *Oxford English Dictionary*. This mentions that from the mid-19th century 'marbles' had to come to mean 'furniture, personal effects.' In this sense it was a corruption of French *meubles* 'furniture.' Elsewhere the dictionary provides evidence that 'furniture' had long been used to mean 'intellectual faculties.' An 18th century commentator on Aristotle is quoted: 'Thus the whole furniture of the human mind is presented to us at one view.' Quotations from the 19th century include: 'His faculty and furniture of mind would have been employed in defending himself', 'Lord Russell had a mental furniture fit for repose.' On this basis, there is surely some justification for supposing that 'lose one's marbles' is indirectly a form of 'lose one's *meubles*.'

Lose One's Thread

Wilfrid Sheed writes in *The Critic*: 'The poor sonofabitch had lost his thread.' *The Group*, by Mary McCarthy, has: 'That's what I started to say. I lost the thread for a minute.' In *Anglo-Saxon Attitudes* Angus Wilson remarks: 'He stopped and, for a moment, he appeared to have lost the thread of his remarks.' The 'thread' in these instances refers to a general train of thought, the sequence of ideas that a speaker has been pursuing. In a similar way the word can refer to what would have been a continuous chain of events, had there not been an interruption. In such cases we talk about 'picking up the thread or threads.' Robert Louis Stevenson writes in *Virginibus Puerisque*: 'We shall take up again the thread of our enjoyment in the same spirit as we let it fall'. George Bernard Shaw, in *John Bull's Other Island*, makes a character say: 'Eighteen years is a devilish long time, Nora. Now if it had been eighteen minutes, or even eighteen months, we should be able to pick up the interrupted thread, and chatter like two magpies.'

'Thread' was no doubt suggested in these instances by the Greek myths, where a thread is often the means of finding the way through a labyrinth or maze. The most famous tale concerns the Greek hero Theseus, who unrolled Ariadne's ball of thread behind him as he progressed to the centre of the infamous labyrinth in Crete to find the Minotaur. After killing the Minotaur he found his way out again by rewinding the thread. To 'lose the thread' of what you are saying means that you have metaphorically found your way to the centre of a maze but have no idea how you got there. (A ball of thread was formerly called a 'clew', which in time became 'clue').

Lost Property Office

'Lost property office' is a curious English phrase, as revealed when it becomes necessary to translate it into a language such as French, German or Polish. In these languages it becomes 'found property office.' English logicians would no doubt argue that people go to the lost property office to recover what they have lost, not what they found. Others might maintain that if property is truly lost then it remains lost. It is only when it has been found that it can take its place in the so-called lost property office. Even the description 'lost and found property office' would not truly cover the situation. Most property that is lost is found by someone, but it is not always handed in to the authorities. Perhaps we should all be referring to the 'returned property office.'

Make a Mountain out of a Molehill

Shakespeare makes use of the mountain\molehill contrast in *Coriolanus*, though not in the modern sense of exaggerating the importance of a trivial matter. Coriolanus is talking about relative social status when he says: 'My mother bows as if Olympus to a molehill should in supplication nod.' The reference was still specifically to Olympus when John Dryden and Nathaniel Lee made a character say, in *Oedipus*: 'Each mole-hill thought swells to a huge Olympus.' *Oedipus* was first performed in 1679; a few years later the satirist Thomas Brown was writing, in *The Saints in Uproar*, about improving 'this mole-hill into a mountain.' People have been accused of making mountains out of molehills ever since. 'Now listen here, Willard, quit making a mountain out of a molehill', occurs in Margaret Laurence's *A Jest of God*. Mary McCarthy, in *The Groves of Academe*, has: 'She had been wondering in secret whether they had not been making a mountain out of a molehill.' In many instances, of course, what is trivial to one person is genuinely of more importance to someone else; one man's molehill is another's mountain.

Writers in the past have occasionally followed Shakespeare's example of making a distinction between a molehill and a mountain for more general purposes. Jeremy Bentham, in one of his works on jurisprudence, makes the scathing remark: 'Of the mountain of their nonsense the magnitude may be measured by the molehill dimensions of their sense.' The phrase has also been interpreted in another way. Professor George R.Stewart mentions in *American Place Names* that a place called Mole Hill in West Virginia probably honoured a family called Mole, but the name failed to satisfy later residents. They voted to change their 'Mole Hill' into 'Mountain.'

Make Both Ends Meet

The idea of trying to make both ends meet is all too familiar in modern times, but there is nothing new about the concept. An early use of the phrase occurs in 1661, in Thomas Fuller's *Worthies of England*. Fuller says of one of his subjects: 'Worldly wealth he cared not for, desiring only to make both ends meet; and as for that little that lapped over he gave it to pious uses.'

We know that this expression refers to balancing one's budget, but what ends are we referring to? Americans in the 19th century seem to have decided that the reference was to the buckle and pin of a belt. 'Beginning without money,' said *Harper's Magazine* in 1888, 'he had as much as he could do to make "buckle and tongue meet", as the phrase goes.' Underlying this, perhaps, was the idea of 'tightening one's belt' in order to live within one's income.

Nevertheless, it is far more likely that we borrowed our 'make ends meet' phrase from French, where the original expression was *joindre les deux bouts de l'année* – 'join the two ends of the year.' For the French, in other words, making ends meet involved spanning another complete year, surviving yet again.

Many Irons in the Fire

People have mixed views about the wisdom of having 'many

irons in the fire.' The image evoked by the expression would have been very clear at a time when a blacksmith working at his forge was a more common sight than it is today. Metals needed to be heated to make them malleable, but the temperatures had to be carefully controlled. Proverbial warnings made the point. 'They that have many irons in the fire, some must cool,' ran one such saying. 'Many irons in the fire, some must burn,' said an alternative version. Individual writers have implicitly supported these views. 'College work is now over and I can get on with fewer irons in the fire,' wrote a 19th century academic. 'He had far too many irons in the fire to find time for original research' said a contemporary.

Some people have chosen to use this phrase more positively, rather as if having many irons in the fire was like having several STRINGS TO ONE'S BOW. Samuel Butler, in *The Way of All Flesh*, describes a carpenter who is a self-taught artist and musician. 'It may be thought,' writes Butler, 'that with so many irons in the fire he could hardly be a very thriving man, but this was not the case.' As others have pointed out, having many irons in the fire is not necessarily a bad thing. The secret of success is to strike them all while they are hot.

Mare's Nest

A 16th century version of this expression was 'horse nest,' used sarcastically of some supposed wonderful discovery that had no real existence. The implication was that anyone who believed such a phenomenon ever could exist was very foolish indeed. A century later the phrase had become 'mare's nest,' though the meaning was unchanged. It has continued in occasional use ever since, at one point becoming a verb. A writer in the 19th century noted: 'He's always mare's nesting.'

Peter de Vries is a writer with an eye for phrases of this kind, and it is no surprise when he uses 'mare's nest' in *Comfort Me With Apples*. He philosophises: 'The worse people are, the easier it is to be objective with them. We fuss at what irritates us, but try to understand real breaches of behaviour. And wasn't the very absurdity of his mare's nest a measure of his need?'

Mind Boggles, The

This phrase was heard on all sides in the late 1960s, but seems to have faded away. The expression was often used jokingly, the mere sound of 'boggles' having a comic appeal. Joseph Heller has fun with it in *Good as Gold*, where the narrator is told by a government representative that he has a gift for 'punchy phrases.' He is pleased about this until he happens to say 'You're boggling my mind.' He is told that this is a 'damned good phrase. I'll bet all of us down here can start getting mileage out of that one right away.'

On the first page of his novel *Other Men's Wives*, Alexander Fullerton has: 'Someone, somewhere, Serge thought, his mind boggling at the idea, loves each one of them.' This leads him later to the deliberately humorous 'the imagination has its limits, the mind its boggle-point.'

Further references to the mind's boggle-point are not easily found, but 'mind-boggling' is common. It may again be significant that the earliest printed example of it discovered by the editors of the *Oxford English Dictionary* was in *Punch*. The humorous magazine referred in 1964 to 'a lot of mind-boggling statistics.' A few years later the *National Observer* told its American readers that 'for the consumer who doesn't understand psychobabble, trying to sort out the various specialties can be downright mind-boggling.'

At the origin of all this is a legitimate word which has been in use for centuries. It was originally horses which 'boggled.' The verb means to 'shy, start with fright, be startled.' In the 16th century horses which boggled were thought to do so because they had seen a 'bogle', some kind of phantom or spectre. The word is therefore connected with the mysterious 'bogey-man.' Scholars think that the ultimate origin of 'boggle' and connected words is to be found in Welsh *bwgwl* 'terror, terrifying.'

In its earliest metaphorical use, 'boggle' meant to 'raise scruples, hesitate.' When Antony tells Cleopatra that she has 'been a boggler ever,' it is not because she boggles men's minds. He means that she has always been capricious. In *All's Well That Ends Well* Shakespeare also uses the verb in its original meaning. The King of France compares Bertram to a startled horse by saying: 'You boggle shrewdly; every feather starts you.'

Mind One's P's and Q's

The origin of this phrase is uncertain, but amateur philologists have dreamed up various explanations. An especially fanciful one involves the keeping of a tally in a pub. A landlord would be told to mind his p's and q's – not chalk up q for 'quart' instead of p for 'pint.' This is nonsense, as is the even more far-fetched story about French dancing-masters supposedly telling their pupils to mind their *pieds* 'feet' and *queues* 'pig-tails.'

The phrase is recorded as early as 1779 in a play by Hannah Cowley, *Who's the Dupe?* 'You must mind your p's and q's with him, I can tell you,' says a character. In modern usage the phrase still means to be on one's best behaviour, not to be socially inept. 'The corvette is carrying their President, so you'll have to mind your p's and q's,' says a naval officer in *Sylvester,* by Edward Hyams. J.I.M.Stewart, in *The Last Tresilians*, has: 'Burntisland realized that he had spoken words angrily and aloud. It was something he had once or twice noticed himself doing of late. I'll gain a reputation, he thought, for eccentricity if I don't mind my p's and q's.'

A possible origin of the expression is hinted at by William Combe in his *Second Tour of Dr Syntax in Search of Consolation*, published in 1820. He writes:

> And I full five-and-twenty year
> Have always been school-master here;
> And almost all you know and see,
> Have learn'd their p's and q's from me.

This suggests young children learning to write, trying to remember the difference between 'p' and 'q' as well as that between 'b' and 'd.' It is easy to understand how the meaning of a phrase which had to do with writing the letters correctly could be extended to cover social behaviour. This is mere conjecture, however, and bar-room philosophers will no doubt continue to seek a more ingenious explanation.

Moot Point, A

H.G.Wells begins his short story, *The Hammerpond Park Burglary*, by saying: 'It is a moot point whether burglary is to be considered as a sport, a trade, or an art.' A 'moot point' is one that is undecided and open to debate. 'Moot' is connected with 'meet,' and its original sense was simply a meeting of people. It was then applied to meetings where those involved formed a court to make legal judgements. One of the specialised meanings of 'moot' that developed still later was a 'discussion of a hypothetical case by law students.'

As the H.G.Wells quotation indicates, 'a moot point' is often used about fairly light-hearted topics. The *Oxford English Dictionary* quotes both Sir Charles Wogan – 'it is a very moot point to which of those causes we may ascribe the universal dulness of the Irish,' and the *Daily Chronicle*, which declared in 1928: 'How much of her success in place-seeking a woman owes to her business-like methods and how much to her milliner is a moot point.' Whether a newspaper would dare to make such a sexist statement today is another moot point.

Mumbo Jumbo

When Europeans visited West Africa in the 18th century they found that the Mandingo tribes worshipped a fearful god whose name sounded something like Mumbo Jumbo. It would have perhaps been more correctly rendered as Mama Dyumbo. One English traveller reported that the idol was 'a thing invented by the men to keep their wives in awe.' In our society, mumbo jumbo is also sometimes used to keep people in awe. Mario Pei, for instance, in his *Words in Sheep's Clothing*, talks of 'mumbo jumbo developed by educators to confound the public in general and inquisitive parents in particular.' M. Franklin, in *All that Swagger*, says: 'The whole world is paralysed by the mumbo jumbo of banking jargon.'

It is easy to understand how mumbo jumbo came to mean verbal nonsense. The chanting used by the Mandingo tribes when worshipping their god would have sounded like gibberish to the Europeans, who would also have dismissed tribal rituals as so much hocus pocus. This dismissive attitude still applies. In 1975 *The Times* newspaper commented sourly that 'Labour's elected representatives mouth the mumbo jumbo of capitalism: the pound must be kept strong, we must all buy British.' Earlier, Nigel Balchin, in *Mine Own Executioner*, had remarked: 'Sometimes I get so fed up with all the mumbo jumbo and abracadabra and making of holy mysteries about simple things that I like to call a spade a shovel.'

Mum's the Word

'Mum's the word,' says a character in Mary Webb's *Gone To Earth*. This is a brief way of saying: 'say nothing to anyone else about what we have just been discussing.' One could also say 'keep mum' – 'remain silent.' Mary McCarthy in *The Group* has: 'Whatever was said about the Apartment, she was going to keep mum; let the others talk.' 'Mum' in this phrase would more accurately be written as 'mmm.' It refers to the inarticulate mumbling sound that can be made when the lips are closed. 'Mum' was used in this sense of a meaningless word centuries before it came into general use as a short form of 'mummy,' or 'mother.' As it happens, the word for 'mother' in many languages begins with an m- sound. Philologists suggest that this may be because it is one of the first sounds a young child is able to produce.

'Mum's the word' now sounds rather inappropriate, since mothers are not renowned for being silent. A similar oddity is the word 'mummy' applied to the embalmed body of an ancient Egyptian, male or female. In this case 'mummy' is ultimately from an Arabic word *mum* which means 'wax.'

Needle in a Haystack, A

In *Call it a Day*, Peter Cheyney writes: 'He thought it was like looking for a needle in a haystack.' The man concerned then decides that 'if you looked long enough for a needle in a haystack you found it,' but this does not change the basic sense of the metaphor. As Charles Kingsley expressed it in *Westward Ho!* – 'it's ill looking for a needle in a haystack.' It is an almost impossible task that is probably a foolish waste of time.

This phrase has a proverbial ring to it which suggests that it has been in use for centuries, but the occurrence in *Westward Ho!* – published in 1855 – is the earliest recorded example in that precise form. In the early 16th century, Sir Thomas More referred to looking for 'a needle in a meadow,' but the usual form of the expression from the end of the 16th century onwards referred to seeking 'a needle in a bottle of hay.' This 'bottle' was not the one that contained liquids, but a different word closely related to 'bundle.' 'Needle in a bottle of hay' was still the form known to Thomas Hood when he published his comic poem 'The Lost Heir' in 1845. In this a London mother whose child has gone missing laments:

Lawk help me, I don't know where to look, or to run, if only I
    knew which way –
A child as is lost about London streets, and especially Seven

Dials, is a needle in a bottle of hay.

I am all in a quiver – get out of my sight, do, you wretch, you
little Kitty M'Nab!

You promised to have half an eye to him, you know you did,
you dirty deceitful young drab.

After a long monologue in similar vein the child is eventually
found watching a Punch and Judy show.

'Needle in a haystack' has become well established as the usual
form of this saying since the mid-19th century, adapted as
necessary to modern technology. The *Scientific American* magazine
reported in 1974 that 'a computer patiently runs the long
repetitive scans looking for tiny needles in microhaystacks.'
Earlier an American critic had used the phrase imaginatively, if
unkindly, when discussing the work of a fellow writer. He had
discovered, he said, 'thin needles of wit buried in unwieldy
haystacks of verse.'

Nine Days' Wonder

We are usually being dismissive when we refer to something or
someone as a 'nine days' wonder.' We mean that whatever is
causing interest at the moment will soon be forgotten. In *Sour
Cream*, Joyce Porter writes: 'The disappearance of Melkin didn't
even rate as a nine-days' wonder.' Winifred Holtby, in *South
Riding*, has: 'It had been a nine days' wonder, a society elopement,
a grand news story.''I didn't want to mention this before,' says
someone in *A Jest of God*, by Margaret Laurence, 'not until we were
more sure of it – sure it would last, you know, and was the
genuine article and not just a nine-day wonder.' Tennyson made
good poetical use of the expression in *Elaine*:

> So ran the tale like fire about the court,
> Fire in dry stubble a nine-days' wonder flared.

This expression has certainly not been a nine days' wonder in itself, having remained in constant use since the 14th century. Chaucer's version of it in *Troylus* and *Cryseyde* is 'Ek wonder last but nine nyght nevere in towne,' which was later rendered by Bishop Guthrie as 'a wonder lasts but nine nights in a town (as we use to say).' By 1579 John Lyly was recording in *Euphues*: 'The greatest wonder lasteth but nine daies.' Shakespeare alludes to the expression in *As You Like It*, where Rosalind remarks 'I was seven of the nine days out of the wonder before you came.' In *Henry VI, Part III*, when King Edward speaks of his impending marriage to Lady Grey, there follows the exchange: 'That would be ten days' wonder at the least.' 'That's a day longer than a wonder lasts.'

Most scholars link this phrase with medieval religious celebrations, which lasted nine days. The wonders would have been the colourful parades that occurred at such times. Others refer to dogs and cats who are blind until they are about nine days old. The complicated thought is that the public is blinded for a few days, then its eyes are opened.

No Love Lost

A charming little verse in Thomas Percy's *Reliques of Ancient Poetry* runs:

> No love between these two was lost,
> Each was to other kind:
> In love they lived, in love they died,
> And left two babes behind.

This may seem a little strange since now, when we say that there is 'no love lost' between two people, we always mean that they do not like each other very much. For several centuries, however, the phrase could be interpreted positively or negatively. In a positive sense it meant that two people gave all their love to each other, so that none was wasted. The negative interpretation was that they kept their love for more worthy recipients, not wasting any on unpleasant people.

The wider context usually makes it clear which of these is meant. A 17th century biography, for example, says that 'Dr. Busby took a particular kindness to him, and there was no love lost betwixt them.' In *Gil Blas*, Smollett writes: 'I have a friendship for you, and I can assure thee, child (said I), there is no love lost.' Goldsmith's *She Stoops to Conquer* has: 'We grumble a little now and then, to be sure. But there's no love lost between us.' There was no sudden change from such favourable comments to the meaning we give the phrase today. Already in 1622 John Taylor, the Water Poet, was writing:

> But there's no great love lost 'twixt them and me,
> We keep asunder and so best agree.

No Man's Land

Most people have heard of the football matches played between British and German soldiers during the First World War. A temporary truce was observed on Christmas Day, and the area that lay between the opposing armies was put to reasonably peaceful use. Normally this 'no man's land' was a place of danger and desolation. One contemporary journalist described it as a 'dreadful wilderness of dead bodies.'

'No man's land' is a very ancient expression. In English villages it was often a piece of land that was left untilled for superstitious reasons, a kind of offering to the devil. To Londoners, many centuries ago, it had a specifically gruesome meaning, since it referred to a plot of waste land outside the north wall of the city used for executions.

In modern times we use this expression in a variety of ways. Tennis players talk about getting 'caught in no man's land,' the area of the court between the service and base lines. It is also used by football commentators to describe an area of the field where there are temporarily no players. In more general terms, we might describe homeless people who sleep rough as inhabiting an urban no man's land. The *Wall Street Journal*, a few years ago, also remarked that 'one aim of the new law was to abolish the so-called no-man's-land between Federal and state authority.'

In such instances, the meaning of 'no man's land' is greatly watered down. Properly speaking, the phrase refers not only to a physical or abstract area of neutrality. Throughout the centuries it has had sinister associations with violent death.

No Soap

In Peter Cheyney's *Call it a Day*, a woman says 'What about coming and having a drink with me tonight, Johnny?' The reply is a terse 'No soap ... I'm going to be busy.' The speaker could equally well have said 'no dice,' 'no chance' or 'no way,' all with the meaning 'nothing doing, absolutely not.' 'No dice' was perhaps directly suggested by 'no chance,' but 'no soap,' which has been in colloquial American use since the 1920's, is the oddest member of this group, and the most difficult to explain.

Laurence Urdang, in his *Picturesque Expressions*, thought that 'soap' might here have its slang sense of 'money used for a bribe,' but this seems unlikely. In situations where 'no soap' is used as an emphatic refusal, the question of bribery rarely arises. Jack Kerouac's *On the Road* shows typical use of the phrase: 'Terry and I tried to find work at the drive-ins. It was no soap anywhere.' Eric Partridge preferred the simpler explanation that 'soap' was a rhyming substitute for 'hope,' but there is no evidence that American speakers ever said 'no hope' where they might now I say 'no soap.' For the moment, the real origin of the phrase remains a mystery.

Nod is as Good as a Wink, A

The 'wink' in this proverbial expression is not necessarily the rapid closing and opening of one eye that we think of today. In former times to wink at, or on, someone referred to giving that person a significant glance, conveying a command or invitation to do something. The look was often accompanied by a nod, and might be answered in that way. 'I therefore wink'd at her,' says a character in Samuel Richardson's *Clarissa*. 'She nodded, to show she took me.' 'Wink' originally had the same meaning of 'significant look' in the phrase 'tip the wink to someone,' which might be paraphrased as 'give someone the nod.' The connection between winking and nodding is even closer than all this suggests. The *Oxford English Dictionary* points out that the meaning of the Old English verb *wincian*, from which 'wink' derives, was 'to nod.'

The saying about a nod being as good as a wink appeared only at the very end of the 18th century. In its full form it was: 'A nod is as good as a wink to a blind horse,' though many writers and speakers quickly began to omit any reference to the 'blind horse.' As Richard Barham implied, in *The Ingoldsby Legends*, the expression usefully replaced a Latin tag. 'The Old Woman Clothed in Grey' has:

> Gentle Reader! – you must know the proverb, I think
> – To a blind horse a nod is as good as a wink!
> Which some learned chap, in a square college cap,
> Perhaps would translate by the words *verbum sap.*

Barham is using the abbreviated form of *verbum sapienti* sat est, 'a word to the wise is enough.' Other short responses, by someone who is quick enough on the uptake for a nod to be as good as a wink, might be 'enough said!' or 'say no more!' – 'I've understood.'

Not Care a Straw

To our ancestors, a piece of straw was the ultimate example of something which had no value. The phrase 'not worth a straw' was already in use by the beginning of the 15th century. To a discerning 19th century writer such as John Ruskin, it was still a useful and respectable phrase. 'No painter who is worth a straw ever will copy,' he says, in *The Political Economy of Art*. The expression could still easily occur in a modern conversation.

An equally ancient phrase is 'not care a straw,' though the number of straws referred to seems to vary with individual users of the language. Anthony Trollope favoured the single straw. 'Mr Baker did not care a straw about it,' he writes in *Doctor Thorne*, and goes on to use the phrase at least six more times in the same book. In *Ulysses*, by contrast, James Joyce has: 'Not that I care two straws who he does it with.' E.F.Benson, in *Trouble for Lucia*, also writes: 'Lucia did not care two straws what "the common people" were saying.' Thomas Hughes, in *Tom Brown at Oxford*, prefers: 'Drysdale, who didn't care three straws about knowing St. Cloud.'

Jane Austen uses the 'three straw' version in *Pride and Prejudice*. Lydia declares that Wickham 'never cared three straws about her − who *could* about such a nasty little freckled thing?' This, incidentally, is as near Jane Austen gets to using what she considers to be bad language. Lydia's sister Elizabeth is 'shocked to think that, however incapable of such coarseness of *expression* herself, the coarseness of the *sentiment* was little other than her own breast had formerly harboured.' Presumably the supposed coarseness lies in 'the nasty little freckled thing.' It is difficult to see how even Jane Austen could object to 'not care three straws.'

Not Have a Bean

'I wanted to marry him for his money,' says a woman in Ruth Rendell's *To Fear a Painted Devil*, 'and he wanted to marry me for mine, and the mad thing is we hadn't either of us got a bean.' This colloquial reference to having no money at all has been in use since the beginning of the 19th century, when a 'bean' became a slang name for a gold guinea coin. In the U.S.A. the same word later came to mean a five-dollar gold piece, though it is now used of a dollar.

It is not clear why 'bean' came to be used for a coin. In his *Dictionary of Historical Slang*, Eric Partridge wonders whether it derived from French *bien*, in the sense of 'something good,' but this seems very unlikely. Presumably there was a vague allusion to a bean's shape. It was this, after all, which was to cause 'bean' to acquire a secondary slang meaning of 'head,' a sense humorously preserved in the vocative 'old bean.' It also survives in an American baseball term. A pitcher who tries to intimidate a batter with a ball aimed at his head is said to have thrown a 'beanball.'

Not have a dog's chance

The origin of this expression is less obvious than it seems. It is not self-evident why a dog should have little or no chance of succeeding at whatever needs to be done, but the reference to a dog may be indirect. When the Romans were gambling with dice, their name for the lowest throw was *canicula* – literally 'little dog.' This was translated into English centuries ago as the 'dog throw' or 'dog chance.' Anyone who threw the dog chance had no hope of winning, 'hadn't a dog's chance' as we now say. The latter expression may well be derived from the former.

Use of the phrase is demonstrated in Martin Armstrong's short story *Calf Love*: '"These people are invincible," said Mr Wilson as he introduced their next opponents to them after tea. "I'm afraid you haven't a dog's chance".' J. B. Priestley offered a suitable reply to such a statement in *Let the People Sing*: 'Don't suppose I've got a dog's chance really, but I have to keep on trying.'

One for the Road

'Can I press you to a drink?' says a man in *A Jest of God*, by Margaret Laurence. 'One for the road, you might say.' The woman to whom this is addressed finds it appropriate, since she is about to leave her home town. 'All right,' she says, 'it'll be a good omen, maybe.' Many would argue that the phrase was often an ominous one in other ways, when drinking and driving were not thought of as such a potentially lethal combination. In these more enlightened times the offer of 'one for the road' is unlikely to be made to someone who is about to drive. 'One for the road. I insist,' says a man in Graham Greene's *The Complaisant Lover*, but he adds: 'While I call a taxi.'

'One for the road' seems to have been launched by a Johnny Mercer song, a great hit in 1943. This called for 'One for my baby (and one more for the road).' Since the word 'road' derives from 'ride,' and originally referred to a journey made on horseback, it was appropriate to use 'road' to mean 'journey.' An early instance of such usage occurs in R.D. Blackmore's *Mary Anerley*, published in 1880: 'He fed him well, and nourished himself, and took nurture for the road.' With the establishment of 'one for the road' as a standard phrase, it became possible to vary it. Thus a conversation in J. P. Donleavy's *The Ginger Man* runs: '"You've had a few." "Five for the road. Never let it be said that I took to the highway or even byway without fuel for me little heart".'

160

On Tenterhooks

To be 'on tenterhooks' is to be in a state of nervous suspense, apprehensive about what is going to happen. Lord Byron plays with the phrase in *Don Juan*:

> Whether Don Juan and chaste Adeline
> Grew friends in this or any other sense,
> Will be discuss'd hereafter, I opine:
> At present I am glad of a pretence
> To leave them hovering, as the effect is fine,
> And keeps the atrocious reader in suspense;
> The surest way for ladies and for books
> To bait their tender or their tenter hooks.

Tenterhooks were originally right-angled hooks attached to a tenter, a wooden framework on which newly-made cloth was stretched so that it could dry evenly. The term was later applied to hooks of this type used in various other trades. *The Pennsylvania Gazette*, for example, carried an advertisement in 1739 which read: 'Just imported and to be sold by John Brientnall, in Chestnut-street, Tenterhooks of several sizes, fit for Butchers, Skinners, Fullers, and for Quilting-Frames.'

The idea of metaphorically stretching a person's nerves like cloth on a tenter was at first expressed by the phrase 'to be on tenters.' 'My very heart-strings are on the tenters,' says a character in John Ford's play *The Broken Heart*, published in 1633. This was still the form preferred by Sir Walter Scott, who told one of his correspondents in 1796: 'Your curiosity will be upon the tenters to hear the wonderful events.' In *The Way of the World*, William Congreve makes Waitwell say: 'Till I have possession of your adorable person, I am tantalised on the rack; and do but hang,

161

madam, on the tenter of expectation.' Other writers preferred to make specific mention of tenterhooks, using the version of the phrase which has survived. 'I left him upon the tenter-hooks of impatient uncertainty,' writes Tobias Smollett, in *Roderick Random*. Walter de la Mare evidently 'saw' the hooks in his mind's eye. In *Desert Islands* he writes: 'Though the tale-teller may well keep his reader on the sharpest of tenterhooks, he is bound to disimpale him in the end.'

On the Nose

This expression means different things to different people. Someone who regularly bets on horses will use it to mean that he is backing a horse to win, not making a place bet. The horse is expected to get its nose past the finishing line before any of the others.

A further meaning of the phrase derives from the early days of radio, when broadcasts were always live rather than recorded. A play would be timed during rehearsals to make sure that it fitted into its time-slot. During the actual broadcast, the director would use hand signals to tell the cast whether they needed to slow down or speed up. If all was going well he tapped his nose. This gesture was later translated into words as 'on the nose.' You can still tell someone, for instance, that you will meet him at 'twelve-thirty on the nose,' meaning that you will be there exactly at that time.

In Australia 'on the nose' was originally used to describe a bad smell. Kylie Tennant's novel *Lost Haven* has: '"Christ! Alec," he complained. "This bait's a bit on the nose, ain't it?" He spat over the side as the reek of fish-heads a week old caught his stomach.'

The phrase is now applied in a more general way to anything which is considered to be offensive, such as someone's behaviour.

On the Tiles

In *Shannon's Way*, A.J.Cronin describes a man who 'seems to exude a careless vitality.' His activities, 'from chain smoking to, in his own phrase, "stopping out on the tiles," made not the slightest inroads upon his constitution.' Cronin seems to suggest that the phrase is a personal one, used only by the individual concerned, but it has been in use since the latter part of the 19th century. It is in Galsworthy's play *The Silver Box*, first staged in 1906, and is regularly found in 20th century novels. In *The Franchise Affair*, Josephine Tey has: 'I'd say she was what is known as "out on the tiles," sir. A very cool customer she was.' Colleen McCullough writes in *The Thorn Birds*: 'They all went out on the tiles. It was some night.' In Fay Weldon's *Leader of the Band*, a husband says to his estranged wife: 'Surprised to see me, I expect. Sneaking home from your night on the tiles.'

The phrase originally alluded to the sexual activities of cats, who were thought to be living it up on the rooftops every night. It may have referred to a specific story, since Mrs Henry Wood, in *Mrs Halliburton's Troubles*, makes someone say: 'Ill reports never lose by carrying: the two cats on the tiles, you know, were magnified into a hundred.' This novel was published in 1862, when human beings were probably first described as being 'on the tiles.' Where people are concerned, the meaning of the phrase has widened to include a considerable consumption of alcohol and the resultant drunken behaviour – what was known in the Royal Navy as being 'on the skite.' Compared to young people who are 'out on the tiles,' most rooftop cats are now relatively well behaved.

A *Times'* sub-editor made a pleasant allusion to this phrase in October, 1996. A pub had been listed by English Heritage as a Grade II building, partly because of its hand-painted tiles. 'Outside,' said the report, 'is a tiled portrait of Sir Henry Havelock, hero of the Indian Mutiny in 1857.' This inspired the sub-editor to head the column: 'Pub honoured for knight on the tiles.'

On the Wagon

The person who is 'on the wagon' is abstaining from alcohol, either temporarily or permanently. The *National Observer* magazine reported in 1976: 'through counseling, they were persuaded to go on the wagon during the last few months of pregnancy.' The reference was to the expectant mothers rather than the fathers-to-be. In James Farrell's *Young Manhood* someone asks: 'Was he oiled when the accident happened?' 'No,' is the reply, 'he was on the wagon again.' A more recent novel, Len Deighton's *Twinkle, Twinkle, Little Spy*, has the comment: 'They dug him out of a bar, stoned out of his mind. He stayed on the wagon for years.'

The original form of this expression, which is first recorded around 1900, is shown in O.Henry's short story *The Rubaiyat of a Scotch Highball*: 'Bob Babitt was "off the stuff." Which means that he had "cut out the booze"; that he was "on the water wagon".' George Bernard Shaw also uses this form in his *Intelligent Woman's Guide to Socialism*, where he says that 'the vast majority of modern drinkers do not miss the extra efficiency they would enjoy on the water wagon.' In Britain a 'water wagon' was more usually a 'water cart,' but it performed the same function. It consisted of a barrel or tank on wheels and was used to spray water onto dusty roads. Long before 'on the water wagon' had come into being, writers such as Dickens had jokingly alluded to the water-cart in quite a different way. In *The Pickwick Papers*, for instance, when Sam Weller says, 'I'm wery much mistaken if that 'ere Jingle worn't a-doin' somethin' in the water-cart way!' the reference is to weeping, not abstaining from alcohol.

On the Wrong Track

An article in the *Guardian* newspaper in 1970 stated that 'much propaganda about personal hygiene is on the wrong track. Why the obsession with stopping fresh perspiration?' C.P.Snow, in *The Affair*, makes use of the same phrase: 'You're really on the wrong track there.' It also occurs in Jerome K. Jerome's *Three Men in a Boat*: 'You know we are on a wrong track altogether. We must not think of the things we could do with, but only of the things that we can't do without.' In these instances the writers are probably referring metaphorically to a railway train which is on the wrong track, though it is just possible that they are thinking of someone following the wrong trail.

Purists might argue that the 'correct' form of this phrase is 'on the wrong tack,' where the allusion is to sailing. 'Tack' refers to the direction in which a sailing ship is moving, as determined by the position of the sails in relation to the wind-direction. Figuratively, 'tack' has long been used to mean 'the course of action a person is taking.' 'On the wrong tack' therefore means 'taking a wrong course of action, going in the wrong direction.' Writers who prefer this form of the phrase include E.F.Benson, in *Queen Lucia*: '"May I enquire the lady's name?" "But, can't you guess?" she said. "Surely I'm not absolutely on the wrong tack?"' and E.M.Forster in *Howards End*: 'I don't feel grave, that's all I can say; you're going quite on the wrong tack.'

It is usually 'tack' rather than 'track' which is used metaphorically in phrases other than 'on the wrong track\tack.' J.I.M.Stewart, in *The Last Tresilians*, writes: 'She went off on another tack – and it was the personal tack I'd been banking on.' *A High Wind in Jamaica*, by Richard Hughes, has: 'Then he went off on a fresh tack.' In *Doctor Thorne*, Trollope makes someone say dismissively: 'He goes on every tack, just as it's wanted.'

Over a Barrel

If you are 'over a barrel' you are in a very weak position, unable to do anything about someone else's action. The phrase is a modern one, the first recorded instance appearing in Raymond Chandler's *The Big Sleep*, published in 1939: 'We keep a file on unidentified bullets nowadays. Some day you might use that gun again. Then you'd be over a barrel.' The origin of the phrase has been linked to the practice of laying a person rescued from the sea over a barrel. This was then gently rocked back and forth until water was expelled from the lungs. The obvious problem with this explanation is that it suggests someone being saved, rather than dominated by, another person.

For different reasons the phrase cannot be linked to the barrel of a gun, as if the meaning was 'in somebody's sights,' and therefore at his mercy. The image evoked by the expression clearly suggests someone being laid over a barrel so that he can be flogged. In this case one might have expected the phrase to have surfaced at a much earlier date, when floggings were relatively common. Nevertheless, in Clarence Major's *Black Slang*, published in 1971, there is an entry for 'barrel punishment.' This is defined as 'placing a prisoner over a barrel and viciously beating him, sometimes to death.' If this treatment was being meted out in the 1930s, as seems likely, it could well account for the phrase. Saul Bellow seems to have some such scenario in mind when he makes someone say, in *Herzog*: 'They'll kill you. Put you over a barrel. Tear your hide off.'

The metaphorical expression is well used in modern times. 'You'll end up paying the increase anyway. They've got you over a barrel,' says a character in Richard Bissell's *The Pajama Game*. The speaker in Barry Hines's *The Blinder* who says: 'Twenty minutes left and we had them over a barrel' is referring to the opposing team in a game of football. Bernard Wolfe, in *The Late Risers*, has: 'He hadn't reported it in his tax returns, and there was a law about that too. Any way you looked at it, he was over the barrel.' In *Comfort Me With Apples*, Peter de Vries couples the phrase with another common expression: 'If you think you've got me over a barrel you've got another think coming.'

Over the Moon

We have become used to sportsmen saying that they are 'over the moon' when interviewed about some recent triumph. Sometimes it seems as if no other way of expressing delight exists. The phrase has become a cliché because of its excessive use, but there is clearly something about the image it evokes that pleases a lot of people. Noel Coward was not above making use of it in his

Middle East Diary. There he notes: 'The Captain is absolutely over the moon with pleasure at having this command.' It also occurs in *Flashman*, by George MacDonald Fraser. The narrator's wife says: 'We shall go out to Lady Chalmers's, and she will be quite over the moon when she hears about this.'

The phrase is not a recent one, though an 18th century speaker would probably have said that he felt like jumping over the moon, an extension of jumping for joy. According to the well-known nursery rhyme, which is thought to date from about 1765, it is the cow which jumps over the moon. A more realistic example of usage occurs in Sheridan's *A Trip To Scarborough*, first produced in 1777. When Miss Hoyd is told that she can do as she wishes she exclaims: 'Oh Lord, I could leap over the moon.'

A Shakespearean phrase that has not survived is 'under (beneath) the moon.' This has nothing to do with being the opposite of 'over the moon,' it simply means 'on earth.' It occurs in *King Lear*, in a cliff-top conversation where Edgar tells the blind Gloucester:

> You are now within a foot of th'extreme verge.
> For all beneath the moon Would I not leap upright.

In *Hamlet*, Laertes talks of a poison that he will put on his sword. It is so powerful, he says, that not even a mixture of all the medicinal herbs 'under the moon' can save someone affected by it.

Paddle Your Own Canoe

In 1854 an American song-writer, Sarah T. Bolton, published a song called 'Paddle Your Own Canoe.' It included the lines:

> Voyager upon life's sea,
> To yourself be true,
> And, where'er your lot may be
> Paddle your own canoe.

In modern times, those who think that they have paddled their own canoes tend to claim: 'I did it my way.' They mean that they have remained independent and been self-reliant.

Sarah Bolton had picked up on a phrase which had already been in use for at least twenty-five years. One popular 19th century writer who made use of it was Captain Frederick Marryat. His *Settlers in Canada* included the comment 'I think that it is much better that as we all go along together, that every man paddle his own canoe.' Perhaps an image of a lone canoeist comes to mind when the phrase is applied to an individual, but it can be used of groups. In 1949, for instance, an article in *Time* said: 'They seem more interested in paddling their own canoes than shaping a strong third force that would be the best weapon against the communism they all hate.' A 1962 article in the *Listener* magazine stated: 'The Labour Party wished, as it were, to paddle its own canoe; to build in Britain a show-house of democratic socialism which the rest of Europe might inspect and then draw the lesson.' Those who do paddle their own canoe must be careful not to find themselves 'up the creek,' in serious difficulty. The military version of this phrase is rather more vulgar, namely 'up shit creek without a paddle.'

Paint the Town Red

This expression was first recorded in an American newspaper at the end of the 19th century. The *Boston Journal* reported that 'whenever there was any excitement or anybody got particularly loud, they always said somebody was "painting the town red".' A few years later, in 1897, an article in the *Chicago Advance* said: 'The boys painted the town red with firecrackers.' By 1922 the expression was well enough known for James Joyce to make a joke in *Ulysses*: 'And there he was at the end of his tether after having often painted the town tolerably pink.'

To paint the town red is to spend a boisterous night out, consuming plenty of alcohol and making a lot of noise. It has been suggested that the kind of behaviour associated with this phrase could lead to a certain amount of blood being splashed about, hence the reference to 'red.' The phrase may merely mean that those concerned attract attention to themselves, as they would if they wandered through the town splashing red paint everywhere.

Pass the Buck

The 'buck' in this expression refers to a knife with a buckhorn handle. In the 19th century, American poker players would pass such a knife around the table to indicate who would be the next dealer. Early instances of the phrase normally refer to the card game. Mark Twain, for example, in *Roughing It* (1872), has: 'I reckon I can't call that hand. Ante and pass the buck.' From this 'pass the buck' came into more general use with the meaning 'pass the responsibility on to someone else.' This is something that anyone who holds a high position in an organization can legitimately do, but 'passing the buck' is more negative than merely delegating a task. It suggests someone who is afraid to make a decision for which he may subsequently be blamed. A junior employee may therefore 'pass the buck' to a senior colleague. This was the reason for the famous sign on the desk of President Truman in the Oval Office: 'the buck stops here.' The phrase seems to have been his own invention and has become as well-known as 'passing the buck' itself.

Other off-shoots of the phrase include 'buck-passing' and 'bucking responsibility.' An American journalist, writing for an Oklahoma newspaper in 1932, commented: 'When America is grappling with things fundamental, tired and disgusted with side-stepping, buck-passing and plain lying, the country must content itself with a stone when it asked for bread.' To 'buck responsibility' for anything is to dodge it.

Pay Through the Nose

To 'pay through the nose' for something – pay an excessive price for it – has been in use since the late 17th century. The origin of the phrase is something of a mystery. Other 'nose' phrases in use at that time included to 'bore someone's nose' and 'wipe a person's nose of something.' The first of these meant to cheat or swindle someone, as when a writer in 1642 reported: 'I have known divers

Dutch gentlemen grosly gulled by this cheat, and some English bor'd also through the nose this way.' The second phrase could also mean to cheat or deprive someone of something. In 1667 Pepys wrote in his *Diary* that 'the King might own a marriage before his contract with the Queen, and so wipe their noses of the Crown.' It is difficult to know whether such expressions influenced the idea of paying through the nose. Since people were no doubt as reluctant in the 17th century as they are today to pay an exorbitant price, there may have been a suggestion of forcing them to do something against their will, of 'leading them by the nose.' The allusion may alternatively have been anti-Semitic in some way, given the hostile attitude in the 17th century to Jewish money-lenders.

Whatever its origin, the phrase is obviously a useful one since it has survived well. Its normal use is demonstrated in Joyce Porter's *Dover One*: 'All he could suggest was that I should go on paying through the nose to keep Juliet Rugg's mouth shut.' Writers have a tendency, however, to link the phrase with other nose expressions. In *David Copperfield* Dickens has: '"He pays well, I hope." "Pays as he speaks, my dear child – through the nose".' In *Abbie*, Dane Chandos comments: 'She looked down her nose, but she had to pay through it.' Lord Lytton's *Lucile* comments on a man who must 'pay through his nose just for following it.'

Penny Drops, The

When we say that 'the penny has dropped' we mean: 'Now, at last, I understand.' Our thought processes have been a little slow, perhaps, but light has eventually dawned. The expression is a relatively modern one, though the penny slot machines which inspired it now seem to belong to the distant past. There are plenty of people, however, who can remember putting a penny into a slot machine to get a small bar of chocolate or something similar. Sometimes the coin would momentarily get stuck, preventing it from functioning. If a thump or a good shaking made the penny drop into the mechanism, all was well. By analogy, something said to a person may fail to register immediately, but when 'the penny drops' the desired result is obtained.

Ruth Rendell is fond of the phrase. In *The Tree of Hands* she writes: 'It was at this point, Barry always remembered, that the penny dropped. At this moment, for the first time, he understood that they thought he had murdered Jason.' She returns to the expression in *To Fear a Painted Devil*: 'As he stood, murmuring assurances to Carnaby, the penny dropped. Not the whole penny, but a fraction of it, a farthing perhaps.' Farthings, alas, have gone the way of penny slot machines, but we shall probably continue to speak of pennies dropping for a long time to come.

Perish the Thought

'Perish the thought!' means 'may that thought perish immediately!' It is said when something which has just been mentioned should not even be considered because it is ridiculous or unpleasant. Colley Cibber made use of the phrase at the end of the 17th century, when he revised Shakespeare's *King Richard the Third*. Shakespeare himself has Lord Rivers say:

> We follow'd then our lord, our sovereign king,
> So should we you, if you should be our king.

Gloucester replies:

> If I should be! I had rather be a pedlar,
> Far be it from my heart, the thought thereof!

In Cibber's version this became, with some justification, 'Perish that thought!'

Use of 'perish the thought!' in modern times is often ironic. 'Had he, perish the thought, been privately soaking?' asked a columnist in the *New Left Review* in 1961. In similar vein, *Time* said in 1977: 'Perish the thought that a shaker and mover should work for the Government.' When the phrase is spoken, the tone of voice or the look that accompanies it shows how seriously it is meant to be taken.

Pie in the Sky

Morris West, in *Proteus*, writes: 'Shareholders, avid always for more profit, grew restive and fell easy prey to flim-flam men peddling pie in the sky.' Other peddlers of pie in the sky, according to the *Sunday Express* in 1959, were candidates for political office: 'With the election moving remorselessly nearer, pie-in-the-sky days are here again. Everything our hearts could desire is promised us by politicians.' American politicians are just as guilty, it seems. In 1962 General Eisenhower attacked the Kennedy Administration as 'a pie-in-the-sky government.' A fuller form of the expression is 'pie in the sky when you die,' alluding derisively to what has been called the 'bourgeois heaven.' The phrase specifically implies that hoping for good things in heaven as a reward for one's suffering on earth is no more than wishful thinking. In a more general way, 'pie in the sky' refers to any extravagant promise that is unlikely to be fulfilled.

'Pie' has long been a symbol of goodness, especially in comparisons such as 'nice as pie,' sweet as pie.' James Joyce uses the former simile in *Ulysses*: 'See him of a Sunday with his little concubine of a wife, and she wagging her tail up the aisle of the chapel, nice as pie, doing the little lady.' Peter De Vries, in *Glory of the Hummingbird*, remarks cynically: 'People were wonderful, nice as pie, glad to see me fallen.' Fay Weldon illustrates the second expression in *Praxis*: 'She's very stubborn. Sweet as pie just so long as she's doing exactly what she wants.' 'Easy as pie' is also popular, presumably because a sweet pie is easy to eat.

Pin-money

Commenting on the origin of 'pin-money,' Brewer's *Dictionary of Phrase and Fable* maintains that 'pins were once very expensive, and in 14th- and 15th-century wills there were often special bequests for the express purpose of buying pins.' The problem with this explanation is that the first reference to pin-money appears to be in the 16th century, by which time phrases such as 'not worth a pin' and 'not care a pin' were firmly established. These make it clear that an ordinary pin had little or no value. It was no doubt for this reason that 'pin-money' – which at first referred to an annual sum of money that was given to a wife for her personal expenses – was re-interpreted to mean 'a trivial amount of money.' That has certainly become its meaning in modern times.

Since pin-money was originally meant to be used to buy such feminine items as jewellery, 'pin' may have been a translation of the French *épingle*. The French word could also refer to the type of pin more usually known as a brooch, which conceals its practical function of pinning a woman's dress in some way by being richly ornamental.

In the 17th and 18th centuries, 'pin-money' still referred to a woman's personal allowance. In Jane Austen's *Pride and Prejudice*, when Elizabeth announces that she is to marry Darcy, her mother's reaction is: 'Oh, my sweetest Lizzy! how rich and how great you will be! What pin-money, what jewels, what carriages you will have!'

There is some evidence, however, that the reference to pins had become obscure. In *A Trip To Scarborough*, Sheridan's adaptation of Sir John Vanbrugh's *The Relapse*, there is a scene in which Miss Hoyden says: 'I must say of my lord, he's as free as an open house at Christmas; for this very morning he told me I should have six hundred a year to buy pins. Now if he gives me six hundred a year to buy pins, what do you think he'll give me to buy petticoats?' The nurse replies: 'Ah, my dearest, he deceives thee foully, and he's no better than a rogue for his pains! These Londoners have got a gibberage with 'em would confound a gipsy. That which they call pin-money is to buy their wives everything in the 'versal world, down to the very shoe-knots. Nay, I have heard some folks say that some ladies, if they'll have gallants, as they call 'em, are forced to find them out of their pin-money too.'

Pleased as Punch

The Punch and Judy puppet show was first seen in England in the 17th century, having been imported from Italy. Punch was earlier Punchinello, or Polichinello in the Neapolitan dialect. Various explanations have been put forward by Italian philologists to account for the name. An early suggestion was that Puccio d'Aniello, a peasant with an unusual face, had inspired the puppet-maker. Others pointed to Paulo Cinella, a well-known 'buffoon at Naples.' Scholars have also connected the name with the word *pollecenella*, which means 'young turkey-cock' in the Neapolitan dialect. Punch's nose resembles the hooked bill of this bird.

The chief characteristics of the puppet character are his cheerful self-satisfaction and his pride. Both are reflected in standard sayings. 'When Sissy got into the school here her father was as pleased as Punch' writes Dickens in *Hard Times*. 'Sergeant Hunter was as pleased as Punch because he got the prize money' occurs in David Walker's *Geordie*. William J.Locke's *Jaffery* has: '"How does Doria take it?" "She's as pleased as Punch".' The latter novel also makes use of the alternative expression: 'You're as proud as Punch of your fame and success and all that it means to you.' This reference to pride was especially common in the 19th century. Charlotte Brontë says in one of her letters: 'Mrs White would be as proud as Punch to show it you.' *David Copperfield*, by Charles Dickens, has: 'I am as proud as Punch to think that I once had the honour of being connected with your family.'

Plus Fours

When Washington Irving published his *History of New York* in 1809, he used the pen-name Diedrich Knickerbocker. This eventually led to Knickerbocker becoming a word applied to any New Yorker of Dutch descent. The illustrations by Cruikshank in Irving's book also caused 'knickerbockers' to become a name for knee breeches, of the type supposedly worn by Dutchmen.

Yet another development caused baggy knee-length drawers for ladies to become known as knickerbockers, then knickers.

'Knickerbocker' was always meant to be a ludicrous name, and it is a tribute to Washington Irving's linguistic skill that mention of the word 'knickers' still seems to be enough in itself to make people laugh. A few people use the word as an exclamation. There are some who advise others to keep calm by saying: 'don't get your knickers in a twist,' though this smacks of contempt.

In the 1920s, especially, sportsmen such as golfers and cyclists regularly wore knickerbockers. They are still occasionally seen, but in Britain are usually known as 'plus fours.' This term originated as tailors' slang, since four inches of material were normally added to the trouser legs to produce the overhang. Had things worked out differently, they might have become known as 'plus threes' or 'plus fives.'

Point Blank

'Had you asked him point blank why,' says a character in John Montague's *The Dark Accomplice*, 'he would have been startled and lost.' Fanny Burney also refers to a 'point-blank question' in her *Diary* of 1779. 'Who but Sir Joshua would have ventured it!' she adds. It is not only questions that are asked in this way – a woman might make a point blank refusal, for example, to an offer of marriage. A writer in the *Edinburgh Review* also once made the interesting comment that 'the dialogues in *Othello* and *Lear* furnish the most striking instances of plain, point-blank speaking.'

'Point blank' in these quotations has all the appearance of a phrase adapted from a French original. As it happens, *point blanc* has never existed in French, where 'point blank' in the sense of 'direct(ly), brusque(ly),' becomes either the similar *de but en blanc* or *à brûle-pourpoint*. However Claude Deneton, in *La Puce à l'Oreille*, mentions that the older French expression, now obsolete, was *de pointe en blanc*. It was clearly this which suggested 'point blank.'

As in English, the French phrase was originally used to describe a shot fired at point-blank range. This would now mean with the gun almost touching the target, but our ancestors understood the phrase differently. A marksman was considered to be within point-blank range if he could aim at the white spot in the centre of a target keeping the barrel of the gun horizontal and not allowing for a curved trajectory. The point-blank range of the gun itself was considered to be the distance a shot travelled before it dipped below the horizontal line of the bore. Ford, in Shakespeare's *Merry Wives of Windsor*, has this meaning in mind when he says: 'This boy will carry a letter twenty mile as easy as a cannon will shoot point blank twelve score.'

Pop the Question

Since the 18th century a man posing the 'formidable' question, as Miss Mitford describes it in *Our Village*, has usually 'popped' it. In theory this means that in the middle of a conversation about other matters the question 'will you marry me?' has suddenly and unexpectedly popped out. It has taken the young lady completely by surprise, no matter how much she may have schemed to ensure that the question was asked. 'Pop out the question' was the form of the phrase in Samuel Richardson's *Sir Charles Grandison*, but the simpler form soon prevailed. 'He was going to take her to dinner,' writes Mary McCarthy in *The Group*, 'and that was where, she expected, if all went well, he was going to pop the question.'

In the 19th century the familiarity of this phrase allowed a speaker to use 'popping' as a synonym of 'proposing marriage.' An example occurs in Trollope's *Doctor Thorne*, when the doctor asks: 'Have you spoken to my niece about this, Sir Louis?' 'I haven't exactly popped to her yet' is the reply. For some reason this usage has died out. A modern young man might say that he intended to propose to his girlfriend, but the statement that he was thinking of 'popping' to her would sound very odd.

As E.F.Benson pointed out in *Miss Mapp*, some speakers are overly fond of the verb 'pop.' He writes: 'Diva had 'popped' into the grocer's. She always popped everywhere just now; she popped across to see a friend, and she popped home again; she popped into church on Sunday, and occasionally popped up to town, and Miss Mapp was beginning to feel that somebody ought to let her know, directly or by insinuation, that she popped too much.'

Pull Someone's Leg

When we pull someone's leg we are metaphorically tripping him up. To 'trip' someone has been used in this sense since at least the 16th century. Edward Hall, in a *Chronicle* published in 1548, remarks: 'The Frenchmen determined to trip and deceive them by their accustomed servant, called master Treason.'

Pulling someone's leg is now a mild form of deceit, not meant to do harm to the victim, but it may originally have been more serious. It is interesting that in *Cocktail Time*, P.G.Wodehouse equates it with 'kidding.' 'You certainly pulled old Morrison's leg last night with that yarn of yours about the secret document,' says a character. 'He believed every word of it. Can you beat it? Never suspected for a moment that you were just kidding him.' 'To kid someone' is now to make harmless fun of him, but a dictionary published in 1811 defined it as: 'to amuse a man or divert his attention while another robs him.'

As it happens, tripping someone up could also be done for unpleasant reasons. In the 1880s, when to 'pull someone's leg' is first recorded, the 'tripper-up' had become a problem in English cities. The tripper-up was the mugger of the period, who kicked his victim's legs from under him and robbed him as he lay on the ground. If 'pulling someone's leg' does derive from the idea of tripping, it may – like 'kidding someone' – have been far less innocent when first used. In modern times, of course, any suggestion of tripping that leg-pulling still carries with it is at the level of a child's prank. The Opies report in their *Lore and Language of Schoolchildren* that this activity still flourishes. An eight-year-old boy is quoted as saying: 'after twelve o'clock, when we come out of school, they say it is tripping up time and they try to trip us over.'

While no one ever physically pulls someone else's leg to make fun of him, we sometimes imagine this happening when we use this phrase. In Graham Greene's *The Heart of the Matter* a character says: 'John used to pull his leg about it, quite gently you know.' The speaker implies that a leg can be pulled with varying degrees of strength. The phrase is also found in shortened form as a single verb or noun. Kate O'Brien, in *Pray For The Wanderer*, writes: 'It's impossible not to suspect you of leg-pulling.' 'I don't leg-pull,' is the reply. 'I'm not at all humorous.' Edith Pargeter's *Most Loving*

Mere Folly has: 'It was not so hard to look a shade sceptical, as if the whole thing were no more than an elaborate leg-pull.' In 1908 a writer in the *Westminster Gazette* remarked: 'I, too, have lived in Australia, where leg-pulling is one of the chief joys of life.'

'Pull someone's leg' has given rise to a new expression which is now much used. Someone who suspects that his own leg is being pulled is likely to retaliate verbally. Dick Francis demonstrates this in *Flying Finish*: 'They are English mares going to be mated with Italian sires,' says a man. 'Pull the other one,' is the scornful reply, 'it's got bells on.'

Pull Strings

Lady Montdore, in Nancy Mitford's *Love in a Cold Climate*, is of the opinion that 'one must be able to pull strings in life, everything depends on that in this world, I'm afraid, it's the only way to be successful. Luckily for me, I like important people best and I get on with them like a house on fire.' There is a rather more involved mention of 'pulling strings' in *Cards of Identity*, by Nigel Dennis. A conversation runs: 'I heard the word "string", did I not, Mr Harcourt? What have you to tell us about string? Are you an authority on string?' 'It was strings, not string,' said Mr Harcourt. 'The plural is of even greater interest. The word that goes with it is "pulling", is it not?'

We have been talking about 'pulling strings' in English since the middle of the 19th century. The allusion, clearly, is to a puppeteer. The metaphorical string-puller is an unseen manipulator of other people, obtaining special favours and privileges from them. He does this by being on good terms with them, or by being markedly superior to them socially or professionally. Typical circumstances in which it becomes possible to pull strings are mentioned by Leslie Thomas, in *Tropic of Ruislip*: 'He said he used to be mayor and he could pull some strings. And he did.' Without such conditions being met, pulling strings becomes difficult. Graham Greene has someone comment on that problem in *The Heart of the Matter*: 'He's cabled that he's pulling strings about the passage. I don't know what strings he can pull from Bury, poor dear. He doesn't know anybody at all.'

The earlier version of this phrase, still sometimes used by American speakers, was to 'pull wires.' 'Wire-puller' was at first a term used in American politics, describing an agent who privately influenced others to further his own interests or those of his party. A New York newspaper commented in 1848: 'Already Philadelphia is filled with wire-pullers, and the whole brood of political make-shifts.' Meanwhile 'pulling wires' had already been exported to Britain, as a private letter to Lord Holland in 1834 reveals: 'Lord Durham appears to be pulling at 3 wires at the same time, not that the 3 papers, the *Times*, *Examiner* and *Spectator* are his puppets, but they speak his opinions.' By 1860 references to 'pulling strings' in the same sense as 'pulling wires' had begun to appear on both sides of the Atlantic. The phrases were also being applied to professions other than politics, such as the academic and publishing worlds.

In modern use 'pulling strings' can be applied in almost any context. Graham Greene, for example, in *Loser Takes All*, writes: 'Rice is still short, but I'm certain Aunt Marion can pull strings with the grocer.' The noun form of the phrase is used by Penelope Gilliatt in *A State of Change*: 'We arranged to have his house requisitioned for billets. We did a little string-pulling.' Some authors 'see' the strings that are to be pulled in their mind's eye. Margaret Kennedy writes, in *The Constant Nymph*: 'With half a dozen strings within her reach, she had not made up her mind which to pull.'

Put a Spoke in Someone's Wheel

Richard Barham, in *The Ingoldsby Legends*, tells the story of 'The Leech of Folkestone.' He includes the comment: 'Others have thought that one José was a personage not unlikely to put a spoke in the doctor's wheel, and that the Sage, wise as he was, would run no slight risk of being bamboozled.' 'Put a spoke in someone's wheel' is not the same as bamboozling, or deceiving, that person. It means rather to make it difficult for him to carry out his plans. A 17th century politician illustrated this well when he wrote: 'Argyle has been very industrious to be chosen, but we have put a spoke in his wheel.' Other examples of usage include Thackeray's remark in *The Newcomes* – 'And thinks I, there's a spoke in your wheel, you stuck-up little old Duchess,' and Josephine Tey's comment in *The Franchise Affair*: 'We can join forces to put a spoke in the wheel of this moppet.'

There is clearly something odd about this phrase. When it was first used in the 17th century it would have referred to a wagon wheel or the helm of a ship, where the spokes are essential. To put a spoke in such a wheel would be a constructive thing to do. This fact is reflected in Smyth's *Sailor's Word-book*, published in 1867, where 'to put a spoke in a man's wheel' is glossed as 'to say something of him to his advantage.' On board ship, in other words, the phrase had the more logical meaning of 'put in a good word for someone.' Nevertheless, this failed to influence the older meaning of the phrase, which has remained in general use.

If the meaning of 'put a spoke in someone's wheel' is illogical, there is at least an easily understood explanation of how it came about. An old Dutch expression is *een spaak in't wiel stecken*, which means literally 'put a bar or pole in the wheel.' The reference was to putting a pole between the spokes of a wheel to act as a primitive brake and stop it turning. Metaphorically the phrase meant to interrupt someone's progress, 'put a spoke in someone's wheel' in the normal English sense. The English phrase no doubt came into existence when someone mistakenly translated Dutch *spaak* as 'spoke.'

Put One's Foot Down

'There's nothing like putting your foot down with them,' says a normally mild-mannered man in *The Purple Pileus*, by H.G.Wells. He is referring to women like his wife, who 'don't respect a man until they're a bit afraid of him.' In his case, putting his foot down has involved shouting and smashing some crockery. Margaret Drabble describes a similar man in *The Middle Ground*: 'He'd put his foot down, turned real nasty.' Ngaio Marsh, in *Death at Dolphin*, has: 'Why hadn't he put his foot down? He should have thrown his weight about.'

A person can of course put his foot down without 'throwing his weight about,' but the phrase does usually imply that someone has tried unsuccessfully to make a point in a mild way and now finds himself forced to be insistent, obliged to take a firm stand. The expression conjures up an image of someone literally planting his foot in a particular spot and making it clear that he will not be moved.

Earlier forms of the phrase, however, seem to have referred to putting one's foot down on something. This suggested that something was being destroyed by being crushed underfoot. The expression was perhaps simplified because of the trouble caused by the *on*. Writers certainly seem to have had difficulty coping with it. 'This is one thing on which I have to put down my foot,' writes Upton Sinclair in *World's End*. Mary McCarthy is equally clumsy in *The Group*: 'You did not have your relations to live with you if you wanted your marriage to succeed; it was the one thing on which you put your foot down.'

Put Someone's Back Up

'I shouldn't talk too much in public about your plans,' says someone in C.P.Snow's novel *The Masters*. 'People might think you were too ambitious. We don't want to put their backs up.' This is yet another phrase that we normally use without thinking about what we are actually saying. Nor do we picture in our minds an irritated person with his back raised. If we did think about it, we would soon realise that observation of a cat's behaviour must have given rise to this expression. We are all familiar with a cat's habit of arching its back when angry.

An early allusion to this habit occurs in *The Provok'd Husband* (1728), a play by Sir John Vanbrugh and Colley Cibber: 'O Lud! how her back will be up then, when she meets me.' Benjamin Disraeli uses a variant of the phrase in *Sybil* (1863): 'But the other great whig families set up their backs against this claim of the Egremonts.' In modern times someone who is becoming angry might talk about getting his or her back up, but we probably refer more often to putting someone else's back up. Sometimes it seems that whatever we do, with however good intentions, it is sure to annoy someone.

Put the Cart Before the Horse

To 'put the cart before the horse' is a preposterous thing to do, in the original sense of 'preposterous,' The word derives from Latin *præ* 'before' and *poster-us* 'coming after.' In its Latin form, this word formed part of a tag which corresponded to our 'cart before the horse' – *currus bovem trahit praepostere,* or 'the plough pulls the ox the wrong way round.' This passed into French, where it still exists, as *mettre la charrue avant* (or *devant*) *les boeufs* 'put the plough before the oxen.' This nearly became the form of the saying in English, since the 13th century monk who translated the *Ayenbite of Inwyt* ('Remorse of Conscience') from French wrote: 'Many religious people set the plough before the oxen.'

The English 'cart before the horse' may well have been influenced by the Latin or French sayings, but it took on a life of its own from the 15th century onwards. Shakespeare was clearly aware of it, making the Fool in *King Lear* ask: 'May not an ass know when the cart draws the horse?' The healthy survival of the phrase seems to indicate that many people are still considered to think or act illogically, putting things in the wrong order. There may be occasions, of course, when the correct order is a matter of debate. Because of the advance of technology, Randle Cotgrave might find himself having to defend his views if he were alive today. His example in a 17th century dictionary of putting the cart before the horse was 'the young instructing the old,' something which is now often all too necessary.

Pyrrhic Victory

One man tells another, in *Comfort Me With Apples*, by Peter de Vries: 'Pete, the game isn't worth the candle. This will be what they call a Pyrrhic victory. A success that's really a setback.' This is a reasonable explanation of 'Pyrrhic victory,' where the victory has been won at too great a cost to the victor. The allusion is to Pyrrhus, king of Epirus in the third century BC. At the battle of Asculum he defeated a Roman army, but the pick of his own soldiers were killed. He is said to have exclaimed: 'One more such victory and we are lost.'

Peter de Vries also mentions that the game is 'not worth the candle.' This expression was in use amongst the gambling fraternity by the end of the 17th century. Gamblers who liked to play for high stakes would treat a small wager with contempt, saying that it was not worth winning because it would not even pay for the candle that provided the lighting. The expression can be used of any enterprise. *The Oxford English Dictionary*, for example, quotes a magazine article: 'When the robbing of banks became difficult we went for the cash in transit, until the professionals got their drill so slick that the game was not worth the candle.'

Quack Doctor

A quack doctor is someone who falsely claims to have medical knowledge and often boasts about the remarkable remedies he has for sale. He is less seldom seen today, but was frequently met with in former times. In the 17th century he was known as a quacksalver – one who 'quacked' about his 'salves,' or ointments. It is normally a duck that quacks, of course, but the verb was sometimes used of loud and uncouth speech. In 1624, for instance, a certain Bishop Smith talked in one of his sermons of 'busy-bodies that will dare to quack against their betters.'

'Quacksalver' was soon abbreviated to 'quack.' By the 18th century George Crabbe was able to write, in *The Village*, of:

> A potent quack, long versed in human ills,
> Who first insults the victim whom he kills.

The meaning of the word was also extended to take in charlatans in other professions, such as the law and the church.

In 20th century military slang, 'quack' became the usual word for the medical officer. This was typical service humour, and there was no implication of fraud or incompetence. In relaxed speech there are still many speakers who would say that they need to consult the quack about a medical problem.

Queer Someone's Pitch

'I suppose you think you've queered my pitch,' says a young scientist to a jealous colleague in A.J. Cronin's *Shannon's Way*. In other words, you think you've spoiled my plans and opportunities. An early use of this phrase occurs in *Stage Reminiscences*, published in 1866 by M. Mackintosh: 'The smoke and fumes of blue fire which had been used to illuminate the fight came up through the chinks of the stage, fit to choke a dozen Macbeths, and – pardon the little bit of professional slang – poor Jamie's pitch was queered with a vengeance.'

The reference to 'professional slang' correctly indicates the origin of this expression. Another 19th century writer, in a book about circus life, explained: 'The spot they select for their performance is their "pitch," and any interruption of their feats, such as an accident, or the interference of a policeman, is said to "queer the pitch".' Nowadays the phrase is normally applied to an individual, and there is nothing accidental about it. As A.J.Cronin indicated, a jealous person is likely to cause trouble for someone else, queer his pitch, as an act of deliberate malice.

Queer Street

A character in George MacDonald Fraser's *Flashman* tells his son: 'We're in Queer Street, Harry. I suppose I've not been taking much account of how the money went.' Similarly, Angus Wilson writes in *Hemlock And After*: 'He enjoys a little flutter, and if he finds himself in Queer Street now and again, I'm sure no one would grudge him his bit of fun.' These references to Queer Street might puzzle American readers, but in Britain they would be generally understood to refer to temporary or permanent bankruptcy.

This meaning has been current since at least the mid-19th century: there is a chapter called 'Lodgers in Queer Street,' for instance, in *Our Mutual Friend*. Dickens clearly assumed that the bankruptcy meaning was already common knowledge.

The editors of the *Oxford English Dictionary* describe Queer Street merely as an imaginary place inhabited by people in difficulties. Yet elsewhere in the dictionary they quote Norman Collins, who refers in *Trinity Town* to 'a man like Mr Broster who might find himself in Carey Street at any moment.' They then explain that Carey Street was 'a street in London, formerly the location of the Bankruptcy Department of the Supreme Court, used allusively to indicate a state of bankruptcy.' Carey Street existed by the early 18th century, having been named for a land-owning family. Surely there is little doubt that Cockney humour changed the name to what must have seemed a more appropriate form?

Rain Cats and Dogs

We know from Jonathan Swift's *Complete Collection of Polite and Ingenious Conversation* that English people were talking about it 'raining cats and dogs' in the early 18th century. Swift considered the phrase an example of the absurd conversation of society 'wits,' but it may have begun as a seaman's expression. In 1766 a writer commented: 'It blows cats and dogs, as the sailors say.' A 19th century seaman's diary contains the remark: 'It blew great guns and poured cats and dogs.' It is possible that seamen used the phrase to mean that it was raining so hard that everything seemed to be falling from the sky, even cats and dogs.

One is forced to make guesses about the origin of the phrase because nothing points conclusively to any one explanation. 'Rain cats and dogs' does not appear to be translated from French or German, though in both languages there are metaphorical expressions related to heavy rainfall. *Il pleut des hallebardes* in French literally means 'it's raining halberds,' a halberd being the long-handled weapon which is a cross between a spear and an axe. More commonly, French people speak about bad weather as *un temps de chien*, literally 'dog-weather,' but this means weather which is only fit for dogs, not that dogs are tumbling from the sky. The German phrase *es regnet Heugabeln* 'it's raining pitchforks' is self-explanatory and has been used in its English form. In *The Island of Jewels*, the minor 19th century playwright James Robertson Planché writes:

> Rain cats and dogs, or pitchforks perpendicular,
> The sky's not mine, and needn't be particular.

The 1852 edition of Roget's *Thesaurus* actually equated 'to rain in torrents' with 'rain cats and dogs, rain pitchforks.'

One explanation that has been offered for the 'cats and dogs' phrase is that heavy rain could quickly cause flooding, especially when drainage systems were less efficient than in modern times. Flood water would drown a number of cats and dogs in a city, so that after torrential rain it might look as if cats and dogs had fallen from the sky. Dr Brewer preferred a link with Norse mythology and the storm god Odin, often portrayed with cat and dog. The latter were said to influence the weather. Dr Brewer did not go on to comment on the likelihood of such an erudite reference suddenly becoming an everyday expression in English. Even more bizarre is the suggestion made by Edwin Radford (in *Crowther's Encyclopedia of Phrases and Origins*) that an obsolete French word *catadoupe* 'waterfall' led to the expression. Perhaps more acceptable would have been a suggestion that Greek words such as *cataclysm* 'violent disaster such as a flood' and *cataract* 'waterfall' became associated with 'cats' in the minds of uneducated people, and that cats were then linked to dogs.

Whatever its origin, 'rain cats and dogs' remains a popular phrase with speakers and writers. 'It was raining cats and dogs and do you think anyone came to meet us?' says a character in Truman Capote's *My Side of the Matter*. In *Flashman*, by George MacDonald Fraser, it is of some significance to the narrator that 'it had been raining cats and dogs.' His wife says that she has 'spent the entire afternoon riding in the Park.' The fact that her riding coat is bone-dry puts uncomfortable doubts into his mind.

Rainy Day, A

It seems to have been Oliver Goldsmith who first used the homely metaphor 'rainy day' to refer to a possible time of trouble or misfortune when extra money is needed. In *The Vicar of Wakefield* the vicar's wife is praising her son Moses when she says: 'Depend upon it he knows what he is about. I'll warrant we'll never see him sell his hen on a rainy day. I have seen him buy such bargains as would amaze one.' Moses, in other words, will never need to dispose of his goods at a time of financial difficulty, he is far too astute. Moments later this same Moses is being assailed by his mother as a 'blockhead' and 'idiot.' He has returned from the market, having been duped into buying a gross of worthless spectacles.

The Vicar of Wakefield was published in 1766 and was widely read. The 'rainy day' comment perhaps inspired Abraham Tucker, who was telling his readers two years later in *Light of Nature Pursued* that 'it behoves us to provide against a rainy day while the sun shines.' Since that time it has been generally accepted that it is sensible to put something by for a rainy day. If the time of need does not arrive, the savings can always be spent on a splurge, but the rain usually comes all too soon. In Thomas Wolfe's *Look Homeward, Angel* a man says that owning property, other than the house one lives in, 'is nothing but a curse and a care, and the tax-collector gets it all in the end.' His wife remonstrates with him: 'That's no way to talk! You want to lay something by for a rainy day, don't you?' 'I'm having my rainy day now,' he says sourly.

Rat Race, The

The 'rat race' is a derogatory term applied to what others might call a middle class way of life. To its detractors the latter is seen as endless competition with one's colleagues in the struggle to 'get on,' and frenzied but unproductive activity. The phrase also hints at the determined response which rats are capable of in a competitive situation. The expression is used especially by those who object to being forced to live their lives in such a way and decide to drop out or refuse to become involved in it at all. Typical uses of the phrase, both drawn from the *Spectator* magazine, are the 1958 comment that 'modern economic life is more like a rat race than a rational way of life,' and the 1959 reference to 'a realism that encourages in its popular press a rat-race morality in the guise of room at the top.' Budd Schulberg's *Waterfront* has: 'He was ready to take life easy in the loft. In the loft you were out of the rat race, you were out from under the shape-up pressure.'

'Rat race' used in this metaphorical sense first seems to have been used in the USA in the late 1930s. A year or two before being recorded in the way that we now understand it, 'rat race' had been for 'jazz addicts,' as H.L. Mencken described them in T*he American Language*, a slang term for a kind of dance. It is therefore possible that it was human threshing about on the dance floor, rather than the frantic activity of laboratory rats on a treadmill, which suggested the adoption of the phrase in its present meaning.

In theory there is another possible origin, though it almost certainly reflects no more than a linguistic coincidence.

An obsolete meaning of 'rat' cited by the *Oxford English Dictionary* is 'a strong or rapid current.' Admiral Smyth, in his *Sailor's Word-book* of 1867, glossed the word as 'a rapid stream or race, derived from sharp rocks beneath, which injure the cable.' This accurately hints at the derivation of 'rat' in this sense, which is from Portuguese *rato* 'a sharp rock.' It also suggests that 'rat race' to a 19th century seaman could have conjured up an image of being caught in a fast-flowing and dangerous current. This is perhaps not far removed from the way we think of the rat race of business life.

Ambitious people were certainly involved in some kind of rat race before that term was used to describe it. A French phrase which was applied to struggles within an organisation was *panier de crabes*, literally a 'basket of crabs.' This is still occasionally used in modern French to define a group of people who are engaged in a struggle for power, the sort of thing Budd Schulberg has in mind when he writes, in the novel quoted above, of 'ecclesiastical in-fighting.'

Real McCoy, The

In a letter written in 1883, Robert Louis Stevenson referred to a man named Johnstone as 'the real Mackay.' This was in the sense of 'the genuine article, something of high quality,' the meaning that we now attach to 'the real McCoy.' Stevenson probably picked up his version of the phrase from advertisements for Mackay whisky. These had claimed since 1870 that their product was 'the real Mackay.' Ngaio Marsh, for one, was clearly convinced that this was the 'correct' version of the phrase. In *Swing, Brother, Swing*, published in 1949, she writes: 'If I could pick my work I'd be in an outfit that went for the real mackay.'

The change to 'the real McCoy' occurred in the U.S.A., where the phrase seems to have been deliberately adapted by a welterweight boxer, Kid McCoy, and his followers. McCoy himself is said to have promoted a story concerning an incident in a bar. When someone asked him to prove who he was, McCoy allegedly obliged by knocking the man to the ground. When the man recovered he is said to have admitted that he had met 'the real McCoy.' An even more unlikely story says that during the time Kid McCoy was champion, from 1898 to 1900, another boxer called McCoy, of inferior quality, was also pursuing his career.

'The real McCoy' is now the normal version of this phrase in all English-speaking countries. It seems to be popular in the musical world. Leonard Bernstein writes, for example, in *The Joy of Music*: 'The operetta score was musically elaborate, closer to opera, even containing finales, with everybody singing his way through the plot, vocalizing different sentiments at the same time; the real contrapuntal McCoy.' In 1972 the music critic of the *Guardian* reported that 'Sadler's Wells is playing host to the regal offspring Royal Ballet, and not, please note, a second eleven but the real Macoy.' The phrase can of course be used in other contexts. Patricia Highsmith, for instance, in *Ripley Under Ground*, has an American commenting on a painting in a discussion about possible forgeries: 'That's a masterpiece. That's the real McCoy.'

Red Herring

Sherlock Holmes hints at the origin of this expression in *The Adventure of the Priory School*. He says: 'It would be well to allow the people in your neighbourhood to imagine that the enquiry is still going on in Liverpool, or wherever else that red herring led your pack. In the meantime I will do a little quiet work at your own doors, and perhaps the scent is not so cold but that two old hounds like Watson and myself may get a sniff of it.'

As Holmes no doubt knew, huntsmen had long needed to train their hounds to follow the scent of a fox, while ignoring any other scents which they happened to come across. Red herrings, with their particularly strong smell, were traditionally used in the training programme. They were drawn across a fox-trail as a distraction, which the more intelligent pack-leaders soon learned to disregard.

'Red herring' now refers to any distracting side issue introduced into a discussion, as C.P.Snow indicates in *The Affair*: 'It seemed incredible to him, not used to academic meetings, that they should have rushed off in chase of this red herring.' Had things worked out differently, Snow might have referred to rushing off in chase of a dead cat. A 17th century writer mentions that dead cats were sometimes used instead of red herrings when hounds were being trained.

Regular Brick, A

Out of context, this phrase appears to be describing a most uninteresting subject – an ordinary brick of regular shape and size. Yet a young man in the 19th century would normally have been delighted to hear himself described by his friends in these terms. The phrase meant that he was a jolly good fellow. The 'brick' allusion no doubt had to do with the idea of dependable solidity, though Barham, in his *Ingoldsby Legends*, hints at a far more ingenious origin. In 'The Brothers of Birchington,' after a glowing description of Father Richard, he says:

> In brief, I don't stick to declare Father Dick –
> So they call'd him, "for short" – was a "Regular Brick,"
> A metaphor taken – I have not the page aright –
> Out of an ethical work by the Stagyrite.

The Stagyrite, or Stagirite, is Aristotle, who lived in Stagira, Macedonia. Barham is thinking of the philosopher's reference to a 'tetragonous man,' a tetragon being a regular four-sided shape. This is meant as a metaphor for 'a man whose name is worthy of commemoration on a monumental stone.'

'Brick' was first applied to persons in a complimentary way around 1840, though it seems to have struck Charles Dickens as rather odd when he was writing *David Copperfield* in 1849. He remarks there that 'Steerforth approved of him highly, and told us he was a brick. Without exactly understanding what learned distinction was meant by this, I respected him greatly for it.' By the time Thomas Hughes came to write *Tom Brown's Schooldays*, in 1857, 'brick' was clearly established in schoolboy speech as a term of approval. Of one of the masters it is said: 'What a brick not to give us even twenty lines to learn.' This sense of 'brick' has survived into modern times and can now be applied equally well to a woman. 'Stella, you're a brick,' says a character in John Sherwood's *The Half Hunter*.

'Regular' in this expression has come a long way from its original meaning of 'living by monastic rule.' When Americans began to refer to 'a regular guy' in the early 19th century they meant someone whose life-style and opinions were like those of most other people. 'I know I'm not a regular fellow,' remarks a man in F.Scott Fitzgerald's *This Side of Paradise*. He continues: 'yet I loathe anybody else that isn't.'

Ring a Bell

We often say that something 'rings a bell' when it calls something to mind. 'The name rang an immediate bell,' writes Ruth Rendell, in *Talking To Strange Men*. Later in the novel a character cannot clearly recall a person who has been mentioned, but says: 'The name does ring a bell, though.' Margery Allingham, in *Coroner's Pidgin*, specifies: 'That's where I saw the name, then. It rang only a very faint bell.' As these examples indicate, it is often a person's name that 'rings a bell,' but there can be other kinds of reminders. 'Do you remember the stage hands who built the set?' asks a character in Pamela Frankau's *Bridge 64*. 'That rings a bell,' is the reply. There is also an old joke which runs: 'Does the name Pavlov ring a bell?'

Laurence Urdang, in his *Picturesque Expressions*, suggests that 'the former practice of ringing church bells to signal the hour or to inform the populace of significant events' might have given rise to this phrase. That would have been more likely had the phrase come into existence in a previous century, but no record of it is found until the 1930s. We must probably look for a more modern association between bell-ringing and people's names, which makes the hotel bell-boy a possibility, ringing his bell as he pages the guests.

To 'ring a bell' continues to be well used, but to 'ring the bell,' in the sense of 'succeed,' is now rare. Edgar Wallace writes in *Strange Countess*: 'You've certainly rung the bell this time, Lois.' 'It seems too good to be true, doesn't it?' Lois replies. In 1945 the *Daily Mirror* reported that 'Leeds Corporation has fifty 'retired' trams to sell. They think a tram would 'ring the bell' as a home, week-end bungalow, or greenhouse.' The origin of this phrase was clearly the 'Try-your-strength' machine of the fairground. As J. B. Priestley explained in *The Good Companions*, with these it was a case of 'down with the 'ammer and up she goes and rings the bell.' Perhaps this phrase has been replaced by 'ring someone's bell,' as heard in soul music of the 1970s. The meaning here varies from 'make an impression on someone' to 'give someone sexual satisfaction.'

Room to Swing a Cat, Not

Authors are rather fond of this expression, though they often add a comment about why anyone would want to swing a cat in the first place. As Nina Bawden puts it, in *George Beneath A Paper Moon*: 'Not much room to swing a cat, I daresay, but then who wants to swing cats?' H.G.Wells, in *Kipps*, makes Mrs Kipps remark 'If we 'ave a smaller 'ouse there won't be room to swing a cat.' The author adds: 'Room to swing a cat, it seemed, was absolutely essential. It was an infrequent but indispensable operation.'

Edna Everage, *My Gorgeous Life*, has: 'The Sylvia Plath Suite was not exactly spacious, in fact there was barely room to swing a cat. That is why I chose it for Mummy. Not that to my knowledge she was likely to swing a cat per se, but in her last days at home she was starting to frighten the animals. Margaret Laurence writes, in *The Diviners*: 'The bathroom is so small you couldn't swing a cat in it (if you should ever desire to engage in such an activity – where do these phrases come from?).'

Most experts would answer Margaret Laurence's question by saying that the 'cat' referred to in this saying is a *cat o' nine tails*, the whip that was used for punishment in the 17th century. It had nine pieces of rope, each about eighteen inches long, attached to a short handle. It was commonly called 'the cat', and had long been in existence when 'room to swing a cat' was first recorded in 1771. There is an alternative theory that 'cat' was the Scottish word for a 'rogue' and that 'swing' meant 'hang from a gallows,' but this explanation has little to support it. It has even been claimed that the phrase originally meant what it said, and that swinging cats by their tails was once a 'sport.' If there is any truth in that report, it probably means that the cat o'nine tails phrase was being maliciously re-interpreted.

Round Robin

In modern times 'round robin' is mostly used to describe an all-play-all chess tournament or some similar competitive event. The phrase can also refer to a document that has been signed by many people. An 18th century magazine defined it more specifically: 'A round robin is a name given by seamen, to an instrument on which they sign their names round a circle, to prevent the ring-leader being discover'd by it, if found.' Another contemporary source talked of the method 'used by sailors when they mutiny, by signing their names in an orbicular manner, which they call a round robin.'

This method of presenting the demands of a ship's crew existed at least a century earlier, though it seems to have had no special name. Jourdain's *Journal*, of 1612, contains the passage: 'The Hectors' boat brought a petition to Sir Henry Middleton, signed by most of them in the manner of a circle, because it should not be known who was the principal of the mutiny.' The phrase 'round robin' was also known in the 17th century. It had nothing to do with documents, but was applied as a disparaging slang term to the consecrated host.

How and why the nautical document became a 'round robin' remains something of a mystery. It is possible that 18th century English sailors gave a new meaning to an old phrase. It has instead been claimed that 'round robin' is a corruption of an old French phrase *ruban rond*, literally a 'round ribbon,' but evidence to support this has yet to be presented. *Ruban rond* is unkown in modern French.

Round the Bend

There are many ways of saying that someone is 'not normal.' Speakers often emphasise their point by using more than one word or phrase at the same time. A conversation between schoolboys in William Golding's *Lord of the Flies* runs: "'If we don't get home soon we'll be barmy." "Round the bend." "Bomb happy." "Crackers".' In *Absolute Beginners*, by Colin MacInnes, a young man says: 'He's round the bend.' He adds, for good measure: 'I said he's flipped, boy.' A speaker in J.I.M. Stewart's *The Guardians* says: 'Right round the bend, I mean, as mad as a hatter.'

The phrase that is common to all these quotations was used by Nevil Shute as the title of a novel. In *Round the Bend* the main character remarks: 'People are saying that I've been out in the East too long, and I've gone round the bend.'

Sea Slang, published in 1929 by F.C.Bowen, listed 'round the bend' as 'an old naval term for anybody who is mad.' This reference to the navy has caused some scholars to wonder whether the bend that is mentioned in the phrase is a knot, a 'bend' at sea being used to tie two ropes together, or to secure a rope to itself after it has passed through a ring. To the landlubber, such knots may merely look twisted, and it is interesting that 'round the twist' exists as an alternative form of 'round the bend.' In the absence of hard and fast evidence, however, all such suggestions must remain speculative. As someone says in *House of Cards*, by Dannie Abse, 'I knew that man was round the twist, sayin' things like that.'

Russian Roulette

In Morris West's *Proteus* a man is threatening to release poison into the water supplies of large cities unless the governments of the countries concerned release their 'prisoners of conscience.' The British prime minister says that he and his fellow leaders are faced with 'an intolerable gamble.' The man wants the governments to play Russian roulette. 'He puts the pistol on the table and invites us to fire it at our own heads or his own.' He is gambling with his own life, in other words, and challenges us to gamble with the lives of our people.

Russian roulette is reported to have been played in the First World War by Russian army officers. It probably stemmed from certain aspects of the Slav character mixed with the Nihilism that became popular amongst Russian revolutionists under the tsarist regime. To the Nihilists, the lives of individuals were of little value, and one's own survival was a matter of unimportant chance. Playing Russian roulette was an act of bravado, to show how little a man cared whether he survived or not. An officer would load one of the six chambers of his pistol with a cartridge, spin the cylinder and snap it back into place. He would then put the gun to his head and pull the trigger.

Modern usage of this phrase is normally metaphoric, though quite what is meant is not always clear. A 1976 article in the *Lancet*, for instance, said that 'abusive parents are often the scarred survivors of generations of reproductive Russian roulette.' One problem with this curious statement is that those who played Russian roulette had usually were not scarred, they were either killed instantly or survived unhurt.

See eye to eye with someone

This expression is mostly used to say that we agree with other people's views, or see things as they do. There is often the implication that any kind of agreement is impossible because of fundamental differences. As William Trevor remarks, in *The Old Boys*: 'cats and birds do not see eye to eye.' Nor are they ever likely to do so.

The phrase is actually a quotation from the bible. In the King James version of the Old Testament, Isaiah 52.8 has: 'they shall see eye to eye, when the Lord shall bring again Zion.' All concerned, in other words, will see the same thing and be in agreement about it. Our ancestors would have first heard these words resounding from the pulpit, but as with many other biblical phrases, they would then have incorporated them unconsciously into their daily speech.

Send Someone away With a Flea in His Ear

This expression has been in regular use since at least the 17th century. Beaumont and Fletcher make use of it in *Love's Cure*, a play first produced in 1625. One of the characters remarks: 'He went away with a flea in's ear, like a poor cur.' Samuel Richardson's famous 18th century novel, *Pamela*, has the heroine remarking: 'I was hurrying out with a flea in my ear, as the saying is.' Rider Haggard's *Jess* (1887) has: 'I sent him off with a flea in his ear, I can tell you,' while Kingsley Amis writes, in *Lucky Jim*: 'If I did try to do something I'd only get sent off with a flea in my ear.'

This phrase refers to scolding someone so sharply that he feels a sharp pain in his ear. In former times an ear-ache was sometimes blamed on a flea which was supposedly inside the ear, biting it. Medical knowledge has moved on, but the metaphorical meaning of this expression has become fossilized. It is still used to mean 'dismiss someone with a stinging rebuff.' 'Didn't I come to your door this morning, Harry, and get sent away with a flea in my ear?' asks a man in *Henry's War*, by Jeremy Brooks. The reply is: 'I didn't send you away with a flea in your ear, Charlie. You came at a bad moment.' The phrase is also alluded to in a slightly different way in *Theirs Was The Kingdom*, by R.F. Delderfield: 'If I were in your shoes I'd own up to it. You may even come off with a flea in your ear. My father has overlooked worse.'

Send Someone to Coventry

'Other passengers sent me to Coventry,' writes Alistair Maclean, in *The Dark Crusader*. The man concerned is being punished for not conforming to the unwritten rules of shipboard life. All normal social contacts with him have been suspended, and it is as if he did not exist.

The significance of 'Coventry' in this expression as opposed to any other city has long been debated, and no conclusive explanation can be given. Most often quoted is *The True Historical Narrative of the Rebellion and Civil Wars in England*, by Edward Hyde, earl of Clarendon. This was first printed 1702-4, nearly thirty years after the earl's death. Clarendon says that the citizens of Birmingham, being especially wicked, had taken to attacking small parties of the king's men. These they either killed or took prisoner and sent to Coventry. Coventry at that time was a Parliamentary stronghold where such prisoners would have been well guarded. There is also a legend that soldiers generally were not liked in the city. If that is so, then Royalist soldiers who were there as prisoners would have had an especially bad time of it.

Thomas Hood jokes with this expression in his 'pathetic ballad' about John Day, an overweight coachman who falls in love with a barmaid. John 'stoutly urged his suit,' but:

> In vain he wooed, in vain he sued;
> The maid was cold and proud,
> And sent him off to Coventry,
> While on his way to Stroud.

Set One's Cap at Someone

In Trollope's *Framley Parsonage* an elderly woman advises: 'Just explain to her that any young lady who talks so much to the same young gentleman will certainly be observed – that people will accuse her of setting her cap at Lord Lufton.' A similar remark occurs in Thackeray's *Vanity Fair*: 'When the ladies had retired after dinner, the wily old fellow said to his son, "Have a care, Joe; that girl is setting her cap at you".' In 'Look at the Clock,' one of Richard Barham's *Ingoldsby Legends*, Miss Davis is said to be 'setting her cap at the curate.' In each case the meaning is that a young lady is making a special effort to captivate a particular man.

Ernest Weekley, in his *Etymological Dictionary of Modern English*, drew attention to the French expression *mettre le cap sur*, 'to turn the head (of a ship) towards.' Professor Weekley believed that the English equivalent of this nautical phrase was applied to young women who were seen, as it were, to be sailing in a particular direction. It was uncharacteristic of Weekley to suggest a complicated explanation for a phrase when a simple one was available, but most commentators have assumed that the 'cap' referred to was the light covering of muslin, worn indoors by a lady and known as a 'mob-cap.' When the lady went outside she was likely to retain it beneath her bonnet. By this interpretation, the expression merely meant that a woman put on her most becoming cap in an effort to attract the man concerned.

In strong support of this 'simple' explanation is the remark in Goldsmith's *She Stoops to Conquer*: 'Instead of breaking my heart at his indifference, I'll set my cap to some newer fashion, and look out for some less difficult admirer.' This pre-dates the earliest uses of 'set one's cap at someone' and confirms that fashionable dress was used as a weapon in sexual warfare as much in the 18th century as it is today.

Seven-year Itch

Movie buffs associate this phrase with Marilyn Monroe, who appeared in the film version of George Axelrod's play, *The Seven Year Itch*, in 1955. Axelrod had cleverly given a new meaning to a phrase that already existed. A correspondent to the *Sun* (Baltimore) pointed out in 1955: 'When I was a boy we called the skin rash from poison ivy "the seven-year itch" and firmly believed that it would reappear every year for seven years.' Carl Sandburg had earlier recalled, in *People, Yes* that the taunt

'May you have the seven-year itch' was answered by 'I hope your wife eats crackers in bed.'

Axelrod gave a specific interpretation to 'itch' in its sense of 'a nagging desire for something, or to do something,' often expressed in the form 'itching for.' In *Hypatia*, for example, Charles Kingsley writes: 'The men's fingers are itching for a fight.' This was an early form of the phrase, where it was always one's fingers that itched to do something. A later writer would simply have said 'the men are itching for a fight.' P.G Wodehouse, in *Laughing Gas*, has: 'I recalled that I had noticed her hand quiver once or twice, as if itching for the slosh.'

In Axelrod's version of the 'seven-year itch,' the nagging desire became a sexual one, the urge of a man to have an extra-marital adventure. It was humorously suggested that this urge was a well-known natural phenomenon, likely to recur at seven-year intervals. Married men throughout the world, needless to say, were grateful to be provided with an excuse for their indiscretions. Since 1955 the phrase has become well established in its new meaning.

Shaggy-dog Story

Shaggy-dog stories became something of a craze in the 1940s. According to the Opies, in *Lore and Language of Schoolchildren*, they sometimes come back into fashion in a particular school just as, on other occasions, limericks or knock-knock jokes suddenly become all the rage. The original shaggy-dog stories were so-called because a shaggy dog was the main character or appeared to deliver the punch line. The description was extended to other long and involved tales, often featuring a talking animal, which had, as one contemporary writer expressed it, a 'logical lunacy' about them. They ended typically with an absurdity or weak pun. Arthur Koestler was of the opinion, expressed in *Arrow in Blue*, that 'the people of Budapest have a peculiar shaggy-dog kind of humour.'

Shaggy-dog stories have to be listened to rather than read. Part of the fun is that one cannot cheat and go straight to the last line. Once the story has begun, the listener is curious in spite of himself to know how it will end, but he is made to suffer along the way. A typical shaggy-dog story concerns Bert, who joins the army. On his first day he meets a friend, a corporal, who says 'Hello, Bert, I haven't seen you for ages. Come and have a drink in the NCO's club.' 'Sorry,' says Bert, 'I'm only a private.' 'No problem,' says his friend, 'I'll lend you my spare uniform.' In the NCO's club-house a sergeant says 'Hello, Bert, you're just the man I need to come with me on my course tomorrow. It's for sergeants, but that doesn't matter. I'll lend you my spare uniform.'

In this manner Bert continues to meet a succession of old friends, of a higher rank each time, who lend him a spare uniform so that he can accompany them. He is eventually found at a Buckingham Palace garden party dressed as a general. The prime-minister is also there and comes over. 'Hello, Bert. Delighted to see you again.' At that moment the Queen and the Duke of Edinburgh emerge to meet their guests. 'Just remind me,' says Her Majesty to the Duke, 'who is that talking to Bert?'

Ships that Pass in the Night

In his *Dictionary of Clichés*, Eric Partridge says that 'ships that pass in the night' is 'particularly hackneyed and objectionable.'

This seems very unfair. The phrase is well used because it so aptly conjures up an image of a brief and rather romantic encounter between two people who are unlikely to meet again. 'Luke was probably no more than a ship passing in the night,' says J.I.M.Stewart, in *The Last Tresilians*, when Luke and Hatty appear to be falling in love. P.G.Wodehouse, in *Uncle Fred in Springtime*, has: 'The thought that they had met and parted like ships that pass in the night was very bitter to him.' A.J.Cronin also uses the phrase in *Shannon's Way*. A woman who has quarrelled with a man tells him: 'It would be a great pity if we stopped being friends ... and drifted apart ... like ships that pass in the night.'

We owe this expression to the poet Henry Wadsworth Longfellow. In *'The Theologian's Tale'*, part of his *Tales Of A Wayside Inn*, occurs:

> Ships that pass in the night, and speak each other in
>   passing;
> Only a signal shown and a distant voice in the
>   darkness;
> So on the ocean of life we pass and speak one
>   another,
> Only a look and a voice; then darkness again and a
>   silence.

These beautiful lines were written in 1873. Many would disagree with Eric Partridge and say that they deserved to make a lasting impact.

Shotgun Wedding

In 1927 the American novelist Sinclair Lewis published *Elmer Gantry*. At one point a Kansas farmer discovers that Gantry, a hypocritical Baptist minister, has seduced his daughter. 'There, there, Lu!' says the father. 'Your dad'll do something about it.' Lewis adds: 'There were, in those parts and those days, not infrequent ceremonies known as "shotgun weddings".' The father and a male relative duly visit Gantry. They are not actually carrying shotguns, but they make it clear that they will beat him to a pulp if he does not set a date for the wedding that night. In the event, Gantry later manages to worm his way out of the engagement, but Lewis was no doubt accurately reflecting a typical event in rural America at the beginning of the 20th century.

Lewis's novel made the phrase 'shotgun wedding' known throughout the English-speaking world. It was taken to mean a marriage where the bridegroom was reluctant to marry, even though the bride's condition made it clear that he had already enjoyed marital privileges. In recent times 'shotgun marriage' has been used in the same sense, as when the *Guardian* newspaper reported that 'shot-gun marriages tend to take place in the registrar's office under the mistaken impression that the church does not marry pregnant brides.' The phrases are also used of enforced marriages for reasons other than pregnancy, and in some instances of a joining-together under duress in a more general sense. *The Manchester Guardian*, for instance, reported in 1958: 'There were references to the possible shotgun marriage of the *Daily Herald* and the *News Chronicle*.' It is likely that it will be with reference to this sort of 'marriage' or business merger that 'shotgun wedding, marriage' will be used in future.

Sitting Pretty

In Joyce Cary's *A Fearful Joy*, a man makes use of several colloquial phrases when he tells his friend: 'You're sitting pretty. She's got to toe the line sooner or later. She knows who pays the piper.' To 'toe the line' in the sense of 'conform' was usually 'toe the mark' in the early 19th century. The allusion was presumably to runners on a starting line or men lining up on parade. 'He who pays the piper may call the tune' has been proverbial since the 17th century. 'Sittin' pretty' suddenly appeared in the USA in 1921 as the title of a musical comedy. The near rhyme of the two words had a simple appeal, and the meaning of 'being in an advantageous position' was clear. The 1921 show was unsuccessful, but the phrase has survived well.

Something about the expression caused it to be well used as a title. P.G.Wodehouse made use of it when he collaborated on a musical comedy in 1924, though this had no more success than the previous production of the same name. In 1933 it became the title of a film comedy about two song-writers hitch-hiking their way to Hollywood. *Sitting Pretty* was finally to achieve success as a title, however, in 1947. In this later film comedy there was a punning allusion to baby-sitting, with Clifton Webb playing the part of Mr Belvedere, baby-sitter extraordinaire.

P.G.Wodehouse continued to use the phrase in many of his novels. In *Cocktail Time*, published in 1958, he equated it with another American expression: 'If we swing it, we'll be sitting pretty, in the catbird seat.' 'To sit in the catbird seat' means much the same as 'sitting pretty.' The reference is to the catbird, an American songbird reputed to perch in advantageous positions.'If you're American,' says a speaker in Wodehouse's *Sam the Sudden*, 'we're sitting pretty, because it's only us Americans that's got real sentiment in them.' There is a similar patriotic remark in Henry

Miller's *Tropic of Cancer*, where an American who lives in France says: I'd rather be a bum in America than be sitting pretty here.'

Sixty-four Dollar Question, The

'Take it or Leave it' was a popular quiz-show on American radio from 1942 onwards. The rewards for contestants increased with each correct answer. At the climax of the show came the sixty-four dollar question, the most difficult of all. The phrase immediately became part of the language, used metaphorically of a crucial question in any situation. 'One of their spokesmen,' writes P. Worsley in *The Trumpet shall Sound*, 'posed the sixty-four dollar question of the segregationist: "Would you let a native marry your daughter or sister?"' A priest in Budd Schulberg's *Waterfront* says: 'A couple of hours ago I asked myself the sixty-four dollar question. Am I just a gravy-train rider in a turned-around collar?' A slight variant of the phrase occurs in *The Uses of Literacy*, by Richard Hoggart: 'All the time he had the sixty-four dollar answer but did not know it.'

For the radio audiences, the challenge of the questions themselves had probably been enough to provide the interest. For the television version of the quiz-show it was decided that money would be the main appeal. The title of the show reflected this: it became 'The $64,000 Question.' The metaphorical phrase is now also found in this inflated form. A 1957 article in the *Observer* reported: 'Mr. Macmillan said there was only one answer to the 64,000-dollar question – to increase production.' Ian Fleming tells us in *Diamonds Are Forever* of another famous speaker who opted for the more impressive sum: 'Bond decided it was time to put the sixty-four thousand dollar question.'

Smart Alec

The expression 'smart Alec' was first used in America in the middle of the 19th century. There is no reason to suppose that there was a specific person named *Alexander* who was generally known as a smug know-all, someone who always thought he knew better than you. Alec was a fairly common name at the time and was probably chosen at random. It had to be a male name, of course. Smart women were smart enough not to earn the label 'smart Alices.'

There seems to have been confusion at first about what was meant by 'smart.' At least one American writer of the time interpreted it as 'smartly dressed.' He equated 'smart Alec' with 'Joe dandy' – showing arbitrary use of another first name.

Since 'smart ass' is also used by American speakers, it is tempting to see 'Alec' as a euphemism for 'ass.' 'Smart Alec' was certainly able to appear in print at a time when 'smart ass' would have been impossible. Whatever the original reason for using the name, a modern Alec need not worry too much. 'Smart alec' is now usually printed with a small 'a,' and the connection with the name is forgotten. 'If MacGregor was going to develop into a real smart alec,' writes Joyce Porter in *Dover One*, 'life was going to get very uncomfortable.'

Smell a Rat

In Bernard Malamud's *The Tenants*, when a man lifts the lid of a garbage can, he is assailed by 'a hot ordurous blast.' He immediately associates the unpleasant smell with a dead rat. In English we have been 'smelling a rat' metaphorically since the end of the 16th century, when rats were probably a familiar part of everyday life. The phrase conveniently sums up a suspicious feeling that all is not well, that there is more going on than meets the eye. Alan Sillitoe, for instance, is describing the prisoners and warders of a remand home when he writes, in *The Loneliness of the Long-Distance Runner*: 'They know we hate their guts and smell a rat if they think we're trying to be nice to them.' Similar uses of the expression are easily found in the works of other writers, including W.Somerset Maugham (*An Official Position*), Angus Wilson (*Anglo-Saxon Attitudes*), and Truman Capote (*Jug of Silver*). Peter Cheyney, in *You Can Call it a Day*, varies the expression to say: 'He's beginning to smell some rats.'

Henry David Thoreau pointed out in *Walden* that there is another possible way of smelling a rat. He talks there of 'the *Smilax herbacea*, carrion flower, a rank green vine. It smells exactly like a dead rat in the wall, and apparently attracts flies like carrion.'

Snake in the Grass

A 'snake in the grass' is someone who pretends to be a friend, but acts treacherously. In *The World According to Garp* John Irving writes: 'We were playing in Dallas, when that snake in the grass came up on my blind side.' In former times, the person who betrayed a friendship in some way was likely to be addressed as 'you snake!' Sheridan took this a step further in *The School for Scandal* by making Snake the name of a character.

'Snake in the grass' is also occasionally applied to a situation in which there is a hidden danger. This is described even more graphically in French as *un serpent caché sous les fleurs* ' a snake hidden beneath the flowers.' One of the nicknames for alcohol in

Russian, as it happens, is 'the green snake.' There is a brand of green vodka which has a strand of grass in the bottle.

This expression is self-explanatory and has a long and respectable ancestry. It was suggested by a line in Virgil's *Third Eclogue*, which dates from approximately 40 BC: *latet anguis in herba* 'a snake hides in the grass.'

Sow One's Wild Oats

The many references in English literature to a young man sowing his wild oats display a great deal of indulgence. The general attitude is that having a number of sexual adventures while he is young and unattached will make a man faithful to his wife when he eventually marries. As Robert Louis Stevenson says in *Virginibus Puerisque*: 'There is some meaning in the old theory of wild oats; and a man who has not had his greensickness and got done with it for good, is as little to be depended upon as an unvaccinated infant.' In *Kipps*, H.G.Wells goes further – the sowing of wild oats is apparently essential: 'He had sown his wild oats – one had to somewhen – and now he was happily married.'

Marriage, of course, puts a stop to the sowing of wild oats. A husband's infidelity falls into a different category, a point made by E.M.Forster in *Howards End*: 'He confused the episode of Jacky with another episode that had taken place in the days of his bachelorhood. The two made one crop of wild oats, for which he was heartily sorry, and he could not see that those oats are of a darker stock which are rooted in another's dishonour. Unchastity and infidelity were as confused to him as to the Middle Ages.'

Trollope appears to condone the youthful sowing of wild oats when a character says, in *Doctor Thorne*: 'Let a young fellow sow his wild oats while he is young, and he'll be steady enough when he grows old.' In this instance, however, Dr Thorne is made to wonder: 'but what if he never lives to get through the sowing? What if the wild-oats operation is carried on in so violent a manner as to leave no strength in the soil for the produce of a more valuable crop?'

'Wild oat' is one of the names of a tall grass that grows as a weed in cornfields. Sowing wild oats instead of good grain would be an example of foolish behaviour, not necessarily apparent at the time but revealed later. Beyond that, it is easy to see why writers as early as the 16th century began to compare the tolerated dissoluteness of young men to the sowing of wild oats. The sowing of seed was an obvious metaphor for their sexual activity; 'wild' was a fitting description of their general behaviour. In a more recent development, 'to get one's oats' has become a slang reference to male sexual gratification.

Respectable young women, needless to say, did not sow their own wild oats. When they married, they were expected to overlook any youthful adventures which their husbands might choose to tell them about. Opinions as to whether they should be told about them tended to differ. Upton Sinclair, in *World's End*, remarks: 'The difference between Robbie Budd and most others was that they didn't consider it necessary to tell their future brides about the wild oats they had sown.' Ivy Compton-Burnett, in *A House and its Head*, offers the view: 'Do you think you could marry me? You know about my wild oats, and that is said to be so important, though I should have thought it would be a mistake. There is nothing for you to find out.'

219

A modern interpretation of 'sowing wild oats' is seen in Peter Gent's *North Dallas Forty*: 'Susan wasn't coming to tonight's party. It was the mutually agreed upon night for Andy to sow his wild oats. They planned to get married after he got it all out of his system.' Another meaning is given to the phrase in George Bernard Shaw's *Man and Superman*: 'He and I and Mr. Sidney Webb were sowing our political wild oats as a sort of Fabian Three Musketeers, without any prevision of the surprising respectability of the crop that followed.'

Spill the Beans

'Spill the beans' was first heard as an American slang term at the beginning of the 20th century, but respectable British authors are prepared to use the expression. 'Tell me the truth,' says a woman in Eric Linklater's *Poet's Pub*, 'spill the beans.' *Anglo-Saxon Attitudes*, by Angus Wilson, has: 'We'll drink a health to the day dear father gets the knighthood he wants so much, because that's the day I shall spill the beans.' 'I don't want them finding me and trying to stop me spilling the beans' is said by Skullion, in Tom Sharpe's *Grantchester Grind*.

The phrase means to reveal a truth that has been deliberately concealed. Although no one is certain of how the saying originated, the most plausible suggestion concerns a popular practice at rural fairs in America. People attending the fairs could win a substantial prize by guessing how many beans were in a large jar. The exact number was only revealed at the end of the day, when the beans in the jar were counted. 'Spill the beans' may have been the exhortation of those who were anxious to know who had made the best guess.

Square Meal, A

Jerome K. Jerome, in *Three Men in a Boat*, makes a character say: 'We'll have a good round, square, slap-up meal at seven.' The interesting point about this is that in this context 'slap-up' serves as a gloss for both 'round' and 'square.' Normally these words describe very different shapes: here they both refer to a 'substantial quantity' of food. The usual modern phrase, needless to say, is 'a square meal.' Thomas Wolfe, in *Look Homeward, Angel*, has a father say of his son: 'I take him up to Sales' with me once or twice a week and give him a square meal.' This expression began to appear in American printed sources in the second half of the 19th century. When the American publication *All Year Round* referred in 1868 to 'roadside hotel-keepers calling the miners' attention to their square meals' it felt obliged to add: 'by which is meant full meals.'

At roughly the same time people began to talk about a 'square deal.' In both cases the underlying sense had to do with 'fairness' and 'honesty.' The provider of a square meal or square deal was giving you value for money. Similar phrases, already in use at the end of the 16th century, included 'square play' and 'square dealing.' 'Squareness' seems to have been associated with 'straightness,' as opposed to dishonest 'crookedness.' A character in William Wycherley's play *The Plain Dealer* says: 'Why, don't you know that telling truth is a quality as prejudicial to a man that would thrive in the world, as square play to a cheat?'

Square Peg in a Round Hole, A

An article in *The Times* newspaper (April 30, 1996) described the work of Trevor Austen, 'the last rakemaker in England using traditional methods.' Mr Austen demonstrates his skills at various country fairs and runs a one-man business. The author of the article, James Kitchenham, mentioned in passing that 'the old rakemakers sometimes left a square end on the tine so that the square edges bit tightly into the round hole for extra grip, giving rise to the saying "a square peg in a round hole".'

It would be truer to say that the old rakemakers merely demonstrated that there are times when a slightly squared peg is exactly what is needed in a round hole. That is the last thing we have in our minds when we talk about a person being a 'square peg.' The latter is someone whose particular skills are totally unsuited for the job he is trying to do. Unlike the squared end of the tine, or peg, this does not lead to greater efficiency but to work badly done.

The 'square peg' metaphor, applied to a person doing the wrong job, was first used in the early 19th century. It can be traced not to a rakemaker's workshop, but to the writings of the clergyman-wit Sydney Smith. In *Sketches of Moral Philosophy*, published in 1806, Smith wrote: 'We shall generally find that the triangular person has got into the square hole, the oblong into the triangular, and a square person has squeezed himself into the round hole.'

By the end of the 19th century 'a square peg in a round hole' had become almost proverbial, a recognition that Smith had identified a widespread human phenomenon. Writers seem to be especially fond of the phrase. W.Somerset Maugham creates a personal version of it in *The Lotus Eater*: 'Most people lead the lives that circumstances have thrust upon them, and though some repine, looking upon themselves as round pegs in square holes, the greater part accept their lot.' Joanna Trollope varies the phrase in a different way in *The Rector's Wife*: 'He concluded by saying that, if ever a priest had been a square peg in a square hole, that priest was Peter.'

Edward Blishen, in *A Cack-handed War*, elaborates on Sydney Smith: 'He was, in every sort of profound sense, an outcast. In his case, the phrase about a square peg in a round hole was laughably inadequate. The labour force at the Quarry was full of pegs merely square. The War Ag knew how to hammer these down, most of the time, into their ill-fitting holes. But it would not be easy to name the shape of peg that might suggest Leonard's unsuitability and crazy awkwardness – and his unhammerability.'

Stalking-horse

A stalking-horse was originally a horse used by fowlers to get within easy range of their game. It was trained to keep its head down, as if it were grazing, so that it caused no alarm. The fowler would either hide behind it or conceal himself under its coverings, gradually edging nearer to the prey. Later the stalking-horse became a portable screen shaped like a horse or other animal, behind which the fowler could hide.

Metaphorically, a stalking-horse is a person used to distract attention from someone who is the real object of interest, or is the real instigator of an action. 'Do you think her fit for nothing but to be a stalking-horse,' says a character in Congreve's *The Double Dealer*, 'to stand before you, while you take aim at my wife?' *The Jewish Chronicle* commented in 1980: 'It raises the fear that the Irish may be acting as a stalking horse for the whole European Economic Community.' *The Times* newspaper had earlier said: 'This meant that the Europeans would regard us as the stalking horse or paid hand of Uncle Sam and would not wish us to participate fully in European affairs.' These latter items accurately reflect the fact that stalking-horse is now most used in political contexts, where concealment of the truth is usually essential.

Steal Someone's Thunder

To 'steal someone's thunder' is to attract attention to yourself by saying or doing what the other person intended to do. In the 1930's it was said of F.D.Roosevelt, for example, that he tried to steal Huey Long's thunder by anticipating his 'soak the rich' tax message. In *The Road to Wigan Pier*, George Orwell says: 'It is important to disregard the jealousy of the modern literary gent who hates science because science has stolen literature's thunder.'

The origin of the phrase would seem rather absurd were it not well documented. The 18th century playwright John Dennis had invented a method of reproducing the sound of thunder on stage for use in his *Appius and Virginia*. The play was not successful, though the imitation thunder impressed other theatre managers. When Dennis heard it being used in a production of *Macbeth* he exclaimed: 'Damn them! they will not let my play run, but they steal my thunder.'

Stew in One's Own Juice

To let someone 'stew in his or her own juice' is to leave that person alone and await developments. In the meantime the person concerned suffers the consequences of his or her own actions. 'Let dear Margaret stew in her own juice,' writes Kingsley Amis, in *Lucky Jim. Georgy Girl*, by Margaret Forster, has the exchange:

'"I'd like you to go and see her." "Well of course, if you want me to, I will. But she'd be best left to stew in her own juice".' Somerset Maugham, in *Ashenden*, writes: 'I left her to stew in her own juice for a week before I went to see her. She was in a very pretty state of nerves by then.' The phrase can also be applied to groups of people. 'Please don't let me bother you if you've got people,' says someone in John Galsworthy's *To Let*. 'Not at all,' is the reply. 'I want to let them stew in their own juice for a bit.'

The earlier version of this expression in English was 'to fry in one's own grease' This came to have the same meaning as 'stew in one's own juice,' which was probably borrowed from the French *cuir dans son jus* 'cook in its juice.' The image evoked by both forms of the phrase appears to be innocently domestic, but there is good reason for the underlying suggestion of suffering. Originally that suffering would have been acute, for the person who 'fried in his own grease' was being burnt at the stake.

Stiff Upper Lip

In Harriet Beecher Stowe's *Uncle Tom's Cabin*, George bids goodbye to Uncle Tom and tells him to 'keep a stiff upper lip.' It seems strange to find in such a context a phrase that is so closely associated with Englishness, yet the earliest recorded examples of 'stiff upper lip' are American. A writer in the *Massachusetts Spy*, for instance, used the phrase in 1815: 'I kept a stiff upper lip, and bought a license to sell my goods.' The original meaning of the phrase may have had to do with being obstinate, but it was interpreted in England as a reference to being courageous and was made the core of a moral philosophy. The typical English boy was taught to show no emotional reaction to stressful situations.

He was not even to allow his lip to tremble as he tried to hold back tears: whatever the circumstances he must keep a stiff upper lip.

The Englishness of stiff-upper-lippery, as it has been called, or stiffupperlippishness as it became on one occasion in *New Society*, has often been mentioned. A.O.J. Cockshut, in *The Imagination of Charles Dickens*, says that Dickens 'oscillated between indignation, self-pity, and reticence of the stiff-upper-lip English school.' 'Machismo,' wrote Graham Greene in *The Honorary Consul*, 'had little to do with English courage or a stiff upper lip.' In the same year that Greene's novel was published, *The Times* was remarking that 'the British owed much of their greatness to their own self-esteem, and to the legend of straight bat, stiff upper lip, probity and detachment.' One suspects that 'British' was substituted for 'English' in this statement for reasons of diplomacy.

The stiff upper lip syndrome is normally associated with men, but an article in the *Listener* in 1958 said: 'She criticizes herself for being too stiff-upper-lipped about the tragedy that she faces.' A few years later the same magazine jokingly remarked: 'It was all very improbable and too stiff-upper-lippish to have been written by anybody but an anglophile Frenchman.'

Storm in a Teacup, A

'Storm in a teacup,' referring to a lot of fuss being made about an unimportant matter, appears to be a very English phrase of an obviously domestic origin, but it is rather more complicated than that. It can ultimately be traced back to Cicero's *De Legibus*, where he refers to an existing saying *excitare fluctus in simpulo*. This is sometimes translated as 'raise a tempest in a ladle,' but it was glossed in Andrews' *Latin Dictionary*, published in 1854, as 'raise a tempest in a teapot.' The latter phrase clearly came into general use, since the *Century Dictionary* of 1891 defined 'tempest in a tea-pot' as 'a great disturbance over a small matter.' American speakers are still likely to refer to a tea-pot rather than a tea-cup when they use a version of this phrase. In 1973, for example, the *Times* newspaper reported: 'Senator Ervin said the issue of whether the subpoenas were continuing was a difference in a teapot.'

By the time the *Century Dictionary* was published many speakers and writers had already changed 'tempest' to 'storm' and 'tea-pot' to 'tea-cup.' The *Pall Mall Gazette* of 1884 told its readers that 'Monsieur Renan's visit to his birthplace in Brittany has raised a storm in the clerical teacup.' In the same year, William E.Norris was writing, in *Thirlby Hall*: 'All she can do is to raise a storm in a tea-cup.' In modern times 'storm in a tea-cup' is well enough established to allow various kinds of allusions. Sport magazine reported in 1951, for instance, that 'a slight teacup storm occurred in Yorkshire Rugby Union circles because a Leeds team were alleged to be wearing shoulder pads.' William Safire referred in the *New York Times Magazine* some years ago to a 'teacup contretemps,' while a writer in *the Times Literary Supplement* remarked that 'those old disputes were no teacup squalls.'

Individual English writers had no doubt been aware of the Latin tag before Andrews' dictionary made it generally known. It probably influenced the Duke of Ormond, who said in his letter to Earl Arlington in 1678: 'Our skirmish seems to be come to a period, and compared with the great things now on foot, is but a storm in a cream bowl.' It is more difficult to explain why the 18th century English statesman Lord Thurlow talked of a campaign against the American colonists as a 'storm in a wash-hand basin.'

Take a Powder

In Saul Bellow's *Herzog* a man writes to a woman friend: 'You mustn't think because I've taken a powder, briefly, that I don't care for you.' The reference is to the man's hurried departure from the city. Similar use of the phrase occurs in Nicholas Blake's *Whisper in Gloom*, where someone asks: 'Where's the Yank?' The answer is: 'Gone. He took a powder.' It is fitting that the phrase is applied here to an American; the meaning of 'take a powder' is understood in Britain but the expression is unlikely to be used by British speakers.

The phrase is recorded in American sources from the 1930s and is something of a puzzle. Since it is sometimes found as 'take a run-out powder,' some scholars have assumed that it refers to a medicinal powder taken as a laxative. This, in turn, supposedly leads to a sudden departure. Others have interpreted 'powder' as the 'dust' raised by running feet. This idea appears to be reinforced by the earlier use of 'powder' both as noun and verb, applied especially to someone riding a horse with impetuous speed. A 19th century *Cumberland Glossary* has: 'Off he went in sic a pooder.' Maria Edgeworth, in *Ennui*, writes: 'You'll take four horses and you'll see how we'll powder along.' Ernest Weekley, in his *Etymological Dictionary of Modern English*, preferred to link 'powder' in this sense with 'pother' and with the first element of 'poltergeist.' Perhaps he had in mind the idea of 'kicking up a dust' in the sense of causing a commotion. The simpler explanation of 'take a powder' is that it refers ultimately to the cloud of dust raised by a horseman departing at speed.

Take Care of Number One

The idea of 'taking care of number one' – putting one's own interests before those of anyone else – has no doubt always existed, though to many it is especially associated with the 1980s. The principle has only been summed up in those precise words since the beginning of the 18th century, though 'one' was earlier used in the same sense. 'I can help one: is not that a good point of philosophy?' asked a writer in the 16th century. By that time the personal pronoun 'I' had settled into its present form. Before 1400 it had been 'ic' or 'ich' and did not immediately suggest the Roman numeral 'one.'

Dickens often refers to people who 'take care of number one.' In *The Pickwick Papers* Lowten says: 'No man should have more than two attachments – the first, to number one, and the second to the ladies.' In *Bleak House* occurs: 'Whenever a person proclaims to you "In worldly matters I'm a child," that person is only a crying off from being held accountable, and you have got that person's number, and it's Number One.' *Oliver Twist* has Fagin explaining to Claypole: 'Some conjurers say that number three is the magic number, and some say number seven. It's neither, my friend, neither. It's number one. It's your object to take care of number one – meaning yourself.' Dickens would probably have agreed with Thackeray, who says in *Pendennis*: 'Almost every person, as it seems to us, is occupied about Number One.'

Talk Turkey

Agatha Christie writes in *Endless Night:* 'Send for a high powered lawyer and tell him you're willing to talk turkey. Then he fixes the amount of alimony.' Most British readers understand that to 'talk turkey' is to talk plainly, to get down to business, but the expression is still one that would be used mainly by American speakers and writers. Peter Cheyney was obviously well aware of this. In *You Can Call it a Day* a character who is supposedly American asks an English woman: 'Do you know what the Americans mean when they say "talking turkey"?' 'Yes,' is the reply, 'it means talking hard sense or the truth, doesn't it?' 'That's right. Any time you feel like talking turkey you ring me up and we'll have another meeting.' Cheyney evidently forgets that no self-respecting American would say 'ring me up' rather than 'call me.' In Henry Miller's *Tropic of Cancer* when the narrator decides to offer a woman money for her sexual services, he says: 'I went back to the bar determined to talk turkey.'

Asked to explain the origin of the phrase, many Americans would repeat a legendary version of the 'heads I win, tails you lose' story. According to this, a Yankee and a native American went hunting together and killed a buzzard and a turkey. They were then faced with the problem of dividing the spoils. The Yankee said: 'You choose. I'll take the turkey and you take the buzzard, or you take the buzzard and I'll take the turkey.' To this the native American replied that the Yankee was not 'talking turkey.'

Like many similar pieces of etymological folklore, this story continues to be passed from one generation to the next, though the chances of its being true are slim, to say the least.

An occasional variant of the phrase is to 'talk cold turkey,' which suggests a meal eaten the day after a feast, without fancy trimmings. This is certainly in line with the idea of a conversation that dispenses with social niceties and gets to the heart of the matter, and is possibly what gave rise to the expression.

Tell it to the Marines

Chapman's *Dictionary of American Slang* explains 'tell it to the Marines' as 'I do not believe what you have just told me.' It goes on to say that 'the usage reflects the contempt in which marines were held by naval seamen, leading to the assertion that they would believe nonsense that sailors would never believe.' Wilfred Granville, in his *Dictionary of Sailors' Slang*, offers a rather different version. The expression derives, he says, 'from King Charles' not believing his attendants at court, who said that when serving in the South Seas they saw flying fish. A Royal Marine officer who was present confirmed this to the king, who remarked to Samuel Pepys: "From the nature of their calling, no class of our subjects can have so wide a knowledge of seas and lands as the officers and men of our loyal Maritime Regiment. Henceforward, ere we cast doubts upon a tale that lacks likelihood, we will first tell it to the Marines".' The implication of this is that if the Marines say a story is true, then it may safely be believed.

The problem with this more flattering explanation is that the phrase does not surface in printed sources until the early 19th century, more than a hundred years after the death of Charles II. It is then readily found. Sir Walter Scott, for instance, quotes it in *Redgauntlet*: 'Tell that to the Marines, the sailors won't believe it.' Thackeray and Trollope are other authors of the time who put it

231

into the mouths of their characters. It continues to occur in more recent writings, such as Somerset Maugham's *The Razor's Edge*: '"*A d'autres, ma vieille*," I replied, which I think can best be translated by: "Tell that to the marines, old girl".' Dick Francis, in *Blood Sport*, has: '"When this is over you can sleep for a fortnight." "Yeah?" he said sarcastically. "Tell it to the marines".'

In another of his works, *Circle*, Somerset Maugham uses an expanded form of the phrase. A woman says 'he's never even kissed me,' and is told: 'I'd try telling that to the horse marines if I were you.' The reference is to an imaginary corps of mounted marine soldiers, typifying men – such as landlubbers on board ship – who are out of their element. Once again the evidence points to sailors having a low opinion of Marines. This, together with the absence of the phrase from 18th century literature, throws considerable doubt on Granville's story about Charles II. s the average sailor would probably say: 'tell it to the Marines.'

Third Degree, The

A conversation in Tom Sharpe's *Wilt* runs: '"You don't think they're giving him third degree or anything of that sort?" "My dear fellow, third degree? You've been watching too many old movies on the TV. The police don't use strong-arm methods in this country".' Sharpe could have specified 'old *American* movies' to identify the usual source for most people's acquaintance with 'the third degree,' the intensive, prolonged and bullying interrogation by police designed to elicit a confession or obtain information. The term is rarely used in a British context, though George Bernard Shaw's *The Apple Cart* has the exchange: '"What do you mean? put me through it? Is this a police office?"

"The third degree is not unknown in this palace, my boy".' Berrey and Van den Bark's *American Thesaurus of Slang* tersely defined 'third degree' in 1942 as 'a going-over.' Another entry in their book was 'gold-fish bowl,' glossed as 'the room in which the third degree is administered.'

In ordinary conversation, anyone who objects to the questions he is being asked is likely to use the phrase in a watered-down sense, saying 'what is this, the third degree?' There was a similar use in the magazine *Automobile Topics*, which reported some years ago that 'each applicant was put through the third degree in order to establish his complete identity and right to the press stand privileges.' This was merely an exaggerated way of saying that applicants were asked searching questions.

The genuine 'third degree,' administered by American police in the early part of the 20th century, bordered on brutality. The interrogation was probably so called because it was like a third degree burn, the most severe of its kind. Burns had long been classified as first, second and third degree by the time references to third degree interrogations began to appear. However, the American lexicographer Charles Earle Funk, in his *Heavens to Betsy and other Curious Sayings*, preferred to link the term to freemasonry. As a 19th century writer pointed out: 'The fellow-craft who is duly qualified by time, on presenting himself as candidate for the third degree, has to submit himself to an examination of his qualifications as a craftsman.' In other words, said Funk, he can only become a Master Mason by undergoing 'a very elaborate and severe test of ability.' However, Funk himself went on to emphasise that this test was 'not even faintly injurious, physically or mentally.' It is therefore difficult to see why he thought that the masonic third degree ceremony suggested a name for the police interrogation.

Thorn in the Flesh, A

Ruth Rendell writes, in *To Fear a Painted Devil*: 'Those begging letters were a continual thorn in his flesh.' Some authors might have preferred to describe a constant annoyance as 'a thorn in his side.' An article in *The Times*, for example, mentioned some years ago that 'Mr Zilliacus is a left winger who has often been a thorn in the side of the party leadership.' Both versions of the phrase were sanctioned by the Authorized Version of the bible, which appeared in 1611. In the Old Testament, at Numbers 35, God tells Moses: 'But if ye will not drive out the inhabitants of the land from before you; then it shall come to pass, that those which ye let remain of them shall be pricks in your eyes, and thorns in your sides, and shall vex you in the land wherein ye dwell.' Church-goers probably heard more often from the pulpit, however, the words of Saint Paul, given in the New Testament at 2 Corinthians 12: 'And lest I should be exalted above measure through the abundance of the revelations, there was given to me a thorn in the flesh, the messenger of Satan to buffet me.'

Before 1611, English writers had referred metaphorically to thorns in other ways. In Chaucer's *Troilus and Criseyde*, Pandarus asks his niece whether she will yield to Troilus and thus 'pull out the thorn' that sticks in his heart. Shakespeare, as it happens, uses much the same image in *Hamlet*, when the prince is told by his father's ghost:

> Taint not thy mind, nor let thy soul contrive
> Against thy mother aught; leave her to heaven,

234

> And to those thorns that in her bosom lodge
> To prick and sting her.

The bawdy possibilities of 'pricking thorns' was not likely to be lost on Shakespeare. It partly accounts for comments like Romeo's:

> Is love a tender thing? it is too rough,
> Too rude, too boisterous, and it pricks like thorn.

Once the Authorized Version had appeared, the 'thorn in the flesh/side' expressions were taken up. In 1649, Jeremy Taylor was proclaiming that 'the pungency of forbidden lust is truly a thorn in the flesh.' A few years later John Bargrave, in *Pope Alexander VII*, was writing: 'Antonio was still a thorn in his side, doing him all the displeasures he could.' Writers this century have perhaps tended to favour the 'flesh' version. 'I can be a thorn in Mr. Turton's flesh' is in E.M.Forster's *A Passage to India*. Somerset Maugham, in *Then and Now*, talks of 'the family that had been for so long a thorn in the flesh of the Vicars of Christ.' For that matter Christ himself, according to Kung and Lapide's *Brother or Lord*, translated by E.Quinn in 1977, 'was undoubtedly a thorn in the flesh' of the Jewish sect known as the Sadducees.

Tickled Pink

To be tickled physically can be a pleasant or irritating experience: when we are tickled metaphorically we are pleased. Since the 17th century we have talked in English about something that 'tickles the fancy.' That thought can be expressed more pompously – one early writer glossed it as 'striking the joyous perception' – but tickling the fancy does rather well and is used by discerning writers. John Lockhart, for instance, in his biography of Sir Walter Scott, remarks: 'Such was the story that went the round of the newspapers at the time, and highly tickled Scott's fancy.'

Once this phrase was established it became possible to speak more simply about being tickled by something or someone. (As every child is fascinated to discover, tickling must always be done by someone else – you cannot tickle yourself). By the beginning of the 20th century it was possible to state more emphatically that one was tickled to death. 'We three boys are going to dance for you in a few minutes,' says an American in Upton Sinclair's *World's End*, 'and we're tickled to death about it.' The alternative expression 'tickled pink' seems to have come into being at the same time, also in America. The pinkness referred to is no doubt the heightened colour that accompanies hearty laughter. 'Tickled pink' is the usual form, but it is recorded that an American who sat opposite William Temple at dinner told him: 'Archbishop, you tickle me pink!' This sounds suspiciously like P.G.Wodehouse, though that writer seems to have confined himself to the conventional wording. In *Nothing Serious* he says: 'Your view, then, is that he is tickled pink to be freed from his obligations?'

Too Big for One's Boots

'Too big for one's boots' is used of someone who is thought to be conceited or arrogant.'I've got too big for my boots,' admits a character in Henry Cecil's *Brothers in Law*. 'He was getting too big for his boots,' writes Ruth Rendell, in *Talking To Strange Men*. The phrase occurs in H.Maxwell's *Life of W.H.Smith*, published in 1893, but the quotation marks used by the author show that he thought it rather novel: 'Sometimes a young man, "too big for his boots", would sniff at being put in charge of a railway bookstall.' Another version of the phrase is nevertheless listed in a glossary of Cheshire words, published in 1887: '"Too big for one's shoon," used of a person whose notions are too high for his station, a conceited person.'

These references to boots and shoes water down the force of the expression in its original form. In 1835, when David Crockett published his *Account of Col. Crockett's Tour to the North and down East*, he wrote: 'When a man gets too big for his breeches, I say good-bye.' This implied that someone with a 'swelled head,' a 'bighead,' also expanded in another specific part of his anatomy. H.G.Wells favoured this version of the phrase. In *Kipps* he writes: 'He's getting too big for 'is britches.' Upton Sinclair, in *World's End*, has: 'All our working men have got too big for their breeches.' William Faulkner evidently thought that 'breeches' or 'britches' were rather too old-fashioned. In *The Sound and the Fury* he writes: 'You're getting a little too big for your pants.'

Turn over a New Leaf

An early instance of this expression occurs in Holinshed's *Chronicles*, published in 1577: 'He must turn the leaf, and take out a new lesson, by changing his former trade of living into better.' The 'leaf' in this case is the sheet of paper in a book which forms two pages. Holinshed's comment implies that a book of moral precepts is being read and that the page is turned to a new lesson; the phrase is more generally taken to mean that someone is turning to a blank page in a diary or journal where one's improved conduct of the future will be recorded. Already in the 17th century a writer was referring to 'turning over a new leaf in one's own history, and amending one's own mistakes.'

In early use the expression was often used of a complete change of life-style, the abandonment of dissolute ways in favour of the straight and narrow path. It might now be applied to something trivial, as when the young hero in Hughes' *Tom Brown at Oxford* says: 'I will turn over a new leaf, and write to you.' Often there is an allusion to the giving up of a bad habit, such as smoking or drinking. Excessive drinking is the topic in Anthony Trollope's *Doctor Thorne*, where a doctor says to his patient 'We must turn over a new leaf, Sir Roger; indeed we must.' The 'we,' needless to say, is a polite substitution for 'you.'

In *You Can Call It A Day*, Peter Cheyney makes someone say: 'I've turned over a new leaf as the English say. I practically never touch the stuff.' This implies quite wrongly that Americans do not use this expression. Examples are easily found in American writing. In Thomas Wolfe's *Look Homeward, Angel*, for example, a fond mother says of her wayward son: 'perhaps he's going to turn over a new leaf now.' In Mary McCarthy's *The Group*, Kay says 'I don't think I'll have anything' when she is offered a drink. Miss McCarthy comments that 'Kay had suddenly decided to turn over a new leaf, but she felt that this was not quite the right moment to announce it.'

Twist Someone Round One's Finger

Manipulating another person so that he does exactly what you want him to do has been referred to as twisting him round your finger since the 18th century. The phrase seems to have been applied at first to masterful men, the metaphor perhaps being drawn from equestrianism. The reference would be to having complete control over a horse even though the reins are held with only one finger. In *King Henry the Fourth Part I* Sir Richard Vernon praises Prince Hal, who can 'turn and wind a fiery Pegasus, and witch the world with noble horsemanship.' That 'turning and winding' could be the notion inherent in twisting a person around one's finger.

By the 19th century it was usually women who were twisting men round their fingers. In *Barnaby Rudge* Dickens has Gabriel say: 'There's my weakness. I can be obstinate enough with men if need be, but women may twist me round their fingers at their pleasure.' William J. Locke, in *Jaffery*, has: 'Of the two, Doria seemed to have unquestionably the stronger will-power. "Surely," said I, "you can twist him round your little finger".' Charles Kingsley, however, in *Westward Ho!* returns to the dominant male: 'The man has twisted the whole council round his finger.'

Upset someone's Apple-cart

This phrase has been in use since the 18th century, when costermongers were probably more frequently seen than they are today. A 'costermonger' was earlier a 'costard monger,' someone who sold costard apples. 'Costard' in turn derived from the Latin *costa* 'rib,' since costards had rib-like lines on them. The meaning of 'upset someone's apple-cart' has varied slightly through the centuries, but is now usually understood as 'upset someone's plans, cause things to go wrong, change the established order of things.' George Bernard Shaw probably had the last of those meanings in mind when he used *The Apple Cart* as the title of a play.

The phrase is a vivid one, instantly evoking a vision of apples rolling chaotically in all directions. Nevertheless, it is normally applied to fairly abstract situations. In 1955, for example, an article in the *Scientific American* remarked that 'names such as ammoniated tincture of valerian can safely be revealed to the patient without upsetting the psychological applecart.' In *The Rector's Wife*, by Joanna Trollope, the rector says of the heroine: 'I've just got all the apples into the cart, and it looks as if Anna has upset the lot.'

Use your Loaf

Hunt and Pringle commented on this expression in their booklet *Service Slang*, published in 1943: 'Use your loaf is the injunction often heard when someone is particularly slow in following orders. But this phrase, in its finer meanings, says: "Use your common sense. Interpret orders according to the situation as you find it, and don't follow the book of words too literally".' This reads rather a lot into three words which have the basic meaning 'use your head.'

George Orwell had earlier remarked in one of his essays, written in the early 1930s, that hop-pickers from London used the expression 'use your twopenny.' He explained that in Cockney rhyming slang, 'loaf of bread' had at first been substituted for 'head.' 'Loaf of bread' was then shortened to 'loaf,' extended to 'twopenny loaf,' then shortened again to 'twopenny.' This would be impossibly obscure in modern times, when loaves cost rather more than twopence, and 'use your twopenny' has disappeared. 'Use your loaf' certainly persists in working-class London speech and is occasionally recorded in fiction. *Maggie*, by Lena Kennedy, has: 'It was the astute young Ginger who told her what to do. "Use yer loaf, Maggie," he said, tapping his ginger head. "Hide it, shove it away till yer need it".'

London Cockneys use less rhyming slang in their ordinary conversations than is generally believed, but some of their expressions have passed into fairly general usage. Because the rhyming word itself is usually dropped, many speakers are probably unaware of terms which derive from this source. They might talk of 'blowing a raspberry,' for instance, without realising that the allusion is to 'raspberry tart – fart.' 'Have a butcher's' means 'have a look,' derived from 'butcher's hook.'

The dropping of a word, incidentally, occurs not only in rhyming slang expressions. Many speakers pride themselves on their economical use of language and will not bother to complete well-known phrases. A footballer will tell a team-mate to 'put him under,' not bothering to specify 'under pressure.' Similarly, 'I haven't the foggiest (idea)' and 'you don't stand an earthly (chance)' are commonly heard.

Walking on Air

Imogen Winn remarks in *Coming to Terms* that 'Kay came to know what the expression "walking on air" meant.' The woman concerned is experiencing that special feeling of exultation known to someone in love. Robert Louis Stevenson seems to have been the first to use the phrase. In his *Memories and Portraits*, published in 1887, he says: 'I went home that morning walking upon air.' Countless writers of romantic fiction were later to borrow those words, unable to think of a better way to describe an ecstatic light-headedness. By the time Frank Sullivan came to write his essay *The Cliché Expert Testifies on Love*, 'walking on air' was firmly established with other phrases, such as 'heart of gold' and 'diamond in the rough,' as essential to the love story. It is the unfortunate fate of many a striking phrase to become too successful for its own good. Over-use makes it a banality.

'Walking on air' successfully describes a mental and emotional state, a feeling of great happiness. In *The Struggles of Albert Woods*, by William Cooper, it is the promise of promotion that causes the hero to feel that he is walking on air. Cooper writes: 'After the first few buoyant moments most men find air is a rather unsubstantial medium for walking on.' This is not true of Albert Woods, who is sustained by the mere promise for a year.

In the 17th and 18th centuries writers sometimes referred to a person who 'danced on air' or 'danced on nothing.' In such instances there was nothing romantic about the allusion, merely the grim humour of former times. The reference was to a criminal being hanged.

Wash One's Hands of Something/Someone

There can be few metaphorical phrases which surpass 'wash one's hands of something/someone' in terms of simplicity and effectiveness. It is difficult to imagine a better way of conveying the notion of disassociation. As it happens, the phrase also has a biblical source that gives it added poignancy. It alludes to a passage in the New Testament, at Matthew 27.22: 'Pilate said to them, "Then what shall I do with Jesus who is called Christ?" They all said, "Let him be crucified." And he said, "Why, what evil has he done?" But they shouted all the more, "Let him be crucified." So when Pilate saw that he was gaining nothing, but rather that a riot was beginning, he took water and washed his hands before the crowd, saying, "I am innocent of this man's blood; see to it yourselves".'

In ordinary speech the phrase is used in less dramatic circumstances and is often extended to 'wash one's hands of the affair.' In *Shannon's Way*, A.J.Cronin has a professor who tells his assistant: 'You are acting with extreme stupidity. But if you persist I can't stop you. I simply wash my hands of the whole affair.' John Stroud, in *On the Loose*, has: 'I'm washing my hands of the whole affair; it's no longer my business.' A slight variation occurs in *Anglo-Saxon Attitudes*, by Angus Wilson: 'If you're going to regard every suggestion I make as a criticism, then I must wash my hands of the whole matter.' Other examples of usage include: 'I wash my hands of it, it is God's doing', in Bernard Wolfe's The Late Risers; 'once you make a formal approach I shall wash my hands of you entirely,' in John Le Carré's *The Honourable Schoolboy*.

Welsh Rabbit

The origin of this phrase has been the cause of countless friendly arguments, and will no doubt continue to be so. Those who maintain that it should be 'Welsh rarebit' are convinced that there is no possible reason for the 'rabbit,' since the basic ingredient of the dish has always been cheese. In its simplest modern form it consists of grilled cheese on bread. Traditionally, cheese and butter were pre-melted, mixed with a little ale, then poured over the toast.

Those who wish to change 'rabbit' into 'rarebit' should also seek a substitute for 'Welsh,' since there is no evidence that links this dish with Wales. There is plenty of evidence, on the other hand, for the use of the word 'Welsh' in the 18th century, when the first references to Welsh rabbit occur, to mean 'inferior substitute for something.' Those who straightened their hair by running their fingers through it were said to be using a Welsh comb. A piece of rock crystal was known as a Welsh diamond, the cuckoo as a Welsh ambassador. Welsh bait was supposedly fodder given to a horse when it reached the top of a hill, but no fodder was involved. The horse was merely allowed to rest for a few moments.

There is also evidence that non-meat dishes could be given 'meaty' names as a joke. A red herring, for example, was known as a 'Yarmouth capon.' Another fish became a 'Bombay duck.'

Originally, therefore, 'Welsh rabbit' was meant to refer humorously to a poor-man's substitute for a meat dish. The 'rabbit' had no special significance; it could as easily have been beef-steak or pork-chop. Early etymologists decided instead that there must be a more complex explanation – 'rabbit' had to be a corrupt form of something else. One suggestion was that it derived from 'rear bit,' since it referred to something eaten at the end of a meal. More ingenious was the 'rarebit' explanation, which has convinced countless people of its authenticity. H.G.Wells, for example, writes in *The Man Who Could Work Miracles*: 'I was always particularly fond of a tankard of stout and a Welsh rarebit.'

For what it is worth, no trace of the word 'rarebit' has ever been found in any other context. The word did not exist before references to 'Welsh rabbit' began to appear. Nowadays it is well established, and often appears in cookery books which offer recipes for English and Irish rabbits or rarebits. The 'English' version is made with red wine, the 'Irish' has added onions, gherkins, vinegar and herbs. Best known is the American 'buck rabbit' or 'rarebit,' which is a Welsh rabbit topped with a poached egg. In many restaurants it is also known as a 'golden buck.'

White Elephant

A 'white elephant' is something that is of little practical value, but which costs a great deal of money to maintain. J.I.M.Stewart provides an example in *The Last Tresilians*, where a coin and art collection is presented to a college. The collection is a valuable one, but the college will have to pay for and maintain the special building that will house it. 'Perhaps, Provost,' says one of the college fellows, 'you will give us some idea of where this monstrous white elephant is to be accomodated?' In Lisa Alther's *Kinflicks* a man says of his large house: 'We just rattle around in that white elephant.'

The phrase originates in a story connected with the former kings of Siam (now Thailand). A white, albino elephant was a rare and valuable creature, normally kept in the royal stables for the king's sole use and treated with veneration. If a king wanted to punish one of his courtiers without appearing to do so, he would present him with a white elephant. The courtier concerned could not, as it were, look a gift elephant in the mouth. He was therefore obliged to keep the animal and pay for its upkeep over a long period, getting nothing in return. It would have insulted the king to treat a white elephant like an ordinary working animal.

This story was circulating in England by the middle of the 19th century, at which time 'white elephant ' began to be used in its figurative sense. A writer in 1851 referred to a man whose 'services are like so many white elephants, of which nobody can make use, and yet that drain one's gratitude, if indeed one does not feel bankrupt.' Typical modern usage is seen in a comment in the *Daily Mail*: 'The new rail link may prove to be ideologically satisfying, but in financial terms it looks like becoming the biggest white elephant in all Africa.' Evelyn Waugh has fun with the phrase in *Work Suspended*: 'It was a large canvas at which he had been at work intermittently since 1908. Even he spoke of it, with conscious understatement, as "something of a white elephant". White elephants indeed were almost the sole species of four-footed animal that was not somewhere worked into this elaborate composition.'

Wild Goose Chase

The 'wild goose' of this expression is the grey lag-goose. It supposedly earned its name because it was the last species of goose to leave Britain each year for the northern breeding-quarters – it lagged behind the others. It could also be said to lag behind its leader when in flight. It flies as part of a V-shaped formation, remaining at a reasonable distance from the other birds, and makes no attempt to overtake the goose it appears to be 'chasing.' A 'wild-goose chase' is thus one which appears never to succeed, one goose never 'catching' another.

Our version of the phrase probably came to us indirectly. In the 17th century a 'wild goose chase' was a kind of 'follow-my-leader' on horseback. It is likely to have been this which led to the figurative use of the phrase, which at first meant an erratic course taken by a person following his own inclinations, possibly followed by others. The phrase has this meaning in *Romeo and Juliet*, when Mercutio says to Romeo: 'Nay, if our wits run the wild-goose chase, I am done: For thou hast more of the wild-goose in one of thy wits than, I am sure, I have in my whole five.'

The modern meaning of a hopeless undertaking, one which can never succeed, came later and remains in common use. In *Waterfront*, by Budd Schulberg, one priest tells another: 'You've got a lot on the ball. Why throw your chances away on a wild-goose chase?' 'He'd found himself on a wild-goose chase' is in Malcolm Lowry's *Under the Volcano*. 'Afraid it was a wild goose chase, doc,' is said by a character in Penelope Gilliatt's A State of Change. Allusions to the phrase also occur. John Le Carré's *The Honourable Schoolboy* has: 'They've got it all wrong. It's a goose-chase.' In *Barnaby Rudge*, Dickens makes a character say:

'He'll have gone away upon some wild-goose errand, seeking his fortune.'

Wild Horses

'There was a time when you had to employ wild horses to drag me from London,' says a character in *Sunset at Blandings*, by P.G.Wodehouse. This is slightly unusual, because wild horses are normally mentioned negatively. A typical example occurs in Alice Dwyer-Joyce's *The Penny Box*: 'Wild horses would never have dragged such words out of her.' E.F.Benson, in *Miss Mapp*, has: 'Wild horses would not have dragged from *Miss Mapp* that this was precisely what she wanted.' Mary Webb has a character in *Gone To Earth* who makes much of this 'wild horses' expression: 'Wild 'orses shanna drag it from me, nor yet blood 'orses, nor 'unters, nor cart-'orses, nor Suffolk punches!' The author comments: 'When he had made a good phrase, he was apt to work it to death.'

Berta Ruck, in her autobiographical *Ancestral Voices*, remarks: 'When I was a child I heard a grown-up man telling someone "wild horses weren't going to drag him" to some party. I was dying to hear about them and where they dragged people... Nobody ever told me.' The adults around her were being kind, not wanting to fill her mind with the horrifying images that lie behind this phrase. A common way of torturing someone in early times was to attach their arms and legs to wild horses, who then pulled in different directions. Sometimes, after a criminal had been hanged, his body was torn to pieces in this way. It was only towards the end of the 19th century, when such barbaric events had faded from memory, that the joking references to wild horses came into being.

Wink is as Good as a Nod, A *see* Nod is as Good as a Wink, A

Woe Betide

This phrase is a linguistic fossil. It would have sounded perfectly normal to an English-speaker in the 14th century, but has somehow survived into modern English. Its literal meaning is 'misfortune will happen to,' though it is now often used to mean no more than 'heaven help.' Lupino Lane, for example, in *How to become a Comedian*, writes: 'What grand comediennes Elsie and Doris Waters are, and Revnell and West: woe betide any comedian who has to follow them on any programme without an interval between.' *Maggie*, by Lena Kennedy, has: 'Her black hair was bound tightly in a bun and never moved while her black button eyes swept the streets as she sailed along – and woe betide anyone who spoke out of turn.'

Apart from its use in this phrase, 'betide' is obsolete. 'Woe' is still heard, though English people no longer exclaim 'woe is me!' when things are not going as they should. The Yiddish equivalent 'oy vay!' might still be used: 'vay' derives from German *Weh* 'woe, pain.' Malcolm Bradbury comments on 'woe' in *Eating People Is Wrong*: 'The absolute refusal of his colleagues to enrich discussion was a matter of some woe to him. He used that word – woe – right there in Treece's office, and Treece supposed that it was the first time the word had been used there, in the ordinary passage of conversation, in forty years.'

In literature the words 'woe' and 'woeful' belong to Shakespeare and *Romeo and Juliet*. The Prince brings that play to a close by saying:

For never was a story of more woe
Than this of Juliet and her Romeo.

Earlier the Nurse, finding Juliet dead, has said in her grief:

O woe! O woeful, woeful, woeful day!
Most lamentable day, most woeful day
That ever, ever, I did yet behold!
O day! O day! O day! O hateful day!
Never was seen so black a day as this.
O woeful day, O woeful day!

Wolf in Sheep's Clothing

A 'wolf in sheep's clothing' is 'someone who appears to be a friend but in reality is completely untrustworthy, likely to do you harm.' Most people would attribute the expression to a fable, but it derives from the New Testament. Matthew 7.15 has: 'Beware of false prophets, who come to you in sheep's clothing but inwardly are ravenous wolves.' The behaviour of such hypocrites will always reveal their true nature, says Matthew. 'You will know them by their fruits. Are grapes gathered from thorns, or figs from thistles?'

Shakespeare alludes to the phrase in *Henry the Sixth Part One*. During an unsavoury slanging match, the Duke of Gloucester berates the Bishop of Winchester as 'thou wolf in sheep's array!' Later literary use is seen in Anthony Trollope's *Three Clerks*: 'Why had this tender lamb been allowed to wander out of the fold, while a wolf in sheep's clothing was invited into the pasture-ground?' The phrase is also well enough established to allow variations. In Derek Jewell's short story *Come In No.1 Your Time is Up* a character remarks: 'His cynicism hides a heart of gold.' 'A sheep in wolf's clothing you'll be telling me next,' is the reply.

Wonders Will Never Cease

'Wonders will never cease' is a comment made when someone says or does something that seems to be out of character, or when something pleasant happens unexpectedly. The words are meant to convey surprise, but they usually add a dash of irony. Sam Weller makes use of the saying in Dickens' *The Pickwick Papers*, mixing his v's and w's as always: 'Vonders vill never cease. I'm wery much mistaken if that 'ere Jingle worn't a doin' somethin' in the vater-cart vay!' This is a convoluted way of saying that Jingle has been reduced to tears.

The earliest instance of this saying known to the *Oxford English Dictionary* comes in a letter by a certain Thomas Creevey, written in February, 1828: 'Well, Creevey, wonders will never cease! I met Lord Bathurst at the Duke of Buccleuch's.' *Everyman's Dictionary of Quotations and Proverbs* cites an earlier example, used by Sir Henry Dudley in a letter dated September, 1776, and addressed to the actor David Garrick. There is no way of knowing whether Sir Henry originated the phrase or merely repeated it. In his favour is the fact that he was a clergyman, and 'wonders' was rather a vogue word at the time in religious circles. Only three years earlier another clergyman, William Cowper, had published a hymn that was to become famous. It contained the line: 'God moves in a mysterious way His wonders to perform.'

Wool-gathering

The wool-gatherers of the 16th century wandered through the fields gathering tufts of wool torn from sheep by bushes and brambles. This menial task was usually assigned to those who were unable to cope with more mentally demanding work; it did at least enable them to feel that they were playing a useful role in village life. Such people often lived in a mental world of their own, pursuing their own fancies. This soon led to anyone who showed signs of absent-mindedness or day-dreaming being accused of metaphorically 'going a wool-gathering.' Later use of the phrase is shown in George Eliot's *Adam Bede*, where a character says: 'It was Seth Bede, as was allays a wool-gathering chap.' The point is emphasised later in the novel: 'There never was such a chap for wool-gathering.'

Modern speakers and writers continue to use 'wool-gathering' as a synonym of absent-minded day-dreaming. 'I drifted into the kind of wool-gathering that music induced in me,' says the narrator of C.P.Snow's *The Affair*. Robertson Davies, in *The Lyre of Orpheus*, writes: 'Darcourt was eating and wool-gathering at the same time, a frequent trick of his.' Peter de Vries makes a verb of the phrase in *Consenting Adults*: 'As she snoozed I wool-gathered about domesticity with such a one.' Another interesting variation was used in 1922 by C. E. Montague in *Disenchantment*. He refers to 'the average German soldier, the docile blond with yellow hair, long skull, and blue, woolgathersome eyes.'

Writing on the Wall, The

'The writing on the wall' refers to anything that warns of impending disaster. Someone whose business has collapsed may say that he failed to see the writing on the wall – he did not realise in time the effect that changing market conditions would have. An employee may have the uneasy feeling that the writing is on the wall for him – there are signs that he will be made redundant. John le Carré uses the phrase in *The Spy Who Came In From The*

Cold, to say: 'It was odd how soon Leamas had realised that Mundt was the writing on the wall.' The arrival of Mundt on the scene means that Leamas's days as a spy are over.

The phrase alludes to a feast given by King Belshazzar, described in the Old Testament at Daniel 5. When the banquet was in progress 'the fingers of a man's hand appeared and wrote on the plaster of the wall of the king's palace, opposite the lampstand; and the king saw the hand as it wrote. Then the king's colour changed, and his thoughts alarmed him; his limbs gave way, and his knees knocked together.' King Belshazzar offers a great reward to anyone who can interpret the writing on the wall. It is Daniel who gives him the bad news: the words mean that 'God has numbered the days of your kingdom and brought it to an end; you have been weighed in the balance and found wanting; your kingdom is divided and given to the Medes and Persians.'

X is One's Middle Name

Sinclair Lewis became world famous in 1920 when he published *Main Street*. One of the American phrases the novel introduced to the rest of the English-speaking world occurred in the brief exchange: '"Like fishing?" "Fishing is my middle name".' This idea of implying that something is as closely associated with someone, or as meaningful to someone, as his middle name was quickly taken up by other speakers and writers, although Agatha Christie pretended to disapprove of it. Her most famous mystery, *The Murder of Roger Ackroyd*, published in 1926, has a character who remarks: 'Modesty is certainly not his middle name.' He is told: 'I wish you wouldn't be so horribly American, James.'

The phrase has continued to serve a useful purpose in one form or another. Examples include: 'Emily's middle name is Loyalty. Emily Loyalty Harrow. She added it the moment she dropped her maiden name.' (John P. Marquand, *Women and Thomas Harrow*); 'Belinda Carroll had a middle name, but you never saw it in print or on a theatre marquee. Her middle name was trouble with a capital T.' (Thomas Tryon, *All That Glitters*); '"Will you wash me?" "What a good idea." "All of me, I mean. No cheating. You're not allowed to concentrate on certain parts." "Thorough is my middle name".' (Guy Bellamy, *The Secret Lemonade Drinker*); 'Tact was far from being the Hon. Con's middle name.' (Joyce Porter,

The Meddler and her Murder); 'You wouldn't know neatness if it was your middle name.' (Margaret Laurence, *The Diviners*); 'I'm tired of kissing women. Everything starts with a kiss and very often the pay-off is a lemon. From now on my middle name's "Hermit".' In her short story *A Memory*, Mary Lavin varies the phrase slightly to say: 'If she said it was so, then it was so. Truth could have been her second name.'

You Cannot Have Your Cake and Eat it

This homely saying dates from the 16th century, though it then had a more logical form. John Heywood's collection of English proverbs, published in 1546, lists it as : 'You cannot eat your cake and have it.' The metaphorical meaning remains the same – you cannot pursue two courses of action which are mutually exclusive – but the change in word-order makes a considerable difference. Once a cake is eaten it cannot be kept because it no longer exists. By contrast, it is possible to keep a cake for a considerable time before eating it, though ultimately, of course, a choice between 'keeping' and 'eating' has to be made.

The change in word order seems to have occurred fairly recently. The Duke of Wellington, in a private letter, was still saying: 'our own government also having got their cake, want both to eat it and keep it.' Today's authors, typified by Margaret Drabble in *The Middle Ground*, reverse the order: 'Kate thinks Judith cannot have her cake and eat it.' Modern writers also often refer to characters who ingeniously try to disprove this proverb. Mordecai Richler, in *Joshua Then and Now*, has: 'You decided to have your cake and eat it too. You would cover your ass and make Kevin the patsy.' Peter Cheyney writes in *You Can Call it a Day*: 'You know Gale. He's an expert in having his cake and eating it.' Thomas Wolfe, in *Look Homeward, Angel*, writes: 'He would have his cake and eat it too – but it would be a wedding-cake.' The meaning here is that the man will have the sexual relationship with an innocent girl that he craves, but will be able to repeat the experience; the girl will have become his wife and their relationship will remain pure.

You've Got Another Think Coming

'If you think that,' we are likely to say, 'you've got another think coming.' In other words, 'you must think about it again, because you're quite wrong.' This informal expression was first recorded in the 1920s, when it hovered for a while between 'another think coming' and 'another guess coming.' Sinclair Lewis, in *Mantrap*, writes: 'If you think that it's any skin off my nose to lose the pleasures of your company, you got another think coming.' This novel was published in 1926, three years before G.Daviot's *Man in the Queue*. The latter has: 'If he thinks he has anything on me, he has another guess coming.' The 'guess' version was clearly in general use for a time. A 1935 caption in *Punch* magazine was: 'If you think I am fool enough to be hoodwinked, you have another guess coming.' A few years later C.Day Lewis was writing, in *Child of Misfortune*: 'If you think that's your doing, you've got another guess coming.'

The modern form of the expression is always 'another think coming,' often spoken with contempt or indignation. A typically irritated statement might be: 'If you think I'm going to stay in all morning waiting for you to call, you've got another think coming.' This does more than make the simple point that the speaker is not going to stay in; it expresses considerable annoyance that such a thing was ever suggested.

Index of Works Cited

Benson, E.F. *Trouble for Lucia* (UK, 1939)

Bernstein, Leonard *The Joy of Music* (1959)

Berrey and Van den Bark *American Thesaurus of Slang* (1942)

Bissell, Richard *The Pajama Game* (1954 as *A gross of pajamas*)

Blackmore, R.D. *Mary Anerley* (1913)

Blake, Nicholas *Whisper in Gloom* (1936)

Blishen, Edward *A Cack-handed War* (1974)

Bowen, F.C. *Sea Slang* (c. 1929)

Boyle, Patrick *Like Any Other Man* (1966)

Bradbury, John *Travels in the Interior of America* (UK, 1817)

Bradbury, Malcolm *Eating People Is Wrong* (1959)

Braine, John *Room at the Top* (1957)

Braine, John *Vodi* (1959)

Brontë, Charlotte *Jane Eyre* (1847)

Brooks, Jeremy *Henry's War* (1962)

Buchan, John *Mr. Standfast* (1919)

Buckeridge, *Anthony Jennings and Darbishire* (1952)

Burney, Fanny *Cecilia* (1782)

Burney, Fanny *Diary* (1889)

Burney, Fanny *Evelina* (1778)

Burton, Robert *Anatomy of Melancholy* (1621)

Butler, Samuel *The Way of all Flesh* (1903)

Byron, Lord *Don Juan* (1819)

Capote, Truman *Jug of Silver* (US, 1949; UK, 1950)

Capote, Truman *My Side of the Matter* (US, 1949; UK, 1950)

Carlyle, Thomas *Frederick the Great* (1873)

Carlyle, Thomas *Past and Present* (1843)

Cary, Joyce *A Fearful Joy* (1949)

Caspary, Vera *Laura* (1943)

Cecil, Henry *Brothers in Law* (1955)

Chandler, Raymond *The Big Sleep* (1939)

Chandos, Dane *Abbie* (1947)

Chapman, Robert L. *Dictionary of American Slang* (US, 1986; UK, 1987)

Chaucer, Geoffrey *Troylus and Cryseyde* (1482, posthumously)

Chetwood, W.R. *The Voyages, Travels and Adventures of W.O.G.Vaughan* (US, 1805)

Cheyney, Peter *You Can Call it a Day* (1949)

Christie, Agatha *Endless Night* (1967)

Christie, Agatha *The Murder of Roger Ackroyd* (1926)

Cicero *De Legibus* (c. 44 BC)

Cockshut, A.O.J. *The Imagination of Charles Dickens* (1961)

Coleridge, Samuel *The Sigh* (1797)

Collins, Norman *Trinity Town* (1936)

Colman, George *John Bull* (1806)

Combe, William *Second Tour of Dr Syntax in Search of Consolation* (1820)

Compton-Burnett, Ivy *A House and its Head* (1935)

Congreve, William *The Double Dealer* (1694)

Congreve, William *The Way of the World* (1700)

Cooke, John *Greene's Tu Quoque* (1913)

Cooper, William *The Struggles of Albert Woods* (1952)

Coward, Noel *Middle East Diary* (1944)

Cowley, Hannah *Who's the Dupe?* (1779)

Crabbe, George *The Village* (1783)

Crockett, David *Account of Col. Crockett's Tour to the North and down* (nd)

Croker, John *Diary* (1884)

Crompton, Richmal *William Again* (1924, 1977)

Cronin, A.J. *Shannon's Way* (1948)

Cronin, Michael *Dead and done With* (1959)

Davies, Robertson *The Lyre of Orpheus* (1988)

Daviot, G. *Man in the Queue* (1929, written by Elizabeth MacKintosh)

Day Lewis, C. *Child of Misfortune* (1939)

de la Mare, Walter *Desert Islands* (1930)

de Quincy, Thomas *Reminiscences of the English Lake Poets* (1907)

de Vries, Peter *Comfort Me With Apples* (1956)

de Vries, Peter *Consenting Adults* (1981)

de Vries, Peter *Glory of the Hummingbird* (1974)

Deighton, Len *Funeral in Berlin* (1964)

Lyly, John *Euphues: the Anatomy of Wyt* (1578)

Lytton, Lord *Lucile* (1860)

MacInnes, Colin *Absolute Beginners* (1959)

Mackintosh, M. *Stage Reminiscences* (1866)

Maclean, Alistair *The Dark Crusader* (1961)

Major, Clarence *Black Slang* (1971)

Malamud, Bernard *The Natural* (1952)

Malamud, Bernard *The Tenants* (1971)

Marquand, John P. *Women and Thomas Harrow* (1958)

Marryat, Frederick *Poor Jack* (1841)

Marryat, Frederick *Settlers in Canada* (1844)

Marryat, Frederick *The King's Own* (1830)

Marsh, Ngaio *Death at Dolphin* (1967)

Marsh, Ngaio *Surfeit of Lampreys* (1941)

Marsh, Ngaio *Swing, Brother, Swing* (1949)

Maugham, W. Somerset *Ashenden* (1928)

Maugham, W. Somerset *Circle* (1921)

Maugham, W. Somerset *Creatures of Circumstance* (1947)

Maugham, W, Somerset *Lord Mountdrago* (1940)

Maugham, W. Somerset *The Razor's Edge* (1944)

Maugham, W. Somerset *Then and Now* (1946)

Maugham, W. Somerset *An Official Position* (1940)

Maugham, W. Somerset *Appearance and Reality* (1951)

Maugham, W. Somerset *Here and There* (1948)

Maugham, W. Somerset *The Lotus Eater* (1940, short story in 'The Mixture as Before')

McCarthy, Mary *Charmed Life* (1955)

McCarthy, Mary *The Group* (1963)

McCarthy, Mary *The Groves of Academe* (1952)

McCullough, Colleen *The Thorn Birds* (1977)

McInnes, G. *Road to Gundagai* (1965)

Mencken, H.L. *American Language* (1919)

Michener, James A. *Chesapeake* (1978)

Collins Dictionary of Allusions
by Julia Cresswell

Why did Tony Benn called Harold Wilson the 'Archie Rice' of politics and why should someone describe Nastassia Kinski as a beautiful 'woodentop'?
If you have trouble with the above references, or can't remember where 'Brave New World' came from, or who 'Skippy' was, or who children mean by the 'Demon Headmaster', help is at hand in this highly entertaining guide to allusions in everyday speech, from classical times to Power Rangers.

ISBN 0 00 472054 7
Price: £5.99

Collins Dictionary of Slogans
by Nigel Rees

'*What passes for culture in my head is really a bunch of commercials*' - Kurt Vonnegut Jr

This classic guide includes unforgettable slogans from the worlds of advertising, politics and cultural history, from 'I'd love a Beer' and 'Black Power' to 'You Too Can Have a Body' and 'A Diamond is Forever'. Includes the famous: 'Beanz meanz Heinz' - the infamous: 'Alas, My Poor Brother' (Bovril) - as well as the undeservedly forgotten: 'We Don't Like Anyone Very Much' (US election sticker).

Compiled and researched over many years by the broadcaster and author Nigel Rees, this is an indispensable reference source for trivia, crossword and quiz buffs.

ISBN 0 00 472042 3
Price: £5.99